TALES OF THE EARLY FRANKS

AUGUSTIN THIERRY

TALES OF THE EARLY FRANKS,

EPISODES FROM MEROVINGIAN HISTORY

translated by
M.F.O. JENKINS

THE UNIVERSITY OF ALABAMA PRESS
University, Alabama

Library of Congress Cataloging in Publication Data

Thierry, Augustin, 1795-1856.
  Tales of the early Franks.

  Translation of Récits des temps mérovingiens.
  Includes bibliographical references and index.
  1. Merovingians.   I. Title.
DC65.T4313   944'.01   76-21314
ISBN   0-8173-8558-4

CONTENTS

TRANSLATOR'S INTRODUCTION

"The Franks or French, already masters of Tournai and of the banks of the Escaut, had spread out as far as the Somme. . . . Clovis, son of King Childeric, came to the throne in 481, and by his victories consolidated the foundations of the French monarchy."

These uninspiring, not to say downright arid, sentences ("and a few others of like impact") nevertheless furnished the fuel for the eager imagination of a fifteen-year-old at the Collège de Blois during the first decade of the nineteenth century. He had learned them by heart, he tells us, from the pages of the official *History of France*, published in 1789 for the Royal Military Academy. Then, one fateful day in 1810, the dry fuel was kindled: he got his hands on a copy of Chateaubriand's prose epic, *The Martyrs*, which had burst into print the previous year, filled with exotic tales about the parallel struggles of early Christianity against paganism, and of third-century Imperial Rome against the encroaching Barbarian hordes.

Among the numerous literary set-pieces in the work, one in particular was to electrify the young Augustin Thierry, sitting all alone in the school study-hall while he read, or "rather . . . devoured the pages." This was the famous account in Book IV of a battle between disciplined Roman regulars and forty thousand Barbarians, "those terrible Franks of M. de Chateaubriand." Thierry became so excited that he began to stride up and down the vaulted room ("making my footsteps ring on the stone floor"), as he declaimed the wild Frankish war-song to himself.

Years later, in 1840, when his own *Tales of the Early Franks* were published, Thierry—in his preface—recalled the never-to-be-forgotten encounter with Chateaubriand as follows: "This moment of enthusiasm was perhaps decisive for my future calling. At the time I was not in the least aware of what had just taken place within me. . . . Today, if I have someone read me the page which struck me so, I recapture the excitement of thirty years ago."

Augustin Thierry was thus, so to speak, virtually programmed to become a historian; and so he did. His two best known works are a *History of the Norman Conquest of England* (1825) and the *Tales of the Early Franks*. Tragically, he had lost his sight long before the publication of the latter work, which was completed with the aid of secretaries and a devoted wife.[1]

The *Norman Conquest* has been translated into English on several occasions,[2] but to my knowledge there exists no current English version of his second major work. Such neglect could no doubt be explained in part by the fact that the English-speaking public is for obvious reasons more interested in William of Normandy, the Conquest of 1066, and its aftermath than in the relatively obscure exploits of the Merovingian kings of the early Dark Ages. This may well be so, but there is another, more fundamental reason for the absence of an English edition of Thierry's *Récits des Temps Mérovingiens*. To put it briefly, his historical methodology fell on evil days even during his own lifetime and was indeed pretty thoroughly discredited—largely, it would seem, because of his desire to make history interesting to the general reader as well as to the professional historian. The preface to the *Tales of the Early Franks* begins: "It has become almost a commonplace to assert that no period of our history is so confusing or so dull as the Merovingian . . . On the contrary, it is teeming with curious facts, eccentric characters, and such a variety of dramatic incidents that *one's only difficulty is to impose some order on the mass of details*" (my italics).

To the austere scholar, Thierry might well appear to have become so entranced with his curious facts and eccentric characters that he never did succeed in imposing any noticeable order on the plethora of dramatic incidents and details that make his work so fascinating and full of life. However, as is often the case, the pedant's poison is the layman's meat, and it is precisely Thierry's failings as a historian, his frequent recourse to vivid local color, his addiction to gripping narrative and to unforgettable character studies, which make him so attractive to the nonspecialist. The book is the very antithesis of what in the preface Thierry himself calls works "of pure erudition, instructive for researchers, tedious for the ordinary reader." This ordinary reader, at least—though of a far less impressionable age than the enthralled boy devouring his copy of *The Martyrs* in 1810—admits to being very nearly as electrified on first reading the *Tales of the Early Franks* (whose continuing popularity with the general public in France is, incidentally, attested by the existence of a 1965 paperback edition[3]). Not the least of Thierry's achievements, it seems to me, is his undoubted success in recreating what Erich Auerbach calls "the strange atmosphere of the Merovingian period"[4] in all its alien, startling, and often appalling reality. The work is above all intensely dramatic in quality. The "terrible Franks" appear before us as real, living, individual people (as do their contemporaries, the Romanized Gauls), and not as some coldly abstract, impersonal entity, as is so often the case in school textbooks—and, indeed, in works of far higher pretensions. This is popularization in the highest and best sense of the term.

One of the outstanding features of Thierry's approach to history which is so dismaying to the professional historian (and, conversely, so engaging to the amateur) is his unabashedly simplistic view of the respective

national characteristics of the aboriginal inhabitants of Roman Gaul and
their Teutonic overlords, the redoubtable Franks. At the royal wedding
of Sigibert and Brunhild, for example, described in the first Episode of
the *Tales*, "there were Gallic nobles, polished and ingratiating;
brusquely arrogant Frankish lords; and genuine savages dressed all in
furs, as uncouth in manner as in appearance" (I, 14). The barbaric
splendor of the nuptial feast is enlivened by "acclamations, bursts of
laughter, and all the uproar of Teutonic merriment," while there follows
"a far more refined form of entertainment, of such a kind as to appeal to
only very few of the guests." The second citation, which refers to the
reading of a highly florid epithalamium by the last of the Roman poets,
Venantius Fortunatus, prompts Thierry to make the following superbly
patronizing observation: "Indeed, among the leading barbarian chiefs
there was no actual bias against civilization; they willingly took in
everything that they were capable of taking in. . . ." (I, 15).

One of the oddest of Thierry's "eccentric characters" is the Frankish
nobleman Guntram-Bose. His *portrait moral* (III, 55), epitomizes the
author's preoccupation with the extreme polarization of the Teutonic
and Gallic psyches. "Though a German, he outdid in ingenuity, resourcefulness, and instinctive knavery . . . the subtlest of the Gallo-
Romans. His was not the ordinary Teutonic bad faith, the crude lie
accompanied by a guffaw; it was something at once more refined and
more perverse, a spirit of intrigue both universal and, as it were,
nomadic, for he practiced it throughout the length and breadth of Gaul."

The main linking characters of the seven Episodes which make up the
work (covering the quarter of a century which elapsed between 561 and
586) are King Chilperic of Neustria, a strange, complex figure, part tribal
chieftain, part civilized ruler, with a taste for architecture, poetry, and
theology, but in whom the ruthless and brutal Barbarian is forever
gaining the upper hand; his queen, the low-born, beautiful, and mon-
strously vindictive Fredegund, a combination of the archetypal wicked
stepmother and Lady Macbeth; and, lastly, the Gallo-Roman Bishop of
Tours, Gregory, Thierry's principal authority and the reluctant eyewitness of many of the horrors and bizarre incidents he relates so graphically
in his *History of the Franks*.

To my mind, Gregory and Thierry are in many ways kindred spirits. At
any rate, the modern historian rarely fails to emphasize the admirably
solid and respectable qualities displayed by the Gallo-Roman chronicler
(a Victorian born out of his century): his dauntless faith; his manly
firmness in the face of ceaseless harassment by the turbulent Frankish
kings, a firmness which on more than one occasion called for personal
courage of a very high order; his touching capacity for being shocked by
what he considered improper or unseemly conduct;[5] and, finally, his
somewhat ponderous sense of humor, much in evidence in a regrettably

acrimonious exchange between Gregory and his confrère, Felix, the bishop of Nantes (v. Fifth Episode, 128-130).

In my translation, I have endeavored to do justice to Thierry's always elegant and urbane style, and to convey some notion of his pervasively subtle irony. I could perhaps do worse than conclude this introduction with a paragraph from the Preface, to give, as Thierry himself intended, at once a résumé and a foretaste of the heady stuff of which the *Tales of the Early Franks* are made:

> The way of life of the Frankish kings, the interior of the royal household, the tempestuous lives of the lords and bishops; usurpation, civil war and private vendetta; the scheming turbulence of the Gallo-Romans and the brutal indiscipline of the Barbarians; the absence of any administrative order and of any moral tie between the inhabitants of the different Gallic provinces in the heart of the same kingdom; the awakening of ancient rivalries and feuds between region and region and between city and city; everywhere a kind of return to a state of nature, and the revolt of individual wills against law and order in whatever shape or form they may appear, political, civic, or religious; a spirit of rebellion and violence reigning even within the convent; such are the diverse scenes that I have attempted to depict from contemporary records, which, in collected form, present a view of the sixth century in Gaul.

San Angelo, Texas
August, 1976

TALES OF THE EARLY FRANKS

PREFACE

It has become almost a commonplace to assert that no period of our history is so confusing or so dull as the Merovingian. This is the age which historians are most inclined to abridge, to slip through, and to pass over with few qualms. Their disdain is the result of laziness rather than reflection; and if the history of the Merovingians is somewhat hard to disentangle, it is certainly not dull. On the contrary, it is teeming with curious facts, eccentric characters, and such a variety of dramatic incidents that one's only difficulty is to impose some order on the mass of details. The second half of the sixth century is particularly rich and interesting in this respect to writer and reader alike, either because it is the period during which the native Gauls and their conquerors first begin to intermingle, which of itself endows it with a certain poetic quality, or else because it owes its lifelike air to the naive talent of its historian, Georgius Florentius Gregorius, known to us as Gregory of Tours.

The impact of the Frankish Conquest and of barbarism, the mores of those who destroyed the Roman Empire and their strange, wild appearance, have often been depicted in our day, and on two occasions by a great master.[1] These portrayals ensure that the historical period that begins with the great invasion of the Gallic provinces in 406 and ends with the establishment of Frankish rule shall henceforth retain its own local and poetic color; but the subsequent period has not been dealt with in any study where art has played a significant role. Its originality lies in a racial antagonism which is already no longer total, obtrusive, or jarring, but is in fact tempered by a host of reciprocal imitations, the consequence of dwelling on the same soil. The change in mentality which appears on both sides in numerous ways and in differing degrees, vastly increases general types and individualized personalities in the history of the time. There are Franks who though in Gaul remain totally Germanic; Gallo-Romans driven to desperation and disgust by the rule of the Barbarians, Franks more or less won over by the mores or manners of civilization, and Romans who have become more or less barbarous in spirit and conduct. The contrast may be traced in all its nuances through-out the sixth century and as far as the middle of the seventh; later on both the Germanic and the Gallo-Roman stamp seem simultaneously to fade away and to become lost in a semibarbarism clad in theocratic forms.

By a fortuitous but singularly happy coincidence, this period, so complex and so motley, is the very one whose primary sources furnish the greatest number of characteristic details. It coincides with a historian wonderfully suited to it in the person of a contemporary, an intelligent and sorrowful eyewitness of that confusion of men and things, of crimes and catastrophes in the midst of which the decline of the old civilization goes irresistibly on. We have to come down to the age of Froissart[2] to find a narrator who equals Gregory of Tours in the art of putting his characters in their proper setting and of portrayal by dialogue. Everything con-trasted or set in opposition on the same soil by the conquest of Gaul—races, classes, different stations in life—appears pell-mell in his narra-tives, which are sometimes humorous, frequently tragic, but always animated and realistic. It resembles a badly organized art gallery: his stories are like disconnected snatches of old folksongs, which could well be rearranged to make a poem, if this word, which nowadays we tend to abuse, may be applied to history.

The idea of undertaking a scientific yet at the same time artistic work devoted to the age of Gregory of Tours was the natural consequence of such thoughts; it came to me in 1833. Having once decided upon my project, I had a choice of two methods: either continuous narrative whose thread would be the sequence of great political events, or narra-tive in isolated segments, whose common denominator would be the life and adventures of some contemporary personages. I did not long hesi-tate between the two methods; I chose the second, first of all because of the nature of the subject, which was essentially to portray in as complete and varied a manner as possible social relationships and human destiny in public and family life; and secondly, because of the particular charac-ter of my principal source of information, Gregory of Tours's *Ecclesiastical History of the Franks*.

And indeed, for that curious book to realize its full potential as a primary source, it must be included in our corpus of narrative history, not for what it tells us of the principal events, for they are mentioned elsewhere, but for the sake of the episodic accounts, local affairs, and characteristic usages which are to be found nowhere else. If these details are linked up with the series of great political occurrences and inserted in their respective places in a unified narrative which is comprehensively elucidated at all points, they will not make much of an impression and indeed will virtually hamper the advance of the narrative at every step. Moreover, such a history would necessarily be of interminable length. This is what Adrien de Valois [1607-1692] has done in his three-volume

Latin compilation in folio of the *Gesta Francorum* [*Exploits of the Franks*], from the first appearance of the name Frank right down to the fall of the Merovingian dynasty. But such a book is a work of pure erudition, instructive for researchers, tedious for the ordinary reader. It would be impossible to translate or to imitate in French the work of Adrien de Valois: and even if this were attempted, the goal, in my opinion, would be unattainable. While giving himself a free hand in his voluminous chronicle, the seventeenth-century scholar frequently prunes and condenses; he smoothes the rougher passages, he expresses vaguely what Gregory of Tours states with precision and either suppresses the dialogue or garbles it. What he has in mind is the substance; the form means nothing to him. But to us, it is of prime interest; its smallest features must be captured; it must be made, through study, more distinct and more vivid. Form must be the medium which introduces the findings of modern historical science on the laws, customs, and social conditions of the sixth century.

This is the plan, self-imposed by every convention of the subject, which appealed to me: to take the culmination of the first period during which Frankish and Gallic customs begin to intermingle, and then, in a well-defined compass to collect and group the most characteristic details, from which to create a progressive sequence of scenes; to vary their settings, while at the same time giving breadth and weight to the various narrative segments; to expand and strengthen the fabric of the original narration, assisted by inductive reasoning from the legends, the poetry, the documents, and the plastic arts of the period. Between 1833 and 1837, I published under an interim title,[3] in *La Revue des Deux Mondes,* six of these episodes or fragments of a history which it would not be feasible to carry through in its entirety. They appear here with their definitive title—*Tales of the Early Franks*—and form the first section of the complete work, of which the second will also have two volumes.

If these isolated histories lack unity of composition, the reader will still find unity of impression. Since the whole series of narratives spans scarcely more than half a century, they will in a way be linked by the reappearance of the same characters, and frequently one narrative will do no more than enlarge on another. There will be one of these isolated narratives whenever I come across facts sufficiently comprehensive to serve as a focus for many subsidiary facts, to give them a general meaning, and to produce a complete action when combined with them. On one occasion it will be the account of the destiny of a particular individual, to which will be added the depiction of the social happenings which had some bearing on it; on another, it will be a series of public actions to which will be connected, in due order, personal adventures and domestic catastrophes.

The way of life of the Frankish kings, the interior of the royal household, the tempestuous lives of the lords and bishops; usurpation, civil war and private vendetta; the scheming turbulence of the Gallo-Romans and the brutal indiscipline of the Barbarians; the absence of any administrative order and of any moral tie between the inhabitants of the different Gallic provinces in the heart of the same kingdom; the awakening of ancient rivalries and feuds between region and region and between city and city; everywhere a kind of return to a state of nature, and the revolt of individual wills against law and order in whatever shape or form they may appear, political, civic, or religious; a spirit of rebellion and violence reigning even within the convent: such are the diverse scenes that I have attempted to depict from contemporary records, which, in collected form, present a view of the sixth century in Gaul.

I have made a minute study of the characters and destinies of the various historical figures, and I have tried to bring reality and life to those most neglected by history. Among these personages, whether famous or obscure nowadays, will predominate four figures who are typical of their age: Fredegund, Chilperic, Eonius Mummolus, and Gregory of Tours himself: Fredegund, the ideal of elemental barbarism, oblivious to any distinctions between good and evil; Chilperic, the man of barbarian stock who acquires a taste for civilization and a surface polish, without any inner reform; Mummolus, the civilized man who turns barbarian and who quite wantonly becomes depraved so as to be at one with his age; Gregory of Tours, the man of a past time—of a time better than the present, which is a burden to him—who faithfully echoes the regret evoked in some noble souls by a dying civilization.

The *Tales of the Early Franks* will, I believe, close the circle of my labors in narrative history; it would be rash to carry my aims and hopes beyond that. While I was attempting in this work to portray Frankish barbarism, mitigated during the sixth century by contact with the civilization which it was devouring, a memory of my first youth often came to my mind. In 1810, I was finishing my studies at the Collège de Blois, when a copy of *Les Martyrs*, brought in from outside, made the rounds of the school. This was a great event for those of us who were already experiencing an appreciation for the beautiful and an admiration for glory. We squabbled over the book; it was agreed that each of us should have it in turn, and my turn came on a holiday, at the usual hour of our walk. On that day, I pretended I had hurt my foot, and I stayed behind at school by myself. I read, or rather I devoured the pages, sitting at my desk in a vaulted room which was our study hall and which in those days seemed grand and impressive. At first I experienced a vague enchantment and as it were a dazzling of the imagination; but when I came to Eudorus' tale, that living history of the Empire in its decline, some indefinable interest, of a less passive and more reflective quality, drew me to the descriptions of the Eternal City, the court of a Roman emperor, a Roman army marching through the mud of Batavia, and its encounter with an army of Franks.

I had read in our textbook, the *History of France* intended for students of the Military Academy: "The Franks or French, already masters of Tournai and of the banks of the Escaut, had spread out as far as the Somme. . . . Clovis, son of King Childeric, came to the throne in 481, and by his victories consolidated the foundations of the French monarchy."[4] My entire medieval archeology consisted of those sentences and a few others of like impact, which I had learned by heart. "French," "throne," "monarchy" were for me the beginning and the end, the substance and the form of our national history. Nothing in it had given me an inkling of those terrible Franks of M. de Chateaubriand, "decked out in the skins of bear, seal, aurochs, and wild boar," of that "fortified camp, with hide boats and wagons drawn by great oxen," of that army drawn up in triangular formation, "where all that could be distinguished was a forest of javelins, of animal skins, and half-naked bodies."[5] As this contrast between the savage warrior and the civilized soldier unfolded so dramatically before my eyes, I was absolutely spellbound; there was something electric about the impression made on me by the Frankish war-song. I left my seat and, striding up and down the room, I repeated it aloud, making my footsteps ring on the stone floor:

"Pharamond! Pharamond! we have fought with the sword.

"We have hurled the two-edged battle-axe: the sweat fell from the warriors' foreheads and streamed down their arms. The eagles and birds with yellow feet uttered screams of joy; the raven swam in dead men's blood; all Ocean was but one wound. Long have the virgins wept.

"Pharamond! Pharamond! we have fought with the sword.

"Our fathers have died in battle, all the vultures groaned because of it: our fathers glutted them with carnage. Let us choose wives whose milk is blood and who fill the hearts of our sons with valor. Pharamond, the war-song is ended, the hours of life are running out; we shall smile when we must die.

"Thus sang forty thousand Barbarians. Their horsemen rhythmically raised and lowered their white shields and, at each refrain, beat their steel-clad breasts with their spearheads."[6]

This moment of enthusiasm was perhaps decisive for my future calling. At the time I was not in the least aware of what had just taken place within me; I did not dwell upon it; I even forgot it for several years: but when, after the inevitable gropings for the choice of a career, I had entirely devoted myself to history, I recalled this incident and its slightest attendant circumstances with remarkable precision. Today, if I have someone read me[7] the page which struck me so, I recapture my excitement of thirty years ago. That is my debt to the writer of genius who opened and who still dominates the new literary age. All those who, in different directions, walk in the paths of this century have also met him at the source of their studies, at the moment of their first inspiration;

there is not one of them who is not obliged to say to him, in the words of Dante to Virgil:

"*Tu duca, tu signore, e tu maestro.*" (*Inferno* II, 140)

Paris, February 25, 1840

FIRST EPISODE
The Four Sons of Lothar I—Their Characters—
Their Marriages—History of Galswinth[1]
(561-568)

A few miles away from Soissons the little town of Braine is situated on the banks of a river. During the sixth century, it was one of those immense farms where the Frankish kings held court, and which they preferred to the finest cities in Gaul. The royal residence had nothing of the military aspect of the medieval castle; it was a vast building, surrounded by porticoes in the Roman style, which were sometimes constructed of highly polished wood and decorated with quite elegant carvings. Around the main building were arranged in order the quarters of the palace officials of both barbarian and Roman descent, and those of the tribal chieftains who, in accordance with Germanic custom, had placed their warriors and themselves in the king's *truste*, i.e., under a special obligation of vassalage and fidelity. Other, less imposing houses were occupied by numerous families whose members, both male and female, practiced all kinds of trades. There were goldsmiths and armorers, weavers and curriers, embroiderers in silk and gold, and even those engaged in the coarsest preparations of wool and linen. Most of these families were Gallic, either born on the parcel of land that the king had appropriated as his share of the spoils of the Conquest, or else taken there forcibly from some of the neighboring towns to colonize the royal domain. However, judging from the appearance of the proper names, there were also Germans among them, as well as other barbarians whose forebears had come to Gaul as workmen or domestics in the wake of the bands of conquerors. Moreover, whatever their origins or type of trade, these families were placed in the same rank and designated by the same name: *liti*[2] in the Teutonic language, and in Latin, *fiscalini,* that is, persons attached to the Treasury. Agricultural buildings, stud-farms, cowsheds, sheep-pens and barns, the huts of the farm laborers and the serfs of the estate completed the royal village, which exactly resembled (though on a larger scale) the villages of ancient Germany. In the very location of these dwellings there was something reminiscent of landscapes beyond the Rhine. Most of them were situated on the edge, some in the middle, of the great forests since mutilated by civilization, forests whose remains we still admire today.

Braine was the favorite residence of Lothar, last of the sons of Clovis, even after the death of his three brothers had given him the kingship throughout Gaul. There it was that he kept under guard hidden away in a secret apartment the great triple-locked chests which contained his wealth in gold coin, plate, and jewels. There too he carried out the principal acts of his royal power. There he convoked the bishops of the cities of Gaul in synod, received the ambassadors of foreign kings, and presided over the great assemblies of the Frankish nation, which were followed by those traditional Teutonic feasts where deer and wild boar were served up whole on spits, and where broached casks occupied the four corners of the hall. So long as he was not summoned abroad by war against the Saxons, the Bretons, or the Goths of Septimania,[3] Lothar would spend his time on progresses from one of his estates to the next. He would go from Braine to Attigny, from Attigny to Compiègne, from Compiègne to Verberie, consuming in turn the provisions stored up on each of his royal farms and engaging with his Frankish *leuds*[4] in hunting, fishing, or swimming, and recruiting his numerous mistresses among the daughters of the *fiscalini*. Frequently, these women would pass from the rank of concubine to that of wife and queen with uncommon ease.

Lothar, whose marriages are not easy to count and classify, married in this way a girl named Ingund, who was of the humblest birth—without, moreover, giving up his dissolute habits, which she tolerated, as wife and as slave, with the utmost submission. He was very fond of her, and they lived together on the best of terms. One day she said to him: "My lord the king has done with his handmaiden what has seemed good to him and has summoned me to his bed. He would fill to overflowing the cup of his favors by granting his handmaiden's petition. I have a sister named Aregund who is in your service; be pleased, I entreat you, to obtain a valiant and wealthy husband for her so that I may not be shamed on her account." This request, by stimulating the king's curiosity, aroused his profligate nature: he set off that very day for the estate on which Aregund lived and where she was practicing some of the crafts which in those days fell to women, such as weaving and dying cloth. Lothar, finding her to be at the very least as beautiful as her sister, took her with him, installed her in the royal bed-chamber, and bestowed upon her the title of wife. Several days later, he returned to Ingund and said to her in the sly, good-natured way which was characteristic of him (and of the German in general): "I have given some thought to granting the favor that you, of your sweetness, desired of me: I have looked for a rich and wise man for your sister, and have found no one better than myself. Know that I have accordingly made her my wife, which will not, I think, displease you." "My lord," replied Ingund with no trace of emotion and without departing in the least from her habitual wifely patience and self-abnegation, "may my lord do what seems fitting, provided only that his handmaiden lose none of his good graces."

In the year 561, after an expedition against one of his sons, whose rebellion he punished by having him burned at the stake together with his wife and children, Lothar, perfectly at ease in mind and conscience, returned to his house at Braine. There he made preparations for the great autumn hunt, which was a kind of solemn ritual among the Franks. Accompanied by a host of men, horses, and hounds, the king made his way to the forest of Cuise, of which the forest of Compiègne, in its present condition, is merely a poor and final remnant. In the midst of this violent exercise, which was no longer appropriate to a man of his age, he fell ill of a fever and, having had himself carried to his nearest estate, died there after a reign of 50 years. His four sons, Charibert, Guntram, Chilperic, and Sigibert, followed his funeral procession to Soissons, singing psalms and carrying wax tapers.

Scarcely was the funeral over when the third of the four brothers, Chilperic, left in great haste for Braine and forced the guardians of that royal estate to hand over the keys of the treasury. Once in possession of all the wealth that his father had accumulated, he began by distributing a part of it to the tribal chieftains and warriors who had their quarters either in Braine or in the vicinity. All swore allegiance to him by placing their hands in his, hailed him by acclamation with the title of *Koning*,[5] and promised to follow him wherever he might lead them. Placing himself at their head, he then marched directly on Paris, the former residence of Clovis I and later capital of the kingdom of his eldest son, Childebert.

Perhaps Chilperic attached some notion of preeminence to the actual possession of a city formerly inhabited by the conqueror of Gaul; perhaps all he had in mind was to take over the imperial palace, whose buildings and gardens ran along the south bank of the Seine, outside the city. There is nothing improbable in this supposition, for the ambitious designs of the Frankish kings scarcely ever went beyond the prospect of immediate personal gain; and besides, while still retaining a strong tinge of Teutonic barbarity, unbridled passions, and a ruthless spirit, Chilperic had picked up some of the tastes of Roman civilization. He liked to build, took pleasure in the shows given in wooden amphitheatres, and above all else, had pretensions to being a grammarian, theologian, and poet. His Latin verse, in which the rules of metre and prosody were rarely observed, found admirers among the Gallic nobles who used to applaud, in fear and trembling, crying that the illustrious son of the Sicambrians[6] surpassed the children of Romulus in eloquence, and that the river Waal[7] set the Tiber to rights.

Chilperic entered Paris with no opposition and billeted his soldiers in the towers guarding the bridges of the city, which was at that time completely surrounded by the Seine.[8] On receiving news of this surprise attack, however, the other three brothers banded together against the one who wanted to award himself his share of his father's inheritance, and made a forced march on Paris with superior numbers. Chilperic did not dare stand up to them, and giving up his enterprise, he submitted to the fortunes of a division by mutual agreement. This partition of the whole of Gaul and of a considerable part of Germany was carried out by the drawing of lots, like that which had taken place half a century earlier among the sons of Clovis. There were four shares, corresponding, with some variations, to the four pieces of territory designated by the names of the kingdoms of Paris, Orléans, Neustria, and Austrasia.

In the drawing, Charibert obtained the share of his uncle Childebert, that is to say the kingdom to which Paris gave its name and which, running from north to south, long and narrow, comprised Senlis, Melun, Chartres, Tours, Poitiers, Saintes, Bordeaux, and the towns of the Pyrenees. Guntram's share consisted, in addition to the kingdom of Orléans (his uncle Chlodomir's portion), of all the territory of the Burgondes[9] from the Saône and the Vosges as far as the Alps and the Sea of Provence. Chilperic received his father's share, the kingdom of Soissons, which the Franks called *Neoster-rike*, or kingdom of the West, and whose boundaries were, to the north, the Escaut river, and to the south, the Loire. Finally, the kingdom of the East, or *Oster-rike*, fell to Sigibert, who combined in his share Auvergne, the entire northeast of Gaul, and Germany as far as the Saxon and Slav frontiers. It seems, moreover, that the cities were doled out one by one, and that their number alone served as the basis for the determination of the four lots; for, quite apart from the whimsicality of such a territorial division, one still comes across a host of enclaves otherwise impossible to account for. Rouen and Nantes go with Chilperic's kingdom, Avranches with Charibert's. The latter possesses Marseilles; Arles is Guntram's, and Avignon Sigibert's. Finally, Soissons, capital of Neustria, is, so to speak, hemmed in by four cities, Senlis and Meaux, Laon and Rheims, which belong respectively to the two kingdoms of Paris and Austrasia.

After the four brothers had been assigned their portions of cities and estates by the draw, each of them swore on the relics of the saints to be content with his own lot and to encroach upon nothing beyond it, whether by force or by trickery. It was not long before this oath was broken. Chilperic, taking advantage of the absence of his brother Sigibert, who was campaigning in Germany, made a surprise attack on Rheims and seized that city, as well as several others within his reach. But he did not long enjoy his conquest; Sigibert returned victorious from his campaign beyond the Rhine, recaptured his towns one by one, and, pursuing his brother to the very walls of Soissons, defeated him in battle and took the capital of Neustria by storm. Like true Barbarians, whose passions are violent but of short duration, they were reconciled, once again swearing to take no action against one another. They were both turbulent, quarrelsome and vindictive by nature; Charibert and Guntram, who were neither so young nor so wild, had a liking for peace and repose. Instead of the rough, warlike manner of his ancestors, King Charibert affected the calm and somewhat heavy bearing of the magistrates who, in the cities of Gaul, dispensed justice according to the laws of Rome. He even had pretensions to being an expert in jurisprudence, and no kind of flattery was more agreeable to him than praise of his ability as a judge in tangled cases, and of the ease with which, although a German by descent and language, he could express himself in Latin. King Guntram, a man of habitually gentle and almost priestly manner, was by an odd contradiction subject to attacks of sudden rage worthy of the forests of Germany. On one occasion, he had several free men put to the torture over a hunting horn which he had lost; another time he ordered the death of a Frankish noble suspected of having killed an ox on the royal domain. During his periods of self-control, he had a certain feeling for rule and order, which was particularly evident in his religious zeal and his submissiveness to the bishops, who in those days were rule incarnate.

King Chilperic was on the contrary a kind of half-savage freethinker, who heeded only his own whim even where dogma and the Catholic faith were concerned. The authority of the clergy seemed intolerable to him, and one of his greatest pleasures was to quash wills made to the advantage of a church or monastery. The character and conduct of the bishops were the principal texts of his jokes and table talk; he would call one hare-brained, another insolent, this one garrulous, that one a lecher. The great, and ever-increasing, wealth enjoyed by the Church, the influence of the bishops in the cities, where since the advent of barbarian rule they possessed most of the prerogatives of the old municipal magistrates, all those riches and that power which he coveted without perceiving any means of getting his hands on it, aroused his keenest jealousy. The lamentations he uttered in his resentment were not altogether unfounded, and he was often heard to repeat: "Just see how our treasury is impoverished and how our wealth is going to the churches! Nobody reigns indeed, except the bishops."

What is more, the sons of Lothar I, with the exception of Sigibert, who was the youngest, all possessed to a very high degree the vice of incontinence, hardly ever being content with one wife at a time, leaving without the slightest scruple the one they had just married, and taking her back later as the fancy took them. The pious Guntram changed wives almost as many times as his two brothers, and, like them, he too had concubines, one of whom, named Veneranda, was the daughter of a Gaul attached to the Treasury. King Charibert took as his mistresses—both at the same time—two sisters of great beauty, who were maidservants of his wife Ingoberghe. One was called Markovefa and was a nun, the name of the other was Meroflede; they were the daughters of a wool-worker of barbarian descent, a *litus* of the royal estate.

Ingoberghe, jealous of her husband's love for these two women, did everything she could to turn him away from them, but did not succeed. Not daring to ill-treat her rivals, however, or to drive them away, she devised what she thought was a fitting strategem for inspiring the king with distaste for a liaison unworthy of him. She sent for the father of the two girls and gave him some wool to card in the palace courtyard. While this man was hard at work, doing his best to show his zeal, the queen, who was standing by a window, called her husband: "Come here," she said, "come and see something different." The king came, looked as hard as he could and seeing nothing but a wool-carder, became angry, thinking the joke a very poor one. The ensuing altercation between husband and wife was violent, and produced quite the opposite effect to that expected by Ingoberghe, for the king repudiated her in order to marry Meroflede.

Before long, finding that one legitimate wife was not enough for him, Charibert bestowed the solemn title of spouse and queen on a girl named Theodohilde, whose father was a herdsman. Some years later, Meroflede died and the king lost no time in marrying her sister Markovefa. He thus found himself guilty of a double sacrilege in the eyes of the Church, both as a bigamist and as the husband of a woman who had taken the veil. Summoned by St. Germain, bishop of Paris, to dissolve his second marriage, he stubbornly refused, and was excommunicated. But the Church did not always get the upper hand in its struggle against the brutal pride of the heirs to the Conquest, for Charibert, unmoved by such a sentence, kept both his wives.

Of all the sons of Lothar, Chilperic is the one credited by contemporary accounts with the greatest number of queens, which is to say women married according to Frankish law, by the ring and the penny. One of these queens, Audovera, had in her service a young Frankish girl named Fredegund, who was of such remarkable beauty that the king fell in love with her at first sight. But this love, however flattering it might seem, was not without danger for a serving-maid whose position left her within reach of her mistress's jealousy and desire for vengeance. Fredegund, however, was not at all frightened; and, being as crafty as she was ambitious, she undertook to find, without compromising herself, legal grounds for the separation of the king and Queen Audovera. If one is to believe a tradition current a century later, she was successful thanks to the connivance of a bishop and to the artlessness of the queen. Chilperic had just joined his brother Sigibert to march beyond the Rhine against the peoples of the Saxon Confederation; he had left Audovera several months pregnant. Before his return, the queen gave birth to a daughter; and, not knowing whether she should have her baptized in her husband's absence, she consulted Fredegund, who, like the consummate deceiver she was, aroused neither suspicion nor mistrust. "My lady," replied the maidservant, "when my lord the king returns victorious, could he see his daughter with pleasure if she were not baptized?" The queen took this advice in good part, and the scheming Fredegund began secretly to prepare the trap that she intended to set.

On the day of the christening, at the hour appointed for the ceremony, the baptistry was adorned with hangings and garlands and the bishop was present in pontifical vestments: but the expected godmother, a Frankish noblewoman, did not appear. The queen, surprised by this contretemps, was in a quandary when Fredegund, who was standing nearby, said: "Why should we worry about a godmother? No lady is as good as you when it comes to standing godmother to your own daughter; if you will take my advice, do it yourself." The bishop, in defiance of his duty, performed the baptismal rites, and the queen withdrew without understanding the consequences for herself of the religious act which she had just accomplished.

On Chilperic's return, all the young girls of the royal domain went to meet him, carrying flowers and singing verses in his praise. When Fredegund met him, she said: "God be praised that my lord the king has gained the victory over his enemies and that a daughter has been born to him! But with whom will my lord sleep tonight? for the queen my mistress is today godmother[10] of your daughter Hildeswinde."

"Well!" replied the king jovially, "if I can't sleep with her, I'll sleep with you." In the portico of the palace, Chilperic found his wife Audovera carrying their child, which she, with mingled joy and pride, was going to present to him; but the king, feigning sorrow, said to her: "Woman, in your simple-mindedness you have committed a criminal act; henceforth you may no longer be my wife." In strict observance of ecclesiastical law, the king punished with exile the bishop who had baptized his daughter, and commanded Audovera to leave him forthwith and to take the veil as if she were a widow. To console her, he gave her several estates of considerable value. She accepted her fate with resignation and chose a convent situated in the city of Le Mans. Chilperic married Fredegund, and it was to the sound of their marriage festivities that the repudiated queen set off for her retreat, where, fifteen years later, she was murdered on the orders of her former waiting-maid.

While Lothar's three older sons were living in such debauchery and marrying domestics, Sigibert, the youngest, far from following their example was ashamed and disgusted. He made up his mind to take but one wife, and one of royal birth at that. Athanagild, king of the Goths[11] who had settled in Spain, had two marriageable daughters, the younger of whom, Brunhild by name, was greatly admired for her beauty; Sigibert's choice fell on her. A large embassy left Metz for Toledo with rich presents, in order to ask the king of the Goths for her hand. The chief ambassador, Gog (or, more properly, Godeghisel), mayor of the palace[12] of Austrasia and a man skilled in all kinds of negotiations, was completely successful in this one, and brought King Sigibert's betrothed back from Spain with him. Everywhere that Brunhild went on her long journey north (according to a contemporary eyewitness account), she was conspicuous for her graceful manner, her charming appearance, and her discreet and pleasant conversation. Sigibert fell in love with her and remained passionately devoted to her all his life. It was in the year 566, with great pomp, that the wedding ceremony took place in the royal city of Metz. The entire Austrasian aristocracy was invited by the king to take part in the day's festivities. Seen arriving at Metz, with their retinues of men and horses, were the counts of the cities and the governors of the northern provinces of Gaul, the patriarchal chiefs of the old Frankish tribes which had remained beyond the Rhine, and the dukes of the Alamans, the Baïwares,[13] and the Thorins or Thuringians. At this outlandish gathering, civilization and barbarity appeared side by side and in varying degrees. There were Gallic nobles, polished and ingratiating; brusquely arrogant Frankish lords; and genuine savages dressed all in furs, as uncouth in manner as in appearance. The nuptial feast was splendid and mirthful; the tables were laid with ornate gold and silver dishes, the spoils of the Conquest; wine and beer flowed unceasingly in bejeweled goblets, or in Teutonic drinking-horns. The vast halls of the palace echoed to the healths and challenges proposed by the drinkers, and to acclamations, bursts of laughter, and all the uproar of Teutonic merriment. The pleasures of the nuptial banquet were followed by a far more refined form of entertainment, of such a kind as to appeal to only very few of the guests.

There was at that time at the royal court of Austrasia an Italian, Venantius Honorius Clementianus Fortunatus, who was traveling in Gaul and was everywhere received with great honor. He was a man of superficial but agreeable intellect, who had brought with him from his native land some remnants of that Roman elegance which had by this time nearly died out beyond the Alps. Commended to King Sigibert by those bishops and counts of Austrasia who still loved and regretted the old urbanity, Fortunatus received a warm welcome at the semibarbarous court of Metz, where the officers of the royal treasury had orders to provide him with board, lodging, and horses. In order to display his gratitude, he had appointed himself court poet, and would offer the king and the nobility Latin poems which, if not always perfectly understood, were well received and well paid for. The marriage festivities could not do without an epithalamium; Venantius Fortunatus composed one in the classical manner, and recited it before the strange audience which crowded around him just as gravely as he would have given a public reading on Trajan's Square in Rome.

In this piece, which has no merit save that of being one of the last pale glimmerings of Roman wit, Venus and Love, the two indispensable characters of every epithalamium, appear with their usual paraphernalia of arrows, torches, and roses. Love shoots an arrow straight to the heart of King Sigibert and goes off to tell his mother about this great triumph. "Mother," he says, "I have put an end to the contest!" The goddess and her son then fly to Metz, enter the palace, and adorn the nuptial chamber with flowers. There, they engage in a disputation as to the respective merits of the bride and groom: Love is for Sigibert, whom he calls a new Achilles, but Venus prefers Brunhild, whose portrait she paints as follows:

"O admirable Virgin, soon to be idolized by your spouse, Brunhild, more brilliant, more radiant than the lamp of Heaven, the fire of precious stones yields before the brightness of your face; you are a second Venus and your dowry is the empire of beauty! Among the Nereids who swim in the seas of Iberia, at the source of Ocean, none can claim to be your equal; no wood-nymph is more beautiful, and the river-nymphs bow down before you! Milk-white and vivid red is your complexion, lilies mingled with roses, purple woven with gold cannot compare with it, and retire from the combat. Vanquished are sapphire, diamond, crystal, emerald, and jasper. Spain has given birth to a new pearl!"

These mythological commonplaces and the jingling of sonorous (but practically meaningless) words pleased King Sigibert and those Frankish lords who, like him, had some little understanding of Latin poetry. Indeed, among the leading barbarian chiefs there was no actual bias against civilization; they willingly took in everything that they were capable of taking in, but this veneer of urbanity came up against such a substratum of savage habits, such violent mores, and such unruly characters, that it could not go very deep. Furthermore, after these exalted personages (the only ones impelled by vanity or aristocratic instinct to seek out the company of the old nobility of the land and to copy their manners) came the throng of Frankish warriors, who suspected any man who could read of cowardice unless he had proved himself in their eyes. On the flimsiest pretext for war, they would begin sacking Gaul all over again, as in the time of the first invasion; they would steal the precious vessels from the churches and melt them down, and would look for gold in the very tombs. In peacetime they were mainly concerned with devising schemes to expropriate their Gallic neighbors, and with going out on the highways to attack with lance or sword those on whom they wished to take revenge. The most peaceful among them spent the days furbishing their weapons, hunting, or getting drunk. By giving them drink, one could obtain anything from them, even promises to use their influence with the king in behalf of this or that candidate for a vacant bishopric.

Constantly harassed by such visitors, always anxious for their property or their lives, the members of the wealthy indigenous families lost that peace of mind for lack of which scholarship and the arts decay; or else, led astray by the example of others and by a kind of instinctive, brutal independence that civilization cannot erase from the hearts of men, they would throw themselves into the barbarian way of life, despising everything but physical strength and becoming quarrelsome and disorderly. Like the Frankish warriors, they would go by night to attack their enemies in their homes or on the highways, and they would never go anywhere without the Germanic dagger called *skramasax*, i.e., safety-knife. Thus, in the space of a century and a half, all intellectual cultivation, all elegance of manners disappeared from Gaul by the mere force of circumstance, ill will and systematic hostility against Roman civilization having in fact had little to do with this deplorable change.

The pomp of Sigibert's marriage, and especially the brilliance conferred upon him by the rank of his new wife, made, according to the chronicles of the time, a deep impression on King Chilperic. In the midst of his concubines and wives married in the style of the old German chiefs—namely, without much ceremony—it seemed to him that he was living a less noble, less kingly life than that of his younger brother. Like him, he resolved to take a high-born wife; and so as to imitate him in every respect, he dispatched an embassy whose mission was to ask the king of the Goths for the hand of Galswinth, his eldest daughter. But this request met with obstacles which Sigibert's envoys had not encountered. Rumors of the king of Neustria's debauchery had traveled as far as Spain; the Goths, more civilized than the Franks and, above all, more thoroughly Christianized, said openly that King Chilperic was leading the life of a heathen. For her part, Athanagild's eldest daughter, who was timid by nature and of a gentle, melancholy temperament, trembled at the thought of going so far away and of belonging to such a man. Her mother Goïswinth, who loved her dearly, shared her repugnance, her fears, and her forebodings; the king was undecided and put off his final answer from day to day. Finally, under pressure from the ambassadors, he refused to make any agreement with them unless their king took an oath to send away all his women and swore to live with his new wife according to the law of God. Couriers set off for Gaul and returned, bearing a formal promise in the name of King Chilperic to forsake all his queens and concubines, so long as he obtained a wife worthy of him, and daughter to a king besides.

A double alliance with the kings of the Franks, his neighbors (and natural enemies), offered so many political advantages to King

Athanagild that he hesitated no longer and, on receiving this guarantee, passed to the articles of the marriage contract. From this time on, all the discussion hinged, on the one side, on the dowry that the future bride would bring with her; on the other, on the jointure that she would receive from her husband after the wedding-night, by way of *morrow-gift*. For in fact it was customary among all Teutonic peoples for the groom to give the bride when she awoke some kind of present as the price of her virginity. This gift could vary greatly in kind and in value; sometimes it was a sum of money or a costly piece of furniture, sometimes teams of horses or oxen; sometimes livestock, houses, or land; but whatever it might be, there was but one term to describe it: it was called *morrow-gift, morghengabe* or *morganeghiba*, depending on the various Germanic dialects. The negotiations pertaining to the marriage of King Chilperic and Brunhild's sister, slowed down by the dispatch of the couriers, were prolonged until the year 567; they were still not completed when an event which had taken place in Gaul made it easier to bring them to a conclusion.

The eldest of the four Frankish kings, Charibert, had left the neighborhood of Paris, his customary residence, to enjoy the climate and produce of southern Gaul on one of his estates, near Bordeaux. He died there almost without warning, and his death brought about a new territorial upheaval in the empire of the Franks. No sooner had he closed his eyes when Theodehilde, one of his wives, who was a shepherd's daughter, sized the royal treasure and, in order to keep the title of queen, sent word to Guntram proposing that he marry her. The king received this message with enthusiasm, and replied with an air of perfect sincerity, "Tell her to hurry here with her treasure, for I wish to marry her and to exalt her in the eyes of the nations; I want her to enjoy even more honors at my side than with my late brother." Overjoyed at this reply, Theodehilde had her husband's wealth loaded on several carts and set off for King Guntram's residence at Chalon-sur-Saône. But on her arrival the king, without taking any notice of her at all, examined the baggage, counted the wagons, and had the chests weighed; then he said to his entourage: "Isn't it more fitting for this treasure to belong to me, rather than to a woman who didn't deserve the honor my brother did her by taking her into his bed?" They all agreed with him, Charibert's treasure was put under lock and key, and the king saw to it that the woman who had, most reluctantly, made him so handsome a present was escorted to the convent of Arles.[14]

Neither of Guntram's two brothers disputed his possession of the money and valuables that he had just appropriated by this ruse: they had much more important concerns to discuss either with him or among themselves. They now had to reduce the partition of the territory of Gaul to three shares, instead of four, and to split up by mutual agreement the cities and provinces which had made up Charibert's kingdom. This new apportionment was carried out in an even stranger and less methodical fashion than the first one. The city of Paris was divided into three equal parts, of which the brothers each received one. To avoid the danger of a surprise invasion, none of them was supposed to enter the city without the consent of the other two, on penalty of forfeiting his share not only of Paris, but of Charibert's kingdom as well. This stipulation was ratified by a solemn oath sworn on the relics of the revered Saints Hilary, Martin, and Polyeuctus, whose judgment and vengeance were called down upon the head of whosoever should break his word.

Like Paris, the city of Senlis was also divided, but into only two parts; out of the remaining cities, three parcels were formed on the basis of the taxes gathered there, but without any regard to their respective positions. The geographical confusion became even greater than before, enclaves multiplied, and the kingdoms were, so to speak, entangled in one another. King Guntram obtained by the luck of the draw Melun, Saintes, Angoulême, Agen, and Périgueux. Meaux, Vendôme, Avranches, Tours, Poitiers, Albi, Conserans, and the cantons of the Lower Pyrenees fell to Sigibert's lot. Finally, Chilperic's share included (along with several cities not named by the historians) Limoges, Cahors, Dax, and Bordeaux, the now ruined cities of Bigorre and Béarn, and several cantons of the Upper Pyrenees.

The eastern Pyrenees were located outside the territory at that time subject to the Franks; they belonged to the Goths of Spain, who used them to keep communications open with their possessions in Gaul, which extended from the Aude as far as the Rhône. The king of Neustria, who had not hitherto owned a single town south of the Loire, thus became the nearest neighbor of the king of the Goths, his future father-in-law. This geographical situation provided a new foundation for the marriage contract, and brought it almost immediately to a conclusion. Several of the cities that Chilperic had just acquired were on the very borders of Athanagild's realm; the others were scattered throughout Aquitaine, a province which had formerly been taken from the Goths by the victories of Clovis the Great. To stipulate that several of the cities lost by his ancestors should be given to his daughter as jointure was an astute political move: the king of the Goths did not fail to make it. Either because he could not grasp the significance of any scheme going beyond an immediate advantage, or because he desired to conclude his marriage with Galswinth at all costs, King Chilperic did not hesitate to promise, by way of jointure and morrow-gift, the cities of Limoges, Cahors, Bordeaux, Béarn, and Bigorre, together with their surrounding territory. The confusion prevalent in the Teutonic nations between the right of territorial proprietorship and that of actual government might well remove these cities from Frankish rule one day, but the king of Neustria was not looking so far ahead. Entirely taken up with a single purpose, he thought only to demand that, in return for what he was about to give up, a considerable dowry in money and valuables should be placed in his hands: when this point was settled, there remained no further obstacles, and the marriage was arranged.

Throughout all the ups and downs of this long negotiation, Galswinth's great aversion to her intended husband and her vague misgivings as to the future never left her. The promises made by the Frankish ambassadors in King Chilperic's name had failed to reassure her. When she learned that her fate had just been irrevocably sealed, she ran, terror-stricken, to her mother, and throwing her arms around her like a child looking for help, she clung to her, silently weeping, for more than an hour. The Frankish envoys presented themselves to pay their respects to their king's betrothed and to take her orders for the departure, but at the sight of the two women sobbing on one another's breast and clutching one another so tightly that they seemed to be lashed together, they were touched, uncouth as they were, and dared not speak of the journey. They let two days slip by, and on the third they came before the queen once again; and this time they announced that they were eager to be off, speaking of their king's impatience and of the distance to be covered. The queen wept and asked for one more day's respite for her daughter: but the next day, when they came to tell her that all was ready for the departure, she replied: "Just one more day, and I will ask for nothing else; don't you know that where you are taking my daughter she will be motherless?" But all possible reasons for delay had been exhausted; Athanagild brought his royal and paternal authority to bear and, despite the queen's tears, Galswinth was entrusted to the care of the men whose mission it was to conduct her to her future husband.

A long file of horsemen, carriages, and baggage-wagons passed through the streets of Toledo and headed toward the north gate. The king rode with his daughter's train as far as a bridge across the Tagus, at some little distance from the city; but the queen could not bring herself to return so soon and wanted to go on. Leaving her own chariot, she sat down beside Galswinth and, stage by stage, day by day, let herself be carried more than a hundred miles. Each day she said: "I want to go as far as such-and-such a place," and when she had reached it, she would go on. As they approached the mountains, the roads became difficult: she did not notice and wanted to keep going. But her retinue, which greatly increased the size of the train, also increased the difficulties and dangers of the journey, and the Gothic lords resolved to prevent their queen from going even one more mile. She had to resign herself to the inevitable parting, and once again affectionate scenes—calmer ones, this time— took place between mother and daughter. The queen gently expressed her sorrow and her maternal fears: "Be happy," she said, "but I fear for you; be careful, daughter, be very careful . . ." At these words, which corresponded only too well to her own misgivings, Galswinth wept, and answered: "It is God's will, I must submit"; and the sorrowful parting was accomplished.

The long procession broke up; horsemen and wagons divided, some continuing to advance, the others returning to Toledo. Before mounting the chariot which was to take her back home, the queen of the Goths stopped by the side of the road and, fixing her gaze on her daughter's wagon, stood motionless as she watched until it disappeared into the distance and the windings of the road. Galswinth, sorrowful but re-signed, continued her journey to the North. Her escort, composed of nobles and warriors of both the Gothic and the Frankish nations, crossed the Pyrenees, then the cities of Narbonne and Carcassone, without leaving the kingdom of the Goths, which extended thus far; next it headed, by way of Poitiers and Tours, for the city of Rouen, where the marriage was to be solemnized. At the gates of every large town, the procession would halt and all would be made ready for a ceremonial entry; the horsemen would cast off their riding-cloaks, uncover their horses' harness, and arm themselves with the shields slung at their saddle-bows; the king of Neustria's betrothed would leave her heavy traveling-cart for a special parade chariot, tall and tower-shaped and completely sheathed in silver. The contemporary poet[15] from whom these details are borrowed saw her enter Poitiers (where she rested for several days) in this manner: he tells us that the pomp of her retinue was much admired, but he says nothing about her beauty.

Meanwhile, Chilperic, true to his promise, had repudiated his wives and sent his mistresses packing. Fredegund herself, the most beautiful of all, the favorite among those upon whom he had conferred the name of queen, could not escape this general banishment; she submitted with apparent resignation, and with a good grace that would have deceived a much subtler man than King Chilperic. She seemed sincerely to recog-nize that this divorce was necessary, that the marriage of a king with a woman like herself could not be a serious one, and that her duty was to give way to a queen really worthy of the title. As a last favor, she asked only not to be sent away from the palace, but to come back, as before, among the women employed in the royal service. Beneath this mask of humility there was a world of female guile and ambition against which the king of Neustria was in no way on his guard. Since the day he had been taken with the idea of marrying a girl of royal blood, he believed he no longer loved Fredegund, and no longer noticed her beauty; for the mind of Lothar's son, typical of barbarian minds in general, was incapa-ble of retaining more than one impression at a time. And so it was due to no ulterior motive or softheartedness, but through downright poor judgment, that he allowed his old favorite to remain near him in the house where his new wife was to live.

Galswinth's nuptials were celebrated with as much pomp and magnificence as those of her sister Brunhild; there were even, on this occasion, unusual honors paid the bride; and all the Franks of Neustria, lords and ordinary warriors alike, swore allegiance to her as though to a king. Standing in a semicircle, they drew their swords in unison and brandished them in the air while uttering an ancient pagan formula giving over to the edge of the sword whosoever should break his word. Next, the king himself solemnly renewed his promise of constancy and marital fidelity; placing his hand on a reliquary, he vowed never to repudiate the daughter of the king of the Goths, and never to take any other wife so long as she should live.

During the wedding festivities, Galswinth attracted favorable attention for the gracious kindness which she displayed to the guests; she welcomed them as though she already knew them; to some she offered gifts, others she addressed in mild and benign language; all assured her of their devotion and wished her a long and happy life. These wishes, which were not destined to be fulfilled, accompanied her to the bridal chamber; and the next day at her rising she received the morrow-gift, with all the ceremonial laid down by Germanic custom. In the presence of selected witnesses, King Chilperic took his new bride's hand in his own right hand, and with his left threw a wisp of straw upon her, while loudly pronouncing the names of the five cities which were in future to be the property of the queen. The deed of this perpetual and irrevocable gift was immediately drawn up in Latin; it has not survived, but up to a certain point its terms can be reproduced, based on the time-honored forms and style used in the other documents of the Merovingian era:

"God having bidden man to leave father and mother, and to cleave unto his wife that they may be two in one flesh and that no man may put asunder what God hath joined together, I, Chilperic, illustrious king of the Franks, to thee, Galswinth, my beloved wife, whom I have epoused according to the Salic law,[16] by the *sou* and the *denier*, give today out of loving kindness, in the name of dowry and of *morgane-ghiba*, the cities of Bordeaux, Cahors, Limoges, Béarn, and Bigorre, together with the lands adjacent thereto and all their population. From this day forward I desire that thou mayst hold and possess them in fee simple, and I yield, convey, and confirm them unto thee by the present charter, as I have done by the wisp of straw and by the *handelang*."[17]

The first months of the queen's marriage were, if not happy, at least peaceful; a gentle and patient girl, she endured with resignation all the savage brusqueness of her husband's character. Besides, for a while Chilperic was genuinely fond of her: at first, he loved her out of vanity, delighted to possess a wife as noble as his brother's; then, when this feeling of self-satisfaction had palled somewhat, he loved her out of

avarice, because of the great sums of money and the quantities of valuables that she had brought with her. But having gloated for a while over
his calculations of all these riches, he stopped finding pleasure in them,
and from then on there was no longer anything to hold him to Galswinth.
Her moral beauty, her lack of pride, her charity to the poor were not of a
nature to charm him, for he had eyes and appetite only for physical
beauty. And so the time came when, despite his own resolutions, Chilperic felt nothing but coolness and boredom in the presence of his wife.

This moment, for which she had been watching, Fredegund exploited
with her customary skill. She had only to show herself, as though by
chance, when the king was passing by, for the comparison of her face
with that of Galswinth to revive in the heart of that sensual man a passion
only half-extinguished by a few transient promptings of vanity. Fredegund was taken back as concubine, and openly paraded her latest
triumph; she even affected haughty and scornful airs towards the slight-
ed wife. Offended both as wife and as queen, Galswinth at first wept in
silence; then she dared to complain and to tell the king that there was no
longer any honor for her in his house, but only insults and affronts that
she could not bear. She asked the favor of being repudiated, and offered
to relinquish everything she had brought with her, provided only that
she be allowed to return to her native land.

The voluntary yielding of a rich treasure, and magnanimous self-
abnegation, were beyond the comprehension of King Chilperic; not
having the slightest conception of them, he could not believe in them.
Therefore, despite their sincerity, the only feelings stirred up in him by
the words of the unhappy Galswinth were dark suspicion and the fear of
losing, through an overt breach, wealth which he considered himself
fortunate to possess. Controlling himself, and concealing his intent with
the cunning of a savage, he suddenly mended his ways, assumed a mild
and affectionate tone, and made professions of remorse and love which
deceived Athanagild's daughter. She spoke no more of separation, and
deluded herself that his change of heart was genuine; then one night, by
order of the king, a trusty retainer was smuggled into her bedchamber,
and strangled her as she slept. On finding her dead in her bed, Chilperic
feigned astonishment and grief; he even pretended to shed tears: and, a
few days later, he restored to Fredegund all her rights as wife and queen.

So perished this young woman, who seems to have had a premonition
of the fate in store for her, a gentle, melancholy figure passing through
the barbarous Merovingian era like an apparition from a different age. In
spite of the weakening of the moral sense in the midst of numberless
crimes and misfortunes, there were still those who were deeply moved
by so undeserved a fate, and in accordance with the spirit of the times,
their compassion took on a superstitious coloring. It was said that a
crystal lamp hanging near Galswinth's tomb had, on the day of her

burial, suddenly come unhooked without human aid, and had fallen to the marble pavement without either breaking or going out. To round off the miracle, it was asserted that the bystanders had seen the marble floor yield, as though it were soft, and the lamp half bury itself therein. Tales of this kind may make us smile, who read them in old books written for men of another age; but in the sixth century, when such legends passed from mouth to mouth like the living, poetic expression of popular faith and sentiment, people became pensive and wept when they were told.

SECOND EPISODE
Sequel to the Murder of Galswinth—
Civil War—Death of Sigibert (568-575)

Among the Franks and in general among Teutonic peoples, whenever a murder had been committed, the victim's next of kin assigned a rendezvous for all his kinsmen and allies, summoning them on their honor to come in arms, because from then on a state of war existed between the murderer and whoever had the slightest degree of kinship with his victim. As husband to Galswinth's sister, Sigibert found himself responsible for performing this obligatory act of revenge. He sent messengers to King Guntram, who, without a moment's hesitation between his two brothers, now enemies, took the side of the offended party, either because national custom left him no choice in the matter or because Chilperic's hateful and cowardly crime had, so to speak, outlawed him from his own family. War was at once declared and hostilities began, but with unequal zeal on the part of the two brothers who were fighting the third. Aroused by the cries for vengeance of his wife Brunhild, who could do anything with him and whose violently passionate temperament had just then come to light, Sigibert wanted to carry the fight to the death; he did not shrink even from the thought of fratricide. Guntram, however, inspired either by Christian feeling or by innate spinelessness, lost no time in dropping his role as co-belligerent for that of mediator. With the help of both entreaties and threats, he dissuaded Sigibert from taking the law into his own hands and induced him to ask peacefully for justice at the hands of the assembly of the people, according to the law.

And in fact, in Frankish law—or rather, Frankish national custom—any man who considered himself wronged had a free choice between private vendetta and public judgment; but once this judgment was handed down, feuding was no longer lawful. The judicial assembly was called the *mâl*, i.e., the council, and in order to exercise the functions of arbitrator one had to belong to the landowning class or, as the German expression has it, to the class of *arimans*[1] or men of honor. The judges, in greater or lesser number, depending on the nature and importance of the cases which they had to argue, came to the assembly armed, and armed they remained as they sat on benches arranged in a circle. Before the Franks crossed the Rhine and conquered Gaul, they used to hold their law-courts in the open air, on hills hallowed by ancient religious rites. After the Conquest, as Christians, they abandoned this practice, and the *mâl* was convened, by the kings or the counts, in covered enclosures of timber and masonry. However, despite this change, the meeting-place kept the name which it had been given in heathen Germany and continued to be called *Mâl-Berg* (i.e., the Council Mountain) in the Teutonic language.

When a proclamation issued in the three Frankish kingdoms had announced that within the space of forty nights (for such was the legal term) a great council would be held by King Guntram to restore peace between Kings Chilperic and Sigibert, the principal chieftains and great landowners came to the appointed place accompanied by their vassals. There was a solemn verdict which the history of the time mentions without going into detail, but its probable circumstances may be reconstructed with the help of various legal texts and judicial records and terminology. Inductive reasoning applied to these texts yields the following facts, which are admittedly mere conjecture, but which can, up to a point, fill in the blanks left by the historical testimony.

When the assembly had convened, King Guntram took his place on a raised seat, with the rest of the judges on ordinary benches, each wearing his sword and with a servant behind him carrying his shield and spear. Summoned as appellant, King Sigibert came forward first and, in the name of his wife, Queen Brunhild, accused Chilperic of having knowingly taken part in the murder of Galswinth, Brunhild's sister. The accused was allowed two weeks to come forward in his turn and swear that he was not guilty.

Frankish law demanded that this oath of self-vindication be ratified by that of a certain number of free men, six in lesser cases, and as many as seventy-two in cases of greater importance, as determined either by the gravity of the facts or the high rank of the parties. The accused had to present himself within the space enclosed by the judges' benches, accompanied by all those who were going to swear with him. Thirty-six would line up on his right and thirty-six on his left; then, when called upon by the ranking judge, he would draw his sword and swear on his weapons that he was innocent; next the co-swearers, drawing their swords in unison, would take the same oath. There is not one passage in either the chronicles or the records of the period which would lead one to believe that King Chilperic tried in this manner to exonerate himself from the crime with which he was charged; in all likelihood he appeared before the assembly of the Franks unaccompanied, and sat down in silence. Sigibert stood up and, addressing the judges, said three times: "Tell us the Salic law." Then he went on, for the fourth time, pointing to

Chilperic: "I charge you to tell us what the Salic law ordains."

Such was the time-honored formula for asking for a verdict against an adversary convicted on his own admission; but in the case in question the response to the summons could come only after long debate, for the Frankish common law was here applicable only by analogy. With a view to forestalling or at the very least shortening private feuds, this law laid down that in the event of murder, the culprit would pay the victim's heirs a sum of money proportional to the victim's station in life. For the life of a domestic slave, the price paid was between fifteen and thirty-five gold *solidi;* for that of a *litus* of Barbarian origin or of a Gallo-Roman dependent, forty-five *solidi;* for a Roman landowner, one hundred *solidi;* twice that sum for a Frank or any other Barbarian living under the Salic law. At each of these levels, the fine was tripled if the murdered man, whether slave or serf bound to the soil and whether of Roman or Barbarian descent, was an immediate dependent of the king either as retainer, vassal, or civil servant. Thus the sum paid was ninety gold *solidi* for a Roman admitted to the royal table and six hundred for a Barbarian who bore an honorary title or was simply *an-trusti,* i.e., a trusted follower of the king.[2]

This fine which, once paid, was supposed to guarantee the culprit against later prosecution and any act of revenge, was called *wer-gheld* (protection-tax) in the Germanic idiom, and in Latin *compositio,* because it put an end to the feud between the offender and the offended party. There was no *wer-gheld* for the murder of persons of royal rank who, in this scale of charges for human life, were placed above and beyond all legal valuation. On the other hand, Barbarian custom in a way gave the sovereign the privilege of homicide; and that is why, without giving a broader interpretation to the stipulations of the Salic law, it was impossible either to say what it ordained with respect to the lawsuit brought against King Chilperic or to state the amount of the settlement which was to be paid to Galswinth's next of kin. Unable to judge in strict accordance with the law, the assembly proceeded by arbitration, and handed down the following verdict, quite authentic as regards substance and reconstructed only as to the form:

"This is the judgment of the most illustrious King Guntram and of the Franks holding court in the Mâl-Berg. The cities of Bordeaux, Limoges, Cahors, Béarn, and Bigorre, which Galswinth, sister of the most excellent lady Brunhild, on her arrival in the land of France, received, as all men know, by way of jointure and morrow-gift, shall become from this day forward the property of Queen Brunhild and her heirs so that, subject to this settlement, peace and charity may be restored between the most illustrious lords Chilperic and Sigibert."

The two kings went towards each other, holding little boughs which they exchanged as tokens of their mutually pledged word, the one swearing never to attempt to take back what he had just lost through the decree of the assembled people, the other vowing not to demand a greater settlement on any pretext. "Brother," said the king of Austrasia then, "I give you hereafter peace and security concerning the death of Galswinth, sister of Brunhild. From this time on you need fear neither accusations nor legal proceedings from me and if, which God forbid, it should happen that, either by me, or by my heirs, or by any other person acting in their name, you should be challenged or summoned once again before the Mâl concerning the homicide in question and the settlement which I have received from you, this settlement shall be restored to you twofold." The assembly dispersed and the two kings, mortal enemies not long since, went out apparently reconciled.

The thought of accepting the verdict against him by way of expiation was not one which King Chilperic could conceive of; on the contrary, he promised himself that one day he would take back his cities, or would seize their equivalent from Sigibert's domains. This design, after maturing in concealment for nearly five years, suddenly came to light in the year 573. Without being any too certain of the respective locations and importance of the five towns whose loss he much regretted, Chilperic knew that Béarn and Bigorre were both the least considerable and the farthest removed from the center of his realm. On giving some thought to the means of recovering by force what he had given up against his will, he found that his plan of conquest would be both more practicable and more profitable if he substituted for the two little towns at the foot of the Pyrenees the large and prosperous cities of Tours and Poitiers, which suited him perfectly. He accordingly mustered troops in the city of Angers, which belonged to him, and gave the command of them to Clovis, the youngest of his three sons by Audovera, his first wife.

Before any declaration of war had been made, Clovis marched on Tours. Despite the strength of that ancient city, he entered it unopposed, for King Sigibert—like the other two kings—kept permanent garrisons only in cities where he resided, and the citizens, who were all or nearly all of Gallic stock, cared little whether they belonged to one Frankish king rather than to another. Chilperic's son, now master of Tours, headed for Poitiers, which opened its gates to him just as readily, and there he established his headquarters, as being at the central point between the city of Tours and those of Limoges, Cahors, and Bordeaux, which still remained to be conquered.

On receiving the news of this unlooked-for aggression, King Sigibert sent messengers to his brother Guntram to request his aid and counsel. The role of peacemaker between the two kings that Guntram had played six years before seems to have invested him in their eyes with a kind of magistracy and with the right to deal severely with whichever of them should break his word and transgress against the verdict of the people.

With this in mind, and acting moreover in conformity with that instinct for justice which was one of the facets of his character, he took it upon himself to repress King Chilperic's hostile endeavor and to compel him not only to abide once more by the conditions of the treaty of partition, but also to submit to the verdict of the Frankish people. Without remonstrating with the breaker of the oath of peace or giving him prior notice, Guntram sent troops into the field against Clovis. They were led by the best of his generals, the Gaul Eonius Mummolus, who equalled the bravest of the Franks in boldness, and surpassed them all in military ability.

Mummolus, whose name, which was famous in those days, will reappear more than once in these Tales, had just vanquished the Langobards[3] in several battles and beaten them back beyond the Alps. These people, who were masters of northern Italy, were attempting to cross over into Gaul and were threatening to conquer the provinces adjacent to the Rhône. With that speed of movement which had won him his victories, Mummolus left Chalon-sur-Saône, Guntram's capital, and set off for the city of Tours by way of Nevers and Bourges. At his approach, young Clovis, who had returned to Tours with the intention of sustaining a siege there, decided to retreat, and went along the road to Poitiers to take up favorable positions not far from that city, and there to await reinforcements. As for the citizens of Tours, they gave a peaceful reception to the Gallo-Roman general, who took possession of the place in King Sigibert's name. In order to make them less indifferent in the future with regard to political matters, Mummolus made them take an oath of loyalty en masse. If, as is likely, the proclamation which he addressed to the count and the bishop of Tours was stylistically consistent with similar instruments, every man of the city and its outskirts, *whether Roman or Frank, or of any nation whatsoever*, was commanded to assemble in the cathedral and there to swear on the holy relics that he would in all sincerity, and like a true leud, keep the allegiance due his lord, the most illustrious King Sigibert.

Meanwhile, the reinforcements awaited by Clovis reached his camp near Poitiers. They were local levies, led by Sigher and Basilius, the former of Frankish, the latter of Roman origin. These men were both influential because of their wealth, and both were zealous supporters of King Chilperic. Their force was large in size, but undisciplined, and consisted mainly of smallholders and peasants, who formed the vanguard of the Neustrian army and consequently were the first to come to grips with the soldiers of Mummolus. Although they put up a gallant and even stubborn resistance, Sigher and Basilius were unable to halt in his advance on Poitiers the greatest, or, to be more exact, the only tactician of the age. Attacked simultaneously head-on and on the flank, they were, after enormous losses, thrown back in disarray against Clovis's Franks, who gave ground and almost immediately broke and fled. The two leaders of the volunteers were killed in this rout, and Chilperic's son, no longer having enough men to defend Poitiers, fled along the road to Saintes. Having won control of the city by this victory, Mummolus considered his mission accomplished; and after administering to the citizenry, as he had at Tours, an oath of allegiance to King Sigibert, departed for Guntram's kingdom, without deigning to give chase to the few remaining Neustrians who were fleeing with their king's son.

Clovis made no attempt to rally his troops and fall back on Poitiers, but, either because he was afraid of finding his road to the north cut, or simply out of youthful bravado, instead of marching towards Angers, he kept going in the opposite direction, towards Bordeaux, one of the five cities he had been ordered to capture. He arrived at the gates of this great city with only a handful of men in sorry array; yet at the very first summons made in his father's name, the gates were opened to him—a curious fact, strikingly illustrative of the administrative impotence of the Merovingian monarchy. There was not sufficient military force in the city to defend Queen Brunhild's right of sovereignty against a band of exhausted fugitives, far from home. Chilperic's son was able, without let or hindrance, to take command and to occupy with his men the buildings belonging to the royal Treasury. These had once been imperial property and had fallen to the lot of the Teutonic kings as part of the heritage of the Caesars.

Young Clovis had been residing in Bordeaux for nearly a month, putting on the airs of a conqueror and assuming the authority of a viceroy, when Duke Sigulf, guardian of the frontier (or Marches) of the Pyrenees, took it upon himself to attack him. The border which had to be defended against the Goths and the Basques then belonged in its entirety to the king of Austrasia, in whose name the proclamation of war was published on both banks of the Adour. Several indications furnished by later actions lead one to believe that, so as not to leave his strongholds unmanned, the duke, or as the Germanic language puts it, the *mark-graf*[4] ordered a mass levy of the local inhabitants: hunters, shepherds, and woodsmen who were almost as wild as their neighbors the Basques, and who frequently banded together with them to plunder freight caravans, hold little towns to ransom, and resist the Frankish governors. Those of the mountaineers who obeyed the call of the Austrasian leader came to the rendezvous—some on foot, some mounted—with their customary weapons, that is to say dressed for the hunt, with boar-spear in hand and hunting-horn or bugle slung at their shoulders. Led by the *mark-graf* Sigulf, they entered Bordeaux, marching at speed as though for a surprise attack, and made for that part of the city where the Neustrians were quartered.

The latter, taken by surprise and outnumbered, barely had time to mount their horses and to make their prince, protected in their midst, do likewise; then they fled northward. Sigulf's men began a hot pursuit, inflamed by the hope of having a king's son at their mercy and holding him to ransom, or perhaps by their instinctive national hatred for the Franks. To spur one another on to the chase, either to increase the terror of the fugitives or simply through a lighthearted whim (which was quite characteristic of the southern Gaul), they blew their bugles and hunting-horns as they galloped along. All that day, Clovis, bending forward over the reins as he clapped spurs to his horse, could hear horns being blown behind him and the cries of the hunters following his trail as though he were a stag rushing headlong through the woods. But in the evening, as darkness came on, the pursuit gradually slackened, and before long the Neustrians were free to go on their way at a normal pace. Thus did young Clovis return to the banks of the Loire and the walls of Angers, which he had so recently left at the head of a large army.

This ludicrous ending to an insolently undertaken expedition filled King Chilperic with black and furious resentment. From then on it was no longer simply the love of gain but also wounded pride which incited him to risk everything in order to get back his conquests and to take up the challenge which was apparently being offered him. With his mind made up to avenge his honor in a striking manner, he mustered another army much larger than the first on the banks of the Loire and put Theodebert, his eldest son, in command. This time the prudent Guntram thought that another intervention on his part would probably be fruitless so far as peace was concerned, whereas it would certainly be very costly for himself. Renouncing the role of arbitrator, he adopted a kind of mediation which, in the event of failure, would allow him to keep aloof and avoid taking sides in the quarrel. He gave an ecclesiastical synod the responsibility of reconciling the two kings, and in obedience to his orders, all the bishops in his kingdom (who were neutral by profession) met in council in Paris, which was a neutral city, and where, according to the provisions of the Act of Partition, none of Lothar's sons might set foot without the consent of the other two. The council most cogently exhorted the king of Neustria not to break the peace he had sworn to keep and not to encroach any more upon his brother's rights. But all their speeches and messages were in vain. Chilperic, paying no heed, went on with his preparations for war, and the members of the synod went back to King Guntram bearing, as the sole fruit of their mission, the announcement that war was inevitable. Meanwhile, Theodebert crossed the Loire and—executing a movement which looks almost like a strategic plan— instead of marching first on Tours, as his younger brother had done, made for Poitiers, where the Austrasian commanders in Aquitaine had just concentrated their forces. Their chief, Gundovald, was imprudent enough to risk an engagement in open country with the Neustrians, who greatly outnumbered him and who, above all, were far more eager for this war than his own troops. He was utterly defeated and lost everything in a single battle. The victors entered Poitiers, and Theodebert, now master of this stronghold in the center of Austrasian Aquitaine, was at liberty to proceed towards any of the cities which he was charged with capturing. He chose the northerly direction and entered that part of the Tours region occupying the left bank of the Loire. Acting either on his father's orders or on his own impulse, he waged a barbarous campaign, carrying devastation and massacre wherever he went. The citizens of Tours were terrified to see from their walls the clouds of smoke which, rising all around them, heralded the burning of the neighboring countryside. Though bound to King Sigibert by an oath sworn on holy relics, they stifled their religious scruples and surrendered unconditionally, imploring the victor to be merciful.

After the submission of Poitiers and Tours, the Neustrian army went on to lay siege to Limoges, which opened its gates; and from there it marched on Cahors. During this long itinerary, its passing was marked by the devastation of the countryside, the looting of houses, and the profanation of holy places. The churches were plundered and set on fire, the priests put to death, the nuns raped, and their convents totally destroyed. With the report of this havoc, universal terror spread throughout the ancient province of Aquitaine, from the Loire to the Pyrenees. This vast and beautiful land which the Franks had entered sixty years before, not as enemies to the native population, but as the adversaries of its first [5] conquerors, the Goths, and as soldiers of the orthodox faith against a heretical power; [6] this favored land, where conquest had twice passed by without leaving any deep scars, where Roman usages were preserved almost intact, and where the Teutonic princes from beyond the Loire were scarcely known save by their reputation as perfect Catholics, was suddenly torn from the repose which it had enjoyed for half a century.

The spectacle of so many acts of cruelty and sacrilege astonished men and saddened them. Theodebert's campaign in Aquitaine was compared to the persecutions of Diocletian; with artless wonder the crimes and acts of brigandage committed by Chilperic's army were contrasted with the pious deeds of Clovis the Great, who had founded and enriched so many churches. Invectives and curses in the Biblical manner poured from the lips of the Aquitanian bishops and senators, whose Christian faith and local patriotism were one and the same thing; or else they would tell one another, with smiles of hope, of the miracles which, according to public report, were being worked in various places to punish the excesses of the Barbarians, as the Franks were called. Incidentally, this term of itself had no injurious connotation; it served in Gaul merely to denote the conquering race, as the name Romans denoted the native population.

Often the merest accident would form the basis for these folk-tales to which awestruck imaginations imparted a superstitious tinge. A few miles from Tours, on the right bank of the Loire, there stood a monastery famous for its relics of St. Martin. While the Franks were plundering the left bank, about twenty of them took a boat to reach the other side and sack this wealthy abbey. Having neither oars nor iron-shod poles with which to steer, they were using their lances, holding the head uppermost and pushing against the river-bed with the other end. Seeing them draw near, the monks, who could not possibly mistake their intentions, came out to meet them, crying: "Beware, you Barbarians, beware of landing here, this monastery belongs to the blessed Martin." Nevertheless, the Franks did land; they beat the monks, smashed the abbey furnishings, and stole all the valuables, which they bundled up and piled in their boat. The badly steered and overloaded craft ran aground on one of the shoals which choke the Loire, and was left stranded. At the jolt caused by this sudden stop, several of those who were poling with all their might to keep the heavy boat moving staggered and fell forward onto their spearheads, stabbing themselves in the chest. The others, overcome simultaneously with terror and remorse, began yelling and calling for help. Some of the monks whom they had handled roughly then came running up, got into a boat, and saw, not without amazement, what had happened. Urged by the looters themselves to take back all the spoils removed from the abbey, they returned to the bank singing the office of the dead for the souls of those who had just perished in so unforeseen a manner.

While these events were taking place in Aquitaine, King Sigibert was gathering all his available forces to march against Theodebert, or to compel Chilperic to recall him and withdraw to the boundaries assigned by the Act of Partition. He called to arms not only the Franks from the Meuse, the Moselle, and the Rhine, but also every other Teutonic tribe living beyond the last-named river and acknowledging the authority or the patronage of the sons of Merovech. Such were the Sweves (or Swabians) and the Alamans, the last vestiges of two once-powerful confederations; the Thorings and the Baïwares, who preserved their independent nationhood under hereditary dukes; and finally, several small tribes from lower Germany, detached willy-nilly from the redoubtable Saxon League, the enemy and rival of Frankish power. These nations from beyond the Rhine (Transrhenane, as they were then called) were completely pagan, or, at any rate, if those nearest the frontier of Gaul had received some seeds of Christianity, they mixed them up in a peculiar fashion with the practices of their old religion, sacrificing animals—and even men—on solemn occasions. In addition to these ferocious propensities, they possessed a thirst for plunder and an instinct for conquest which were driving them westward and spurring them to cross the great river to go and take their share of the territory and spoils of Gaul, as the Franks had done before them.

The Franks knew this and kept a suspicious eye on the slightest movements of their blood-brothers, who were always ready to emigrate in their wake and try to conquer them. It was to ward off this danger that Clovis the Great fought the united Swabians and Alamans at the famous field of Tolbiac. Other victories, won by Clovis's successors, followed the defeat of this vanguard of the Transrhenane peoples. Theoderic tamed the Thuringian nation and several Saxon tribes, against whom Sigibert himself displayed his energy and courage. As king of eastern France and guardian of the common frontier, he had kept the Germanic peoples in awe and respect of the Frankish royal power; but by enlisting them in his army and leading them under his colors to the very center of Gaul, he was inevitably to revive in them their old jealousy and lust for conquest and to raise up a storm threatening Gaul and Frank alike.

Therefore, at the news of this great arming of Austrasia, a feeling of anxiety spread abroad, not only among Chilperic's subjects, but also among Guntram's, and he himself shared their fears. Despite his natural disinclination for picking a quarrel without long and bitter provocation, he had no hesitation about regarding the mass levies of the heathen nations across the Rhine as an act of hostility against every Christian in Gaul, and he responded favorably to Chilperic's request for aid. "The two kings had an interview," says the contemporary narrator,[7] "and forged an alliance, each swearing that neither would let his brother perish." Foreseeing that Sigibert's plan would be to march toward the southwest and to win some point on the highway between Paris and Tours, Chilperic took his forces to the eastern half of the course of the Seine, to prevent Sigibert from crossing there. For his part, Guntram garrisoned his northern border, which was unprotected by any natural defences, and he himself came to Troyes, where he settled down to observe.

It was in the year 574 that the Austrasian king's troops reached a point near Arcis-sur-Aube, after a march of several days. Sigibert halted here and waited, before going on, for the reports of his scouts. In order to enter Chilperic's kingdom without changing direction, he was obliged to cross the Seine a little above its confluence with the Aube, at a place then called Twelve Bridges (now Pont-sur-Seine); but every bridge had been broken, every boat removed, and the king of Neustria was encamped not far off, ready to do battle if an attempt was made to ford the river. Less than twenty-five miles to the south, the Seine and the territory on both its banks formed part of Guntram's states, or portion, as the term then was. Sigibert made no bones about summoning Guntram to grant the right of way across his lands. The message which he sent him was curt and to the point: "If you do not let me ford the river through your territory, I will march against you with my entire army."

The presence of this formidable host made the strongest possible impression on King Guntram, and the same fears which had induced him to combine with Chilperic led him to break both the alliance and his word. Every piece of information which he received from his spies and the local inhabitants concerning the number and appearance of the Austrasian troops disclosed in a terrifying light the danger to which a refusal must expose him. And indeed, if the armies of the Merovingian kings were customarily undisciplined, Sigibert's excelled in fierce unruliness anything seen since the period of the great invasions. The crack battalions were composed of the least civilized and least Christianized of all the Frankish peoples, namely those who lived closest to the Rhine; and the great mass of the troops consisted of a horde of Barbarians in the fullest sense of the term. There were strange figures like those who had wandered through Gaul in the days of Attila and Clovis, and who were no longer met with except in folk tales; warriors with drooping mustaches and a tuft of hair on the tops of their heads, who hurled their battle-axes into their adversary's face or harpooned him from a distance with their hooked javelins. Such an army was incapable of going without brigandage even in friendly territory; but Guntram preferred exposing himself to some short-term depredations to the risk of being invaded and conquered. He yielded the right of passage, probably by way of the bridge at Troyes, and in this same city had an interview with his brother Sigibert, to whom he pledged undying peace and sincere friendship.

When he received word of this betrayal, Chilperic hastily abandoned his positions on the left bank of the Seine and retreated headlong towards the interior of his kingdom. He marched nonstop as far as the environs of Chartres and made camp on the banks of the Loir, near the little town of Avallocium, which is now called Alluye. During this long journey, he was continually followed, with the enemy troops always close on his heels. More than once Sigibert, thinking that he was going to call a halt, challenged him to name a day of battle, in accordance with Teutonic custom, but instead of replying, the king of Neustria would increase the pace and march on. Scarcely had he taken up his new positions when a herald from the Austrasian army brought him the following message: "If you are not a man of no account,[8] prepare a battlefield and agree to fight." Never had such a challenge made to one of Frankish stock remained unanswered; but Chilperic had lost all his original self-respect. In desperation, after vain attempts to elude his enemy, and lacking the courage of the wild boar at bay, he resorted to entreaty, and asked for peace in return for promises of satisfaction.

Despite his violent nature, Sigibert did not lack generosity; he agreed to overlook everything on condition that the cities of Tours, Poitiers, Limoges, and Cahors were restored to him forthwith, and that

Theodebert's army returned to its own side of the Loire. Chilperic, who on his own admission was vanquished and whose dreams of conquest had been blighted for the second time, appeared to have become altogether meek and mild. To his ostensible resignation he even joined scruples—true or false—of justice and charity. He became anxious over what would befall the inhabitants of the four cities which had surrendered to him: "Pardon them," he said to his brother, "and do not lay the blame on them, for if they have failed in the loyalty they owed you, it is because I compelled them to do so with fire and sword." Sigibert was humane enough to heed this recommendation.

The two kings seemed well pleased with one another, but the Austrasian army was seething with discontent. The men enrolled in the Transrhenane regions complained that an unexpected peace had cheated them of the booty which they had looked forward to amassing in Gaul. They were indignant at having been led so far from home only to have no fighting and no spoils. They accused King Sigibert of having withdrawn from the game just when he should have given battle. The entire camp was in an uproar, and a violent insurrection was in the making. The king, with no sign of emotion, mounted his horse and galloped towards the groups where the most mutinous soldiers were bawling. "What is the matter?" he asked them. "And what do you want?" "Battle!" the yell arose from all sides. "Give us a chance to fight and get rich, otherwise we won't go home." This threatened to bring about a new territorial conquest in the heart of Gaul and the dismemberment of the Frankish empire; but Sigibert was in no way intimidated, and, combining a steadfast bearing with mild speech and promises, succeeded without too much difficulty in calming the anger of these savages.

They struck camp and the army began to march back towards the banks of the Rhine. It took the Paris road, but did not actually pass through that city, whose neutrality Sigibert, faithful to his commitments, respected. All along their path, the Austrasian columns looted the places they went through, and the Paris region long felt the effects of their passing. Most of the small towns and villages were set on fire, the houses sacked, and many men led away into slavery, while the king was powerless to forestall or prevent excesses of this kind. "He would speak to them and entreat them to stop such things from happening," says the old chronicler. "But he could not prevail against the rage of the men from across the Rhine."

These pagans entered churches only to rob them. In the wealthy basilica of St. Denis, one of their captains took a piece of silk, gold-brocaded and studded with gems, which covered the tomb of a martyr; another did not scruple to climb up on the tomb itself to reach and knock down with his spear a golden dove which was hanging from the chapel ceiling as a symbol of the Holy Spirit. Both as king and as Christian,

Sigibert was outraged by these acts of looting and desecration, but, feeling that he could do nothing with the minds of his soldiers, he behaved towards them as his grandfather Clovis had done towards a man who had smashed a vase at Rheims. So long as the army was on the march, he let well alone and concealed his resentment; but when he was home again, and these unruly men had dispersed, each returning to his own tribe and house, he had those who had been the most conspicuous by their disobedience and lawlessness seized one by one and put to death.

It appears that similar destruction occurred when the Austrasians crossed the northern borders of Guntram's kingdom, and that this grievance, which sorely rankled with him, was the cause of the falling-out he had with Sigibert. And in any case, the king of Neustria's peaceable frame of mind was not long-lived; as soon as he found himself out of danger, he came back to his obsession and once more looked covetously at the Aquitanian cities which he had briefly possessed. The coolness which had arisen between his two brothers seemed to him a favorable opportunity for the resumption of his plans for conquest; he lost no time in making the most of it, and less than a year after the conclusion of peace he sent word to Guntram: "Let my brother come with me, let us be friends, and, with one accord, let us harry our enemy Sigibert." This proposal was very well received; the two kings had an interview, gave one another presents in token of friendship, and concluded an offensive alliance against their brother of Austrasia. Chilperic confidently dispatched fresh troops to the Loire under the command of his son Theodebert, who crossed that river for the second time in the year 575. He himself, with another army, entered the territory of Rheims, the western frontier of the kingdom of Austrasia. His invasion was attended by the same devastation as Theodebert's campaign in Aquitaine; he burned the villages, destroyed the crops, and plundered everything that could be carried off.

The news of these lawless acts reached Sigibert at the same time as that of the coalition formed against him. He had forgiven Chilperic and resisted the supplications of his wife, who wanted neither peace nor truce with Galswinth's murderer. His was the indignation of a simple-hearted, hot-tempered man who discovers that his good faith has been trifled with. He exploded with invectives and curses, but his seething anger, like a fever which could well subside again once the enemy had submitted, was too uncertain to satisfy Brunhild. She exerted all her influence over her husband to implant in his soul a more deliberate desire for vengeance, and to channel all his animosity towards a single goal: fratricide. Put an end to the murderer; this was the cry of Galswinth's sister: and this time Sigibert heeded it. Accordingly, he was thinking in terms of a duel to the death when he once again proclaimed his ban of war against Chilperic among the eastern Franks and the Transrhenane tribes.

In order to encourage so intractable a people to fight resolutely, the king of Austrasia promised them everything: money, booty, even lands and cities in Gaul itself. He marched due west to succour the province of Rheims, which relieved him of worrying about how to cross the Seine. On his approach Chilperic, avoiding battle as he had done in the previous campaign, retreated along the course of the Marne and went towards the lower reaches of the Seine in search of favorable positions. Sigibert gave chase as far as the walls of Paris, but there he halted, tempted by the idea of occupying that city (which was in those days considered to be virtually impregnable) and of making it his strong point and, if need be, place of refuge. However prudent this idea might seem, by giving way to it the king of Austrasia committed an act of foolhardiness which he would doubtless have recoiled from had not his passion for revenge stifled his every scruple and fear.

By virtue of the treaty of partition concluded eight years before, Paris, divided into three zones, was for all that a neutral city, forbidden to each of Lothar's sons by the most sacred of oaths and by all the terrors of religion. Not one of them had thus far dared to violate his oath and face the maledictions decreed against whosoever should break it. Sigibert had the courage to do so, preferring to risk his salvation rather than to neglect a single means of success in the pursuit of his aims. Paris was indeed indispensable to him as *point d'appui* and, to use an entirely modern expression, as a base for his future operations, whether he wanted to take action against Chilperic to the west or Theodebert to the south. Therefore, calling upon the city to let him in, in defiance of the treaty, he entered it unopposed.

After establishing his headquarters in Paris, King Sigibert first of all saw to it that troops were sent against Chilperic's son, who, taking the same route in Aquitaine as he had the previous year, had just arrived in Limoges. Between the cities of Tours and Chartres there was a strip of land, comprising the regions of Châteaudun and Vendôme, which belonged to the kingdom of Austrasia: Sigibert resolved to raise an army there so as to husband the forces that he had brought with him. His messengers went from village to village, issuing a proclamation charging all free men to appear at the rendezvous equipped to the best of their ability with weapons of some kind. But in neither town nor country did they respond to the call; and despite the penalty incurred by anyone disobeying royal decrees, the inhabitants of Châteaudun, Vendôme, and the country to the north of Tours neither took up arms nor left their homes. These people were well aware that their district was included in Sigibert's portion and that taxes raised there went to the Austrasian Treasury, but that was as far as it went; and since the king whose subjects they were only rarely made his administrative authority felt—this command being the first of its kind that they had received from him—they paid little attention to it.

This passive resistance, if prolonged, would have compelled the king of Austrasia to divide his forces, and so he dispatched his two most skillful negotiators to the place to put a stop to it promptly and without violence. These were Godeghisel, mayor of the palace, and Guntram called Bose, i.e., the cunning one, a scheming, knowledgeable man, endowed, despite his Teutonic extraction, with a versatility uncommon in those not of Gallo-Roman stock. The two Austrasians were successful in their mission and before long reached the Loire at the head of a native army, poorly equipped but of sufficient size to have no fear of coming to grips with Theodebert's Franks.

These latter, already much alarmed at the news of Sigibert's invasion, were even more so when they learned that troops were advancing against them and that their line of retreat was cut off. But no matter how discouraged his soldiers, Theodebert, like a real Teuton chief, resolved to advance against the enemy. He marched out of Limoges and took up positions on the banks of the Charente eight or ten miles from Angoulême; on the way there, many of his men deserted, with the result that, when he gave battle, he was almost completely forsaken. He nonetheless fought with great gallantry and was killed in the melee.[9] The Gallic peasants who made up the army of Godeghisel and Guntram-Bose did not, like the Franks, have a sort of cult for the descendants of Merovech; regardless of the distinctively long hair of Chilperic's son, they stripped him like the other dead and left him naked on the battlefield. However, an Austrasian chief named Arnulf was appalled at this profanation and, although Theodebert's enemy, had the young prince's body reverently taken up; then, having washed it in accordance with the custom and dressed it in costly garments, he had it buried at his own expense in the city of Angoulême.

In the meantime, King Guntram, again yielding to his taste for peace and quiet (or perhaps to the impression made on him by fear), had just come to terms with Sigibert. Chilperic learned of this latest betrayal at the same time as the death of his son and the loss of his army in Aquitaine. Reduced by this double misfortune to a state of utter despair and thinking only of saving his life, he left the banks of the Seine and went to take refuge within the walls of Tournai with his wife, his children, and the most loyal of his warriors. The strength of that city, which had been the first Frankish capital in Gaul, was what induced him to take shelter in it. Expecting a siege, he busied himself recruiting soldiers and collecting munitions, while Sigibert, with complete freedom of movement throughout Neustria, was seizing that kingdom's cities.

Having occupied those to the north and east of Paris, he proceeded westward, determined to hand over what he had just conquered, land and cities alike, as payment to his Transrhenane warriors. This plan caused all the Franks, even those of the kingdom of Austrasia, the gravest misgivings. The Austrasians were far from eager to have people whom they considered to be their natural enemies as their neighbors in Gaul, while for their part the Neustrians saw themselves faced with expropriation, political subservience, and all the other evils following in the wake of a territorial conquest. The former expressed their protests and complaints to the king; the latter came to terms with him. After deliberating as to what ought to be done in such perilous circumstances, the nobles or *arimans* of Neustria sent Sigibert a message worded thus: "The Franks who once looked to King Childebert and who have since become the liegemen of King Chilperic now desire to turn to you, and mean to set you up as their king, if you will come to meet them."

Thus did the Franks exercise their right to leave the prince governing them and to go over to the allegiance of another of Merovech's descendants. For each of Lothar's sons, royal authority lay far less in the extent and prosperity of his kingdom than in the number of fighting-men who had placed themselves under his patronage and who, to use the Teutonic expression, obeyed his mouth. [10] There was nothing fixed or stable in the distribution of the Frankish population among the kings whose strength it constituted; it did not correspond exactly to territorial divisions, and one of the rulers might well have vassals in another's kingdom. Among these vassals or leuds, the most devoted, the most useful (as the expression then was) were those who, living close to the king and forming his permanent bodyguard, received in lieu of pay subsistence at his table or from the revenues of the royal domain. Less trustworthy was the allegiance of those who, residing far away and living in their own homes, enjoyed, by royal grant, the *feod* or remuneration in land. It was this latter class which, to save its property, deserted Chilperic's cause and offered the crown to Sigibert; the former, more loyal but less numerous, had followed the fugitive king within the walls of Tournai. The Neustrian message and offer were joyfully received by Sigibert, who solemnly pledged that not one city would be turned over to his soldiers, promising to go to the assembly where he was to be inaugurated in accordance with ancestral custom. Next he went as far as Rouen to carry out a kind of military reconnaissance, and returned to Paris after making sure that no fortified city of the west was disposed to hold out against him.

To protect her husband against a return of brotherly affection, and to attend personally the fulfillment of her revenge, Brunhild left the city of Metz to go to Sigibert's side. Such was her confidence in the certainty of her triumph that she wanted to make the journey accompanied by her two daughters, Ingund and Chlodoswinde, and her son Childebert, then a child of four. Her baggage wagons carried great riches, as well as her most precious golden ornaments and jewels. It would seem that, with feminine vanity, she wanted to dazzle the eye of the beholder, to appear arrayed in all her magnificence, and at the same time, to strike her enemies with terror. Far more than other Merovingian royal women, this princess, who was still young and remarkably beautiful, embodied the Gallic idea of what a queen should be, an idea going back to Roman imperial tradition. As a king's daughter born in a land where royalty, though of Barbarian origin, had a most imperial bearing, she commanded respect through her dignified manner and the nobility of her birth. On the day she arrived in Paris, the diocesan clergy and members of the senatorial families hurried to pay their respects; but the man who was by virtue of both ecclesiastical and civic rank the leading citizen did not appear. This was Bishop Germanus, today honored as St. Germain.

He was as much a civilized man as he was a Christian, one of those sensitive natures filled with unbelievable repugnance at the spectacle of the Roman world being governed by Barbarians, and wearing themselves out in a fruitless struggle against the brute force and passions of the kings. From the very beginning of the civil war, St. Germain had tried to interpose himself as mediator between Chilperic and Sigibert, and when the latter arrived had vainly renewed his entreaties and expostulations. Fatigue and despondency undermined his health; he fell ill, and in the midst of his physical sufferings, the present and future of Gaul appeared even blacker than before. "Why," he exclaimed, "why can we not have a moment's peace? Why cannot we say, like the apostles between two persecutions, 'here at last are endurable days.' " Confined to his bed by sickness and unable to declare his exhortations in favor of peace in person to Brunhild, he addressed them to her in writing.[11] This letter, which was delivered by a Frankish cleric named Godulf (and which has come down to us) begins with respectful excuses and protestations of devotion to Brunhild. Then it goes on in the following manner:

"Shall I repeat the rumors abroad among the people? They fill me with dismay, and I would like to be able to conceal them from the knowledge of your piety. They say that it is on your advice and at your instigation that the most glorious King Sigibert persists so obstinately in ruining this land. If I report talk of this kind, it is not because I lend credence to it, but only to implore you not to provide any pretext for such serious accusations. For a long while, this country has been far from happy. Still we do not despair of the divine mercy which can stay the arm of vengeance, provided that our rulers do not let themselves be dominated by thoughts of murder, by greed, which is the root of all evil, and by wrath, which drives men out of their wits.

"God knows it, and that is enough for me; I have wished to die so that their lives might be lengthened, I have wished to die before them, so that these eyes of mine might not see their ruin and that of this land. But they never weary of quarreling and making war, each throwing the blame on the other, taking no heed of God's judgment, and not wanting to leave anything to be decided by the divine omnipotence. Since neither of them will condescend to listen to me, it is to you that I address my entreaties, for if, because of their dissensions, the kingdom falls in ruins, there will be no great triumph in it for you and your children. Let this land have reason to congratulate itself on having made you welcome; show that you are come to save it and not to destroy it; by calming the king's anger, by persuading him to await the judgment of God in patience, you will reduce to nought the wicked talk of the people. . . .

"It is with sorrow that I write these things, for I know how kings and nations are cast down through offending God. Whosoever relies on the strength of his own arm will be confounded and will not obtain the victory; whosoever puts his trust in the number of his people, far from remaining secure, shall fall into danger of death; whosoever shall pride himself on his riches in gold and silver shall suffer disgrace and desolation before his avarice be appeased. That is what we read in the Scriptures. . . .

"It is a victory without honor to vanquish one's own brother, to bring one's own kinsmen into humiliation, and to ruin property founded by our ancestors. By fighting with one another it is against themselves that they are warring: each of them is working to destroy his own good fortune, and the foeman who watches them and who comes nearer rejoices to see that they are undoing one another. . . . We read that Queen Esther was God's instrument for the salvation of an entire people; let your prudence and the sincerity of your faith shine forth, by turning King Sigibert aside from an undertaking condemned by the divine law, by causing the people to enjoy the blessing of peace until in his justice the everlasting judge delivers his verdict. The man who would put aside brotherly affection, who would scorn the words of a spouse, who would refuse to yield to truth, all the prophets raise their voices against him, all the apostles curse him, and God himself in his omnipotence will judge him."

The sense of melancholy which pervades every line of this letter, the somewhat lofty gravity of the style, even that disdainful way of speaking about the two kings without actually naming them, in all of this there is something impressive; but it was all to no avail. Brunhild possessed in the highest degree that vindictive and relentless character whose archetype is personified by the old Germanic poets in a woman bearing the same name.[12] She took no account of either the threats of religion or those ancient warnings about the instability of fortune furnished by human experience. Far from giving thought to the truly critical position she would be in if her husband were to suffer some setback, she showed herself more impatient than ever to see him set off for Tournai to give the coup de grâce and complete his victory by murdering his brother.

Sigibert first sent some of his troops to invest the fortress of Tournai and to begin the siege; he himself made ready to go to the place where he was to be inaugurated as king of the western Franks. Neither Paris nor any other city was suitable for this ceremony, which was supposed to take place in the middle of an encampment. One of the Neustrian royal estates, at Vitry sur la Scarpe, was chosen for the meeting-place, either because it was not far from Tournai or because its northerly site made it a convenient rendezvous for the Frankish population, which became denser the further north one went. At the moment of his departure, when the king was setting out escorted by a detachment of picked horsemen, all uniformly armed with lances and painted shields, a pale man in priestly vestments appeared before him: it was Bishop Germain, who had just dragged himself from his sickbed to make one last, solemn attempt. "King Sigibert," he said, "if you are leaving with no intention of killing your brother, you will come back alive and victorious; if, however, you have different plans, you will die: for the Lord has said through the lips of Solomon, 'Whoso diggeth a pit shall fall therein . . .'" [13] The king was not troubled in the least by this unexpected speech; his mind was made up and he believed himself certain of victory. Without a single word of response he went on his way, and soon lost sight of the city where his wife and three children were to await his return.

Sigibert's progress through the kingdom which was about to belong to him by election was like a triumph before the event. The Gallic population and the diocesan clergy came in solemn procession to greet him; the Franks mounted their horses to join his train. Everywhere he was loudly hailed in both Teutonic and Latin. From the banks of the Seine as far as those of the Somme, the Gallo-Romans were numerically speaking predominant; but from the Somme northward an ever-stronger Germanic strain began to appear. The further one went, the more numerous became the Franks among the indigenous masses; they did not merely form little bands of idle warriors quartered far apart, as in the central provinces of Gaul; here they constituted entire tribes, living in farming settlements, on the edges of the marshes and the forests of the Belgian province. Vitry, near Douai, was more or less on the boundary of these two regions; the northern Franks, farmers and smallholders, and the southern Franks, military vassals, could easily come together there for the inauguration of the new king. Of all the great landowners and chieftains of the kingdom of Neustria, only one, named Ansowald, was not present at the rendezvous; his absence was conspicuous, and earned him a great reputation ever after for loyalty in misfortune.

The ceremony took place on a plain lined with the tents and huts of those who, unable to find lodgings in the buildings of the domain of

Vitry, were obliged to bivouac in the fields. The armed Franks formed a vast circle in whose center was seated King Sigibert, surrounded by his officers and great lords. Four sturdy soldiers came forward holding a shield on which they seated the king, and then lifted it shoulder-high. Sigibert went around the circle three times on this kind of traveling throne, escorted by the nobles and hailed by the multitude, who applauded by striking their iron-studded shields with the flat of their swords to make their acclamations more clamorous. After the third circuit, in accordance with the ancient Teutonic rite, the royal inauguration was complete, and from that moment on Sigibert was entitled to style himself king of the Franks, of the *Oster* as well as of the *Neoster-Rike*. The rest of that day and several of the following were spent in merrymaking, mock combats, and sumptuous banquets, during which the king, squandering the supplies of the Vitry farm, did the honors of his new kingdom to all comers.

A few miles away, Tournai, blockaded by the Austrasian troops, was the theater of very different scenes. Insofar as his gross constitution left him capable of mental anguish, Chilperic was suffering the distress of a betrayed and ousted king; Fredegund, in her fits of terror and despair, gave way to transports of bestial rage. She was pregnant and almost at term when she arrived within the walls of Tournai; she was soon delivered of a son in the midst of the tumult of the siege and the obsessive fear of death which never left her. Her first impulse was to abandon the child and let him perish for want of care and feeding, for she considered him a new source of danger. However, this wicked thought was of brief duration, and her maternal instinct soon regained the upper hand. The newborn child, taken to be baptized with the bishop of Tournai standing godfather, received, contrary to Frankish custom, an un-German name—Samson—which his parents in their distress chose as a portent of deliverance.

Judging his situation to be almost hopeless, the king was awaiting the outcome more or less impassively, but the queen, who was less slow-witted, racked her brains in a thousand ways, formed escape plans, and was constantly on the lookout for the least glimmer of hope. Among the men who had come to Tournai to share their ruler's fate, she noted two who by their looks and words displayed a deep feeling of sympathy and devotion. These were two young men of Frankish descent born in the Térouanne country and temperamentally predisposed to that fanatical loyalty which was to be the point of honor of the medieval vassal. Fredegund brought to bear all her cunning and all the prestige of her rank to win them over. She sent for them and told them of her woes and of her lack of hope; to her gracious words she added intoxicating drink, and, when she thought that she held them, as it were, spellbound, she suggested that they go to Vitry to assassinate King Sigibert. The young soldiers promised to do anything that the queen commanded; she then personally gave each of them a long sheath-knife, or as the Franks called it, a *skramasax*, whose blades she had (to make assurance double sure) poisoned. "Go," she said, "and if you come back alive I will load you and your posterity with honors: if you succumb I will distribute alms for your souls in all the holy places."

The two young men left Tournai and, passing themselves off as deserters, crossed the Austrasian lines and took the road leading to the royal domain at Vitry. When they arrived there, all the halls were still echoing with the merriment of the festivities and banquets. They said that they were from the kingdom of Neustria, that they had come to pay their respects to King Sigibert and to speak with him. In these early days of his kingship, Sigibert was obliged to be affable and to give audience to any man coming to claim protection or justice at his hands. The Neustrians requested a moment's private talk, which was readily granted; the knife that each carried at his belt did not arouse the slightest suspicion, being as it was part of the usual Germanic costume. While the king was benevolently listening to them, with one of them on his right and the other on his left, they simultaneously drew their skramasaxes and stabbed him twice between the ribs. Sigibert cried out once and fell dead, whereupon his chamberlain, Hareghisel, and a Goth named Sighila came running up sword in hand; the former was killed and the latter wounded by the assassins, who defended themselves in a kind of ecstatic frenzy. But other armed men immediately arrived, the room filled, and the two Neustrians, assailed from all sides, succumbed in an unequal fight.

On hearing of these events, the Austrasians besieging Tournai made haste to decamp and set off for their own country. Each of them was in a hurry to go and see what was happening at home, for the unexpected death of the king was bound to give the signal for a host of disorders, of acts of violence and lawlessness, in Austrasia. The large and formidable army thus melted away towards the Rhine, leaving Chilperic without an enemy and at liberty to go wherever he wished. Having escaped practically certain death, he left the walls of Tournai to go and take possession of his kingdom again. The domain of Vitry, witness to so many events, was the first place he went to. He did not find the resplendent Neustrian assembly still there (all the Neustrians having gone off about their business), only some Austrasian servants who were guarding Sigibert's body. Chilperic viewed the corpse without either remorse or hatred, and desired that his brother should have a burial fit for a king. At his command, Sigibert was dressed, as was the custom, in costly garments and arms, and buried in state in the village of Lambres sur la Scarpe.

Such was the end of this long drama, which begins with a murder and ends with a murder; a genuine tragedy in which nothing is lacking, neither the passions nor the characters nor that somber inevitability which is the soul of ancient tragedy and which bestows upon the fortuitous events of real life all the grandeur of poetry. On no other history is the seal of an irresistible destiny more deeply impressed than on that of the kings of the Merovingian dynasty. These sons of half-savage conquerors, born with their fathers' ideas in the midst of the enjoyments of luxury and the temptations of power, had neither rule nor measure in their passions and their desires. In vain did men more enlightened than themselves with regard to the affairs of this world and the conduct of life raise their voices to counsel moderation and prudence: they paid no heed. They were destroyed for want of understanding; and men said, "God's hand is in it." Such was the Christian formula; but at the sight of them, like drifting boats, blindly following the current of their brutal instincts and reckless lusts, it did not take a prophet to divine and predict the end which was in store for nearly all of them.

One day when Chilperic's family, restored to greatness, was residing in the palace of Braine, two Gallic bishops, Salvius of Albi and Gregory of Tours, after being received in audience, were walking together around the palace. In the middle of their conversation, Salvius, as though struck by an idea, suddenly broke off and said to Gregory: "Do you not see something above the roof of that building?" "I see," replied the bishop of Tours, "the new belvedere that the king has just had erected." "And you perceive nothing more?" "Nothing at all," replied Gregory; "if you can see something more, tell me what it is." Bishop Salvius sighed deeply and went on: "I see the sword of God's wrath hanging over this house." Four years later, the king of Neustria had died a violent death.

THIRD EPISODE
History of Merovech, Second Son[1]
of King Chilperic (575-578)

Since King Sigibert's departure, Brunhild, left alone in Paris, had each day seen her ambitious hopes grow greater; she believed that she was already queen of Neustria and mistress of the fate of her enemies when she learned of Sigibert's death, an event which suddenly plunged her from the highest fortune into extreme and imminent danger. Chilperic, who owed his victory to fratricide,[2] was advancing towards Paris to take possession of his brother's family and treasure. Not only were all the Neustrians without exception coming back to him, but the leading Austrasians were also beginning to be won over and, going to meet him on his march, were swearing allegiance to him, hoping to receive crown lands in return or to secure his patronage for themselves in the disorders threatening their country. As a reward for his defection, a nobleman named Godin or Godwin received great estates in the Soissons area; and the keeper of the royal signet-ring or great seal of Austrasia, the referendary Sig[3] or Sigoald, set the same example, which was followed by many others.

Stunned by her misfortunes and by these melancholy tidings, Brunhild did not know what to do and could not rely on anyone: the old imperial palace where she lived on the banks of the Seine had become a prison for her and her three children. Although she was not closely watched, she did not dare leave the palace to return to Austrasia, for fear of being stopped or betrayed in her flight, thereby aggravating an already highly perilous situation. Convinced that it would be impossible to flee with both her family and her baggage, she conceived the idea of saving at least her son who, though but a child, cast too great a shadow on Chilperic's ambition for his life to be spared. Young Childebert's escape was prepared in the greatest secrecy by the only devoted friend his mother still had; this was the same Duke Gundovald who two years before had so bungled the defence of Poitou against the Neustrian invaders. The child, placed in a large basket used for household provisions, was let down from a window and taken out of the city by night. Gundovald—or, according to other accounts, a mere retainer, less likely than he to arouse suspicions—traveled alone with King Sigibert's son and took him to Metz, to the great astonishment and delight of the Austrasians. His unforeseen arrival changed the face of the land; defections ceased and the eastern Franks hastened to set up their national kingship once more. A great assembly of the nobles and warriors of Austrasia was held in Metz; Childebert II, scarcely five years old, was there proclaimed king, and a council chosen from among the great lords and bishops took over the government in his name.

When he heard this news, which snatched from his grasp all hopes of combining without warfare his kingdom and his brother's, Chilperic, furious at seeing his most cherished design thwarted, made all speed to reach Paris and to secure at least Brunhild's person and fortune. King Sigibert's widow soon found herself in the presence of her mortal enemy, with no protection other than her beauty, her tears, and her woman's coquettishness. She was barely twenty-eight; and whatever the malevolent intentions of Fredegund's husband might have been toward her, the grace of her manner, that grace extolled by her contemporaries, would without doubt have made an impression on him, if other charms—those of the rich treasure, equally renowned—had not long since preoccupied him. But Merovech, the older of Chilperic's two sons (who were accompanying him) was deeply touched by the sight of this woman, so attractive and so unfortunate, and his pitying and admiring glances were not lost on Brunhild.

The young man's sympathy may have been a consolation for the captive queen, or, with the practiced eye of a woman skilled at intrigue, she may have glimpsed a means of salvation; at any event, she used all her art to gratify this budding passion, which became almost at once the blindest and most reckless of loves. By giving way to it, Merovech would necessarily become the enemy of his own family, the tool of an implacable hatred directed against his father and all his friends. Perhaps he did not clearly realize how criminal and how dangerous for him this violent situation would be; perhaps he did foresee everything but stubbornly went his own way and followed his own inclination despite the danger and his own conscience. But, however great Merovech's attentions to his uncle's widow, Chilperic noticed nothing, completely taken up as he was in having an inventory made of the sacks of gold and silver, the chests full of jewels, and the bales of precious cloth. It so happened that their number exceeded his hopes, and this happy discovery, all at once influencing his mood, made him milder and more lenient toward his prisoner. Instead of exacting a cruel vengeance for the harm that she had tried to do him, he was content merely to banish her; and he even left her, as a sort of courtesy, a small part of the treasure of which he had just despoiled her. Brunhild, treated more humanely than she would have dared hope, left under escort for the city of Rouen, which was her appointed place of exile; the only truly painful thing that she had to endure after so many fears was to be separated from her two daughters, Ingund and Chlodoswinde, whom King Chilperic, for reasons known only to himself, ordered to be taken to Meaux and kept under guard.

Her departure left young Merovech tormented by sorrow, made all the more bitter since he dared not confide in anyone; he followed his father to the palace at Braine, which already seemed to him a rather dismal place, and which now especially he must have found unbearable. Fredegund felt for her husband's children a true stepmother's hatred, which, if no other examples were known to us, might well have become proverbial. Any affection or kindness shown them by their father aroused her jealousy and spite. She longed for their deaths, and that of Theodebert, killed the previous year, had overjoyed her. Merovech, as future head of the family, was now the principal object of her aversion and of the countless persecutions that she excelled in stirring up against those she hated. The young prince would have liked to leave Braine and go to Rouen to find the woman whose eyes (and possibly words) had led him to believe that she loved him; but he had neither the means nor the excuse to undertake this journey safely. But soon, his father, without realizing what he was doing, gave him the opportunity himself.

Having settled the affairs of Neustria to the best of his ability, Chilperic, whose stubborn attachment to his schemes was due less to native energy than to slowness of mind, turned his thoughts to making a new attempt on the cities which had caused a two-year war between his brother and himself. These cities, recaptured by the Austrasian generals shortly before Sigibert's death, had all just acknowledged the authority of his son Childebert II: all, with the exception of Tours, that is, whose inhabitants—the more apprehensive about what the future held for them as they were less distant from the center of Neustria—pledged allegiance to King Chilperic. It was therefore a question of once more undertaking his campaign, so frequently launched anew, against Poitiers, Limoges, Cahors, and Bordeaux. Of the two sons remaining to him since Theodebert's death, Chilperic chose Merovech—the one who had not so far been beaten—as commander of the new expedition. His father put him in charge of a small army and ordered him to set out for Poitou.

This was not the direction that the young man would have chosen had he been free to march as he pleased, for in his heart he had an object of passion quite other than glory and battle. While journeying by easy stages towards the Loire with his horse and foot, he was thinking about Brunhild and regretted not finding himself on a road which might at least bring him closer to her. Ceaselessly taken up with this idea, he soon lost sight of the purpose of his journey and of his commission. When he reached Tours, instead of merely halting, he stayed in the city for more than a week, giving as a pretext his desire to celebrate Easter at St.

Martin's basilica. During this rest period he was engaged, not in making leisurely preparations for his campaign, but in arranging escape plans and amassing, by every possible means, an easily portable treasure composed of articles of great value and inconsiderable bulk. While his soldiers were roaming through the environs of the city, ransacking and ravaging, he wrung every last penny from a zealous supporter of his father: Leudast, count of Tours, who had received him in his home with every mark of respect. Having stripped this man's house of all its valuables, he now had at his disposal a sufficient sum to put his plans into effect. He left Tours, pretending that he was going to see his mother, who had been a nun at Le Mans ever since Chilperic had repudiated her to marry Fredegund. But instead of performing this filial duty and then rejoining his army, he kept going, and made for Rouen by way of Chartres and Evreux.

Whether or not Brunhild expected such a token of affection, or whether Merovech's arrival took her by surprise, she was so delighted, and their love progressed so rapidly, that a few days later she had completely forgotten Sigibert and agreed to marry Merovech. The degree of kinship between them made this marriage fall within the class of unions forbidden by the laws of the Church; and although religious scruples had little hold on the lovers' consciences, they were quite likely to see their desires thwarted for lack of a priest willing to exercise his ministry in defiance of canon law. The metropolitan bishop of Rouen at that time was a Gaul, one Praetextatus, who, by a curious coincidence, happened to be Merovech's godfather and who, by virtue of this spiritual paternity, had ever since the day of his baptism retained a genuine fatherly affection for him. This softhearted, weak-willed man was unable to withstand the earnest entreaties (and possibly the passionate outbursts) of the young prince he called his son; and, despite the obligations of his office, he let himself be induced to solemnize the marriage of the nephew with the uncle's widow.

During the decline of Gaul into barbarism, impatience and neglect of all rules constituted the sickness of the age, and private whim or the inspiration of the moment tended to replace law and order even among the most enlightened of men. The natives of Gaul were only too ready to follow the example set by their Teutonic conquerors, and the laxity of the former competed with the brutality of the latter for the same ends. Blindly obeying an impulse of sympathy, Praetextatus secretly celebrated the nuptial mass of Merovech and Brunhild; and, holding the hands of the bride and groom in accordance with the rite, pronounced the sacramental form of words of the marriage benediction. This act of condescension would one day cost him his life, and its consequences were no less fatal to the foolhardy young man who had wrested it from him.[4]

Chilperic was in Paris, full of hopes for the success of the Aquitanian expedition, when he received the strange news of his son's flight and marriage. To his violent outburst of rage were added suspicions of treason and fears of a plot against his authority and his life. In order to foil it, if there was still time, and to remove Merovech from Brunhild's influence and evil counsels, he immediately set out for Rouen, quite determined to separate them and to have their marriage annulled. Meanwhile the newly wedded couple, completely absorbed in the joys of the first days of marriage, had till now thoughts only for their love, and consequently, despite her ready and resourceful wit, Brunhild was taken unawares by the arrival of the king of Neustria. So as not to fall into his hands during the first heat of his anger, she hit on the idea of taking refuge with her husband in a little church dedicated to St. Martin on the city ramparts. It was one of those wooden basilicas then common throughout Gaul, whose slender structure—its pillars formed of several lashed-together tree-trunks and its arches necessarily sharp-pointed, because of the difficulty of making round ones with such materials—in all probability furnished the prototype of the Gothic style which was to dominate great architecture several centuries later.

Although such a sanctuary was very uncomfortable owing to the poverty of its lodgings, which, adjoining the walls of the little church and sharing in its privileges, served as living quarters for the refugees, Merovech and Brunhild settled down there, determined not to leave the place so long as they believed themselves in danger. In vain did the king of Neustria try all kinds of subterfuges to lure them outside; they were not in the least taken in by them, and since Chilperic dared not resort to violence, fearing to call down upon himself the redoubtable vengeance of St. Martin, he had no alternative but to come to terms with his son and daughter-in-law. Before surrendering, they demanded that the king should promise, on oath, not to make use of his authority to separate them. Chilperic did indeed make this promise, but in a slily perfidious manner which left him perfectly free to act as he saw fit: he swore that, if such was the will of God, he would not separate them. Despite the ambiguity of the terms of this pledge, the refugees were satisfied, and overcome partly by weariness and partly by persuasion, they left the privileged enclosure to which St. Martin's church transmitted its right of asylum. Chilperic, somewhat reassured by his son's submissive demeanour, prudently restrained his anger and let no outward sign of his suspicions appear; he even embraced the husband and wife and sat down at table with them, affecting an air of paternal geniality. After spending two or three days in perfect dissimulation, he suddenly took Merovech away with him to Soissons, leaving Brunhild in Rouen under a stricter guard.

A few miles before reaching Soissons, the king of Neustria and his young traveling companion were stopped by the most sinister news. The city was being besieged by an Austrasian army; Fredegund, who was there awaiting her husband's return, had barely time to flee with her stepson Clovis and her own son, who was still a babe in arms. Increasingly positive accounts left no room for doubt as to the circumstances of this unexpected attack. It was the Austrasian renegades, and at their head Godwin and Sigoald, who, deserting Chilperic for the young King Childebert II, were signalling this change of heart by an audacious *coup de main* against the capital of Neustria. Their small army was made up mostly of inhabitants of the Rheims area, turbulent folk who, at the first rumor of a war with the Neustrians, crossed the border to go plundering on enemy territory. King Chilperic had no trouble marshalling a more considerable force than this between Paris and Soissons. He at once marched to the relief of the beleaguered city; but instead of making a sharp attack on the Austrasians, he was content to show them his troops and to send word to them, hoping that they would retire without a battle. Godwin and his companions replied that they were there to fight: but they fought badly, and Chilperic, victorious for the first time, joyfully entered his capital.

His joy was short-lived, and it was not long before serious reflections made him uneasy and anxious. It occurred to him that the Austrasian attempt against Soissons was the result of a conspiracy instigated by Brunhild, that Merovech had known about it, that he had actually been a party to it, and that his air of obedience and good faith was merely a mask of hypocrisy. Fredegund venomously seized the opportunity to magnify the youth's imprudent conduct through false insinuations. She credited him with great designs of which he was incapable, the ambition to unseat his father and to rule over the whole of Gaul with the woman who had just been joined to him in incestuous marriage. Thanks to these skillful maneuvers, the king's misgivings and mistrust increased almost to the point of panic. Imagining that his life was endangered by his son's presence, he had his weapons taken away and commanded that he be kept under close guard until he had made a definite decision about him.

Some days later, an embassy sent by the lords governing Austrasia in the name of the young King Childebert, and charged with disavowing Godwin's endeavor as an act of private warfare, presented itself to Chilperic. The king of Neustria feigned so great a love of peace and so much affection for his nephew that the envoys did not scruple to join to their apologies a request whose success was highly problematic, namely, the setting at liberty of Brunhild and her two daughters. Under any other circumstances, Chilperic would have taken good care not to release at the first appeal an enemy who had fallen into his clutches; but, struck by the notion that Merovech's wife would disrupt his kingdom, and seizing the opportunity to perform a prudent act with a good grace, he readily agreed to what was asked of him.

At this unhoped-for repeal of the orders keeping her in exile, Brunhild made as much haste to leave both Rouen and Neustria as if there had been an earthquake. Fearing the slightest delay, she hurried the preparations for her journey and even resolved to set off without her baggage, which, despite the grievous diminution it had suffered, was still of great value. Several thousand gold pieces and several bales containing jewels and precious fabrics were at her command left with Bishop Praetextatus, who, by agreeing to hold these riches in trust, compromised himself for the second time—even more seriously than the first—for love of his godson Merovech. Having left Rouen, the mother of Childebert II went to fetch her two daughters at Meaux; then, avoiding the approaches to Soissons, she made for Austrasia and arrived there without hindrance. Her presence, eagerly desired in that country, before very long aroused the jealousy of the powerful and ambitious chieftains who wanted to remain solely responsible for the tutelage of the young king.

Brunhild's departure did not put an end to either King Chilperic's suspicions or the harsh treatment meted out to his eldest son. Merovech, deprived of his weapons and his military shoulder-belt (which, by Germanic custom, was tantamount to loss of civil rights) was still under close arrest. As soon as the king had gotten over the agitation produced by so many events in such rapid succession, he returned to his perennial plans for the conquest of the five cities of Aquitaine, of which Tours alone was actually in his possession. No longer having to choose between his two sons, he handed over the command of his new expedition to Clovis, despite his former misadventure. The young prince's orders were to make for Poitiers and to collect as many men as he could in Touraine and Anjou. Having raised a small army, he took Poitiers unopposed and there joined up with a much larger force which was being brought to him from the south by a great Gallic nobleman called Desiderius.

Desiderius was a man of high birth, with great property near Albi; he was unruly and ruthlessly ambitious (as was not uncommon in those days) but surpassed his rivals of Barbarian extraction by a certain breadth of outlook and considerable military aptitudes. As governor of a district adjoining the frontier with the Goths, he had made himself feared by that nation, which was hostile to the Gallo-Franks, and had acquired by his brilliant feats of arms much renown and influence among the southern Gauls, thus accounting for the large number of well-equipped men who came, under his command, to link up with the Neustrian troops. From the moment the two armies united, it was Desiderius who assumed command. Both as warrior and statesman, he judged Chilperic's plan for the piecemeal subjugation of four cities separated by considerable distances to be a paltry one, and substituted his own strategy for the conquest of all the territory included between the Loire, the Atlantic, the Pyrenees, and the Cévennes. Since this projected invasion admitted of no distinction between the cities dependent upon Austrasia and those belonging to Guntram, Desiderius did not spare the latter, and began by taking Saintes, which opened the road to Bordeaux for him.

At this most unlooked-for aggression, King Guntram for the second time abandoned his habitual lethargy; in great haste he dispatched, with sufficient forces, the celebrated Provençal patrician Eonius Mummolus, who had at that time a universal reputation for invincibility. Mummolus, advancing by forced marches across the plain of Auvergne, entered the territory of Limoges and forced Desiderius to abandon the west country to come and meet him. The two armies, each commanded by a Gaul, soon confronted one another; there took place between them a pitched battle of a kind not seen in Gaul since Roman tactics had given way to skirmishing and guerilla warfare, which was all the Barbarians understood. The victory was keenly contested, but Mummolus was victorious, as usual, and compelled his adversary to retreat after fearful carnage. The chronicles tell of five thousand dead on one side and of twenty-four thousand on the other; this is hard to believe, yet the very exaggeration demonstrates how greatly contemporaries were impressed.

Seeing the Neustrian army utterly destroyed, Mummolus returned home, either because such were his orders or because he believed he had done enough. Although victorious, he conceived a high regard for the skill of the man who had just crossed swords with him, and this opinion later served to unite them in an enterprise which aimed at nothing less than the founding of a new kingdom in Gaul. Desiderius soon found himself at the head of a large army once more, and, helped by racial sympathy, and by the personal credit which he enjoyed with the Gallo-Romans, he resumed his military operations with a success that was thenceforth unbroken. Five years later, every city from Dax to Poitiers and from Albi to Limoges belonged to the king of Neustria, and the Roman responsible for this conquest, now established in Toulouse with the title of duke, was exercising a kind of viceroyalty.

Merovech had already spent several months under house arrest when sentence was passed upon him by the family tribunal, in which his stepmother Fredegund had the deciding vote. The sentence, against which there was no appeal, condemned him to lose his hair: that is to say, to be cut off from the Merovingian dynasty. In accordance with an ancient custom, probably once connected with some religious teaching, the special attribute of that dynasty and the symbol of its hereditary right to kingly rank was in effect a long head of hair, preserved intact from the moment of birth and forever untouched by scissors. The descendants of the original Merovech could thus be distinguished among all the Franks;

in the most commonplace clothes, they could always be recognized by their hair, which, now tied in a braid, now hanging loose, covered their shoulders and hung to their waists. To cut off the smallest part of this adornment was equivalent to the profanation of their persons, the taking away of their right to consecration, and the suspension of their title to the sovereignty, a suspension tacitly limited by custom to the time needed for the hair to grow to a certain length again.

A Merovingian prince could suffer this temporary degradation in one of two ways: either his hair was cut in the ordinary Frankish style, i.e., so that it reached the collar; or else it was cropped very close in the Roman fashion—and this type of degradation, more humiliating than the first, was generally accompanied by the ecclesiastical tonsure. Such was the severe decision taken by King Chilperic in his son's case; at one stroke the young man lost both the right to rule and the right to bear arms. He was ordained priest against his will in defiance of canon law, compelled to surrender the sword and shoulder-belt which had been given to him in solemn Teutonic ceremony, to take off every piece of his national costume and to put on Roman clothes, which was the dress of the clergy. Merovech was ordered to mount his horse in this attire, so little suited to his tastes, and to set out for the monastery of St. Calais near Le Mans, where he was to be instructed—in complete seclusion—in the monastic rule. Escorted by armed horsemen, he began his journey with no hope of escape or rescue, but perhaps consoled by the familiar saying, composed for members of his family who had been the victims of a similar fate: "Green is the wood, the leaves will grow again."

There was just then in the basilica of St. Martin of Tours—the most highly respected of religious sanctuaries—a refugee whom King Chilperic was trying to have driven out so that he could get his hands on him. This man was the Austrasian Guntram-Bose, commonly rumored to have personally killed young Theodebert, or at the very least to have allowed his soldiers to butcher him when, as a generous enemy, he might have spared his life. Taken by surprise right in the middle of Aquitaine by the terrible news of Sigibert's murder, and afraid (not without reason) of falling into the clutches of the king of Neustria, he had come to seek safety under the protection of St. Martin. To this mystical shield was joined—further guaranteeing Duke Guntram's security—the more visible but no less effective intervention of the bishop of Tours, Georgius Florentius Gregorius, who staunchly saw to it that the rights of his church, and especially the right of asylum, were upheld. Whatever the peril, in those days when society was turned upside down, of defending the cause of the weak and the outlawed against the brute force and bad faith of the mighty, Gregory displayed in this ever-renewed struggle an unwearying steadfastness and a prudent yet intrepid dignity.

Since the day Guntram-Bose had installed himself with his two daughters in one of the houses lining the courtyard of St. Martin's basilica, the bishop of Tours and his clergy no longer had a moment's rest. They were obliged to resist King Chilperic who, thirsting for revenge on the refugee but not daring to take him from his asylum by violent means, wanted—thus sparing himself the crime and the dangers of sacrilege—to coerce the clerics to expel him from the privileged enclosure themselves. First of all there came a friendly request from the king, next menacing hints, and finally, since words remained ineffective, comminatory measures apt to strike terror into not just the clergy, but the entire population of Tours.

A Neustrian duke called Rokkolen pitched camp at the city gates with a troop of men levied in the territory of Le Mans. He established his headquarters in a house belonging to the metropolitan church of Tours, and from there dispatched this message addressed to the bishop: "If you do not send Duke Guntram out of the basilica, I will burn the city, outskirts and all." The bishop calmly replied that such a thing was not possible. But he received a second, even more ominous message: "If you do not expel the king's enemy this very day, I am going to destroy all the vegetation for a league around the city, so that a plough can be driven through there." Bishop Gregory was no more moved than he had been the first time, and Rokkolen, who to all appearances had too few men with him to make any serious attempt against the population of a great city, had to be content, after such a deal of boasting, with sacking and demolishing the house which had served as his lodging. This was built of timbers joined and fastened with iron pins, which the soldiers from Le Mans carried off with the rest of the booty in their leather knapsacks. Gregory of Tours was just congratulating himself on seeing the end of this trying ordeal, when fresh troubles came upon him, brought about by a quite unpredictable sequence of events.

Guntram-Bose was a notably strange character. Though a German, he outdid in ingenuity, resourcefulness, and instinctive knavery (if this word may be used here) the subtlest of the Gallo-Romans. His was not the ordinary Teutonic bad faith, the crude lie accompanied by a guffaw; it was something at once more refined and more perverse, a spirit of intrigue both universal and, as it were, nomadic, for he practiced it throughout the length and breadth of Gaul. No one knew better than this Austrasian how to push others into a tight corner and to extricate himself just in time. It was said of him that never had he pledged his word to a friend without immediately betraying him, which in all likelihood explains his Teutonic nickname.[5] While under the protection of St. Martin of Tours, instead of living the usual life of a refugee of distinction—i.e., spending the day eating and drinking with no concern for anything else—Duke Guntram was on the lookout for all the latest news, and would inquire about the smallest event in order to turn it to his advantage. He learned both swiftly and accurately about Merovech's misadventures, his forced ordination and his banishment to the monastery of St. Calais. The idea occurred to him of using this as a foundation for a plan of deliverance for himself; of inviting Chilperic's son to join him, to share his asylum, and to come to some agreement with him as to means of getting both of them into Austrasia. Guntram-Bose was counting on increasing his own chances of escape by the far more numerous ones open to the young prince thanks to the prestige of his rank and the devotion of his friends. He confided his plan and his hopes to a subdeacon of Frankish origin named Rikulf, who out of friendship undertook to go to St. Calais and, if possible, to have an interview with Merovech.

While Rikulf was making his way towards the city of Le Mans, Gaïlen, a young Frankish warrior bound to Merovech by ties of vassalage and the brotherhood of arms, was lying in wait near St. Calais for the arrival of the escort which was supposed to hand the new cloistered monk over to his superiors and jailers. As soon as the escort appeared, a troop of men posted in ambush swooped down on it in superior numbers, forcing it to take flight and to give up its prisoner. Merovech, restored to freedom, joyfully took off his clerical dress and put on his national costume once more. This was wholly military, the footgear fastened by long leather cross-garters, the tight, short-sleeved tunic, barely reaching the knee, and the fur jerkin, over which was worn the shoulder-belt from which hung the sword. Such was the attire in which Guntram-Bose's messenger found Merovech, wondering which way he should go to be completely safe. Rikulf's proposal was accepted without much scrutiny, and Chilperic's son, escorted this time by his friends, immediately set out for Tours. A traveling cloak with a deep hood protected him from the astonishment and derision that would have been caused by the sight of a priestly head on a warrior's shoulders. When he reached Tours, he dismounted at the foot of the walls and, with his head still muffled up in his hood, strode straight towards St. Martin's basilica, all the doors of which were standing wide open at that moment.

It was a solemn feast day, and the bishop of Tours, who was celebrating pontifical high mass, had just given the faithful communion in both kinds. The loaves of bread remaining after the consecration of the eucharist covered the altar, placed on cloths beside the large two-handled chalice containing the wine. Custom dictated that at the end of the mass these loaves, which had not been consecrated but merely blessed by the priest, should be cut up and distributed among those present; this was called "giving eulogias."[6] The entire assembly, with the exception of the excommunicated, took part in this distribution performed by the deacons (as that of the eucharist was performed by the priest or bishop officiating). After having gone the length of the basilica, giving to each his portion of the holy bread, the deacons of St. Martin saw near the doors a stranger whose half-concealed face seemed to indicate that he had no intention of making himself known: they passed him by suspiciously without offering him any bread.

Young Merovech's temper, naturally violent, had been made yet more fiery by the worrying and exhausting journey. Finding himself deprived of a favor that everyone else had obtained, he gave way to an outburst of bitter resentment. Pushing through the crowded nave, he went right into the choir where Gregory was sitting with another bishop, Raghenemod, a Frank who had just succeeded St. Germain in the metropolitan see of Paris. When he came up to the dais on which Gregory was seated in full pontificals, Merovech said to him in a sharp, imperious tone: "Bishop, why don't they give me eulogias like the rest of the faithful? Tell me if I am excommunicated."[7] Thereupon, he threw back his hood and disclosed to the onlookers his face, flushed with anger, and the strange figure of a tonsured soldier. The bishop of Tours had no difficulty in recognizing King Chilperic's elder son, for he had often seen him and already knew his entire history. The young fugitive appeared before him guilty of a double infraction of canon law, marriage at one of the forbidden degrees, and renunciation of the priesthood, a sin so grave that strict casuists gave it the name of apostasy. In the state of flagrant culpability in which his secular costume and his weapons placed him, Merovech could not, without undergoing the ordeal of an ecclesiastical trial, be admitted to the communion of consecrated bread and wine, or even to that of bread which had simply been blessed (which was in a way the figure of the other). This is what Bishop Gregory said in his usual calmly dignified way, but his grave and gentle speech only exasperated the young man's fury. Flinging aside all restraint and all respect for the sanctity of the place, he cried: "You have no power to suspend me from Christian communion without the assent of your brother bishops, and if you do cut me off on your own private authority, I will behave like someone who has been excommunicated and kill somebody here and now." These grimly uttered words appalled those who heard them and greatly saddened the bishop. Fearing to drive this frenzied young Barbarian to the breaking point, thus causing some great misfortune, he gave in under duress and, for the sake of legal form at least having conferred a while with his colleague from Paris, had the eulogias which Merovech claimed given to him.

As soon as Chilperic's son, his brother-warrior Gaïlen, his youthful companions, and numerous servants had taken lodgings on St. Martin's square, the bishop of Tours made haste to comply with certain formalities required by Roman law,[8] of which the main one was to notify the competent magistrate and the plaintiff of the arrival of each new fugitive. In the present case, there was no judge and no interested party other than King Chilperic himself; accordingly, he had to be notified, quite apart from the need to assuage the bitterness of his resentment by a display of deference. A deacon of the metropolitan church of Tours set off for Soissons, the Neustrian royal capital, with the mission of giving an exact account of all that had just occurred. His associate in this embassy was Nicetius, a kinsman of the bishop who was going to Chilperic's court on private business.

Having reached the palace of Soissons and been admitted to an audience with the king, they were beginning to set forth the reasons for their journey when Fredegund arrived unexpectedly and said: "These men are spies, they have come here to find out what the king is doing so that they can tell Merovech." Her words were enough to excite Chilperic's suspicious mind; the order was at once given to arrest Nicetius and the deacon who was the bearer of the message. They were robbed of all the money they had on them and taken away to a remote part of the kingdom, from which neither of them returned until they had spent seven months in exile.

While the messenger and Gregory's relative were being treated so roughly, Gregory himself received a dispatch in the king's name which read as follows: "Drive the apostate out of your basilica, otherwise I will destroy the entire region by fire." The bishop simply replied that such a thing had never happened, not even in the time of the Gothic kings, who were heretics, and that therefore it would not happen in a time of true Christianity. Compelled by this response to proceed from threats to deeds, Chilperic made up his mind, but only halfheartedly. At the instigation of Fredegund, who had not the slightest fear of sacrilege, it was resolved that troops would be collected and that the king himself would lead them to chastise the city of Tours and to force St. Martin's sanctuary.

On hearing of these preparations, Merovech was gripped with a terror which he expressed in terms tinged with religious feeling: "God forbid," he cried, "that the holy basilica of my lord Martin undergo any violence, or that his land be laid waste on my account." He wanted to leave at once with Guntram-Bose and attempt to reach Austrasia, where he deluded himself that he would find a sure refuge with Brunhild, as well as tranquillity, wealth, and all the pleasures of power. However, they were by no means ready for so long a journey; as yet they had neither enough men nor sufficient outside contacts. Guntram's opinion was that they must wait and not, for fear of the present danger, plunge into a much greater one. Incapable of undertaking anything without the cooperation of his new friend, the young prince sought a cure for his anxieties in an uncharacteristically fervent piety. He resolved to spend a whole night praying in the sanctuary of the basilica, and having had his most valued belongings brought in, he placed them on St. Martin's tomb as an offering; then, kneeling down near the sepulchre, he entreated the saint to come to his relief, to grant him his favors, to see to it that his liberty might quickly be restored to him, and that one day he might become king.

For Merovech these two desires were inseparable, to all intents and purposes, and the latter, it would appear, played quite an important part in his conversations with Guntram-Bose and in their joint plans. Guntram, full of confidence in his own resourcefulness, rarely invoked the protection of the saints; but, on the other hand, had recourse to fortune-tellers in order to test the soundness of his machinations by means of their art. Leaving Merovech to pray alone, therefore, he dispatched one of his servants to consult a woman he claimed to be very clever, who had, among other things, foretold the year, the day, and the hour of King Charibert's death. Questioned in Duke Guntram's name about what the future held for him and for Merovech, the witch (who probably knew all about both of them) gave this reply, addressed to Guntram himself: "It will come to pass that King Chilperic will die within the year, and that Merovech will obtain the royal power to the exclusion of his brothers; as for you, Guntram, for five years you will be senior duke of the realm, but in the sixth year, through the favor of the people you will receive the rank of bishop in a city located on the left bank of the Loire; and you will leave this world at last old and full of days."

Guntram-Bose, who spent his life making fools of people, was himself duped by the rascally tricks of sorcerers and fortune-tellers. He was overjoyed at this preposterous prophecy, which was unquestionably consistent with his ambitious dreams and innermost desires. Thinking that the city so vaguely indicated could be none other than Tours, and already seeing himself in his mind's eye as Gregory's successor on the pontifical throne, he took pains to inform Gregory—with mischievous satisfaction—about his coming good fortune, for the title of bishop was much coveted by the Barbarian chiefs. Gregory had just arrived at St. Martin's basilica to celebrate the evening services when the Austrasian duke, like a man convinced of the infallible knowledge of his prophetess, let him into his strange secret. The bishop replied: "It is of God that such things must be asked," and could not help laughing. But this foolish and insatiable vanity brought his thoughts painfully back to the men and the miseries of his day. Gloomy reflections preoccupied him in the midst of the psalm-singing, and when, after the evening devotions, wishing to take a little rest, he had gone to bed in a lodging near the church, the crimes of which this church was apparently to be the theatre in the unnatural war between father and son, all the misfortunes which he foresaw but was powerless to avert pursued him almost until he fell asleep. As he slept, the same ideas, transformed into ghastly images, still came into his mind. He saw an angel hovering over the basilica and crying in a doleful voice: "Alas! Alas! God has smitten Chilperic and all his sons! Not one of them will survive him and possess his kingdom!" This dream appeared to Gregory to be a revelation of the future far more worthy of credence than all the responses and marvels of the soothsayers.

Merovech, who was temperamentally frivolous and irresponsible, soon turned to amusements more in keeping with his unruly habits than vigils and prayers at the tombs of the saints. The law consecrating the inviolability of religious sanctuaries was intended to guarantee the fugitives complete freedom to procure supplies of every kind, so that it would not be possible for their pursuers to starve them out. The priests of St. Martin's basilica themselves shouldered the burden of providing the basic necessities of life for those of their guests who were poor and without servants. The wealthy were served sometimes by their own retainers, who came and went quite freely, sometimes by men and women from the outside world, whose presence often gave rise to troubles and scandals. At all hours, the courtyards and colonnades of the basilica were filled with a bustling crowd or with idle and curious strollers. At mealtimes, the din of drunken feasting occasionally drowned out the singing in church and disturbed the priests in their choir-stalls and the monks in their cells. Sometimes too the diners, flown with wine, would quarrel to the point of coming to blows, and bloody brawls took place at the doors and even within the church itself.

If similar disorders did not actually follow in the wake of the banquets at which Merovech was trying to drown his sorrows with his fellow-refugees, there was no lack of noisy merriment: roars of laughter and coarse witticisms echoed in the hall, especially when the names of Chilperic and Fredegund were mentioned. Merovech did not spare the one any more than the other. He used to recount his father's crimes and his stepmother's dissolute behavior, calling Fredegund an infamous whore and Chilperic an imbecile husband, the persecutor of his own children. "Although there was a good deal of truth in all this," says the contemporary historian, "I do not think that it was pleasing to God that such matters should be divulged by a son." As a guest at Merovech's table one day, this historian (Gregory of Tours himself) heard the young man's disgraceful remarks with his own ears. At the end of the meal, Merovech, who alone remained with his pious guest, felt himself in a devout mood and begged the bishop to read him something for the instruction of his soul. Gregory picked up the book of Proverbs and, opening it at random, happened upon the following verse: "The eye that mocketh at his father, . . . the ravens of the valley shall pick it out." [9] The bishop took this passage, which he had so felicitously encountered, for a second revelation of the future, just as ominous as the first.

Meanwhile, Fredegund—a more determined hater and in any case more energetic than her husband—resolved to forestall the expedition then being prepared and to have Merovech murdered by means of an ambush. Leudast, count of Tours, who was eager to secure the queen's favor and who moreover had the previous year's ransacking of his house to avenge, volunteered with alacrity to do the deed. Counting on the want of foresight of the man he intended to surprise and kill, he tried various strategems to lure him outside the prescribed bounds of sanctuary, but failed. Through either savage spite or the desire to arouse the young prince's anger and make him lose all sense of caution, he had armed men attack his servants in the city streets. Most of them were massacred, and the infuriated Merovech would have charged headlong into the trap if the prudent Guntram had not restrained him. His rage knew no bounds, and he said that he would not rest until he had most bloodily punished Fredegund's toady. Guntram advised him to take reprisals in a quarter where the danger would be nonexistent and the gains considerable, and to exact payment for the attack not from Leudast, who was on his guard, but from another—any other—of King Chilperic's friends or familiars.

Marileïf, chief physician to the king, who was a very rich and unwarlike man, happened to be in Tours at that time on the way from Soissons to Poitiers, his birthplace. He had very few people with him but a great deal of baggage; and nothing was simpler for Merovech's young warrior companions than to abduct him from his inn. They burst in unexpectedly, in fact, and cruelly beat the peaceable physician, who, fortunately for himself, managed to escape and take refuge, almost naked, in the cathedral—leaving his gold, his silver, and the rest of his baggage in the hands of his assailants. All this was considered fair game by Chilperic's son, who, content with the trick he had just played on his father and thinking himself sufficiently avenged, was pleased to show mercy. At the bishop's request, he had poor Marileïf (who did not dare leave his sanctuary) informed that he was at liberty to continue his journey. But just as Merovech was congratulating himself on having for his chance companion and bosom friend a man as sagacious as Guntram-Bose, the latter was making no bones about selling his services to the mortal enemy of the thoughtless youth who trusted him implicitly.

Far from sharing King Chilperic's hatred for Duke Guntram on account of the murder of Theodebert, Fredegund was grateful to him for the deed which had rid her of one of her stepsons (as she desired to be rid of the other two). Her favorable interest in the Austrasian duke had become still keener since she had glimpsed the possibility of using him as the instrument of Merovech's destruction. Guntram-Bose did not willingly undertake perilous errands, but the bad success of the ventures of Count Leudast—who was more violent than clever—induced the queen to turn to the man who, while not actually performing the assassination with his own hand, could nevertheless make it foolproof by his cunning. She therefore sent a trustworthy person to Guntram to give him this message in her name: "If you succeed in having Merovech come out of the basilica so that he may be killed, I will give you a magnificent present." Guntram-Bose gladly accepted the proposition. Convinced that the crafty Fredegund had already made all necessary arrangements and that assassins had been posted to lie in wait in the vicinity of Tours, he went to find Merovech and said in the most playful fashion: "Why are we living a cowardly, slothful life here, and why do we stay cowering like idiots near this basilica? Let us send for our horses, let us take our hawks and hounds with us and go hunting, to get some exercise, breathe the fresh air, and enjoy a fine view."

The need for space and open air felt so keenly by prisoners went to Merovech's heart, and his easily influenced character made him approve without question of everything his friend suggested. He welcomed this alluring invitation with all the vivacity of youth. The horses were at once brought into the basilica courtyard, and the two fugitives went out in complete hunting array, with their hawks on their wrists, escorted by their servants and followed by their hounds on the leash. They took as the goal for their outing an estate belonging to the church of Tours which was situated at the village of Jocundiacum (nowadays Jouay), not far from the city. They spent the whole day thus, hunting and coursing together, without Guntram's giving the least sign of abstraction or looking as if he were thinking of anything other than enjoying himself as best he might. But what he was expecting did not take place; neither during the day's riding nor on the return journey did any armed band appear to pounce on Merovech, either because Fredegund's emissaries had not as yet reached Tours, or because her instructions had been bungled. So Merovech returned peacefully to the enclosure which served as his place of refuge, happy to have spent some hours at liberty and not in the least suspecting that he had been in danger of perishing through the most arrant treachery.

The army which was supposed to march on Tours was ready, but when it actually came to setting out, Chilperic all at once became irresolute and timorous: he would have liked to know exactly what there was to fear from the resentment of St. Martin against those who infringed upon his privileges: and since no one could give him any information about that, he hit on the curious notion of writing a letter to the saint in person, requesting a plain and positive reply. He accordingly drew up a letter, setting out in the manner of a forensic address his paternal grounds for complaint against the murderer of his son Theodebert, and appealed to the justice of the holy confessor against this great sinner. The petition concluded with the following request: "Is it or is it not lawful for me to take Guntram out of the basilica?" Even more peculiar is the fact that there was a ruse in all this and that King Chilperic wanted to trick the saint, promising himself that if permission were granted with respect to Guntram, he would also make use of it to seize Merovech (whose name he did not mention for fear of being thought a wicked father). This singular missive was taken to Tours by a Frankish cleric named Baudeghisel, who placed it on St. Martin's tomb with a blank sheet of paper beside it so that the saint could write his reply. Three days later the messenger came back and, finding the sheet still on the stone sepulchre just as he had left it, without the smallest trace of writing on it, he was of the opinion that St. Martin refused to explain himself, and returned to King Chilperic.

What the king feared above all else was that Merovech might go to join Brunhild in Austrasia and that, with her advice and her money, he might succeed in creating a large following among the Neustrian Franks. Such fears even prevailed over his hatred for Guntram-Bose, whom he was half-inclined to pardon, provided he in no way furthered the departure of his companion in refuge. This gave rise to a new plan in which Chilperic once more reveals the same constitutionally ponderous and painstaking shrewdness. The plan consisted in extracting from Guntram (without whom Merovech, for lack of resourcefulness and determination, was incapable of undertaking his journey) his sworn promise not to leave the basilica without first notifying the king. Chilperic expected in this manner to be warned early enough to be able to cut off communications between Tours and the Austrasian frontier. He sent emissaries to hold secret talks with Guntram, who was not backward in this duel of double-dealers. Trusting little in the words of reconciliation sent him by Chilperic, but thinking that in them lay a possible last chance for safety if all else failed him, he took the required oath in the very sanctuary of the basilica, with one hand on the silk cloth covering the high altar. This accomplished, he was no less busy than before in getting everything ready, in the greatest secrecy, for a sudden escape.

Since the stroke of luck which had caused the money of the physician Marileïf to fall into the fugitives' hands, their preparations for leaving had been going on apace. Professional cutthroats, a class of men created by the Conquest, came forward in droves to serve as their escort all the way to their destination: there were soon more than five hundred of them. With such a force, escape was easy and it was more than likely that they would reach Austrasia. Guntram-Bose no longer saw any reason for delay, and—taking good care, despite his oath, not to give the king any advance warning—he told Merovech that they had to think about leaving. Merovech, weak and irresolute when not buoyed up by passion, wavered on the brink of this great enterprise, and relapsed into his anxieties again. "But don't we have the soothsayer's predictions in our favor?" said Guntram. The young prince was not reassured, and in order to take his mind off his gloomy forebodings, he wanted to make inquiries about the future at a better source.

There was at that time a method of religious divination forbidden by Church Councils, but practiced in Gaul, in defiance of this prohibition, by even the wisest and most enlightened of men. Merovech took it into his head to have recourse to it. He repaired to the chapel where St. Martin's tomb was, and placed on the sepulchre three books of the Bible: the Book of Kings, the Psalms, and the Gospels. All night long he prayed to God and the holy confessor to let him know what was going to happen and whether or not he should hope to obtain his father's kingdom. Next, he fasted for three whole days, and on the fourth, returning to the tomb, opened the three volumes one after the other. First of all, in the Book of Kings, which he was especially eager to consult, he came upon a page at the top of which was the following verse: "Because they forsook the Lord their God . . . and have taken hold upon other gods . . . therefore hath the Lord brought upon them all this evil."[10] On opening the Book of Psalms, he met with this passage: "Thou castedst them down into destruction. How are they brought into desolation . . . ."[11] Finally, in the Book of the Gospels, he read this verse: "Ye know that after two days is the feast of the Passover, and the Son of man is betrayed to be crucified." [12] For one who believed that in each of these utterances he saw the reply of God himself, it would be hard to imagine anything more sinister: it was enough to unsettle a braver spirit than that of Chilperic's son. He was overwhelmed by the burden of this triple threat of betrayal, ruin, and violent death, and wept long and bitterly beside St. Martin's tomb.

Guntram-Bose, who was sticking to his oracle, and who in any case found no cause in all this why he himself should be afraid, persisted in his resolve. With the help of what might almost be called the magnetism that determined men exert over weak and impressionable natures, he restored his young companion's courage so thoroughly that their departure took place forthwith, and Merovech mounted his horse both calmly and confidently. Guntram, at that crucial moment, had to do violence to his own feelings in quite another way; he was about to be separated from his two daughters, who had taken refuge with him in St. Martin's basilica, and whom he dared not take with him because of the hazards of so long a journey. Despite his profound egotism and his imperturbable double-dealing, it cannot be said of him that he was absolutely devoid of good qualities, and among his many vices he did have at least one virtue, paternal love. His daughters' company was exceedingly dear to him. In order to rejoin them when he was far away, he would not hesitate to jeopardize his own life; and if it was a question of defending them from some danger, he would become pugnacious and daring to a reckless degree. Obliged to leave them behind in a sanctuary that King Chilperic, if enraged, might well cease to respect, he promised himself that he would come in person and fetch them, and it was with this in mind, the only good thought of which he was capable, that he crossed the hallowed boundary, galloping along beside Merovech.

Almost six hundred horsemen, recruited, to all appearance, from among the soldiers of fortune and vagabonds of the land, Franks and Gauls alike, accompanied the two fugitives. Following the left bank of the Loire in a northerly direction, they traveled in good order across King Guntram's territory. When almost at Orléans, they turned eastward, in order to avoid passing through Chilperic's realm, and they reached the vicinity of Auxerre unopposed; but it was there that their luck ran out. Erp, or Erpoald, governor of the city, refused to let them pass, possibly because he had received some dispatch from King Chilperic claiming his friendly assistance, or perhaps he simply acted on his own impulse to maintain peace between the two kingdoms. It would seem that this refusal caused a battle in which the troops of the two exiles had very much the worst of it. Merovech, no doubt driven by anger to some ill-advised act, fell into Erpoald's hands, but Guntram, always skilled at getting out of tight corners, beat a retreat with the wreckage of his little army.

No longer daring to venture northward, he made up his mind to retrace his steps and to reach one of the cities of Aquitaine belonging to the kingdom of Austrasia. The approaches to Tours were extremely dangerous for him; he had to fear that the rumor of his flight had impelled Chilperic to give his troops the order to march, and that the city was full of soldiers. But all his prudence did not prevail against a father's affection; instead of giving Tours a wide berth with his small band of ill-equipped runaways, he went straight to St. Martin's basilica. It was guarded; he forced his way in and came out again immediately with his daughters, whom he wished to leave in a safe place outside Chilperic's kingdom. After this daring foray, Guntram took the road to Poitiers, a city which had become Austrasian again since the latest victory of Mummolus. He arrived there without mishap, installed his two daughters in St. Hilary's basilica, and left them to go and see what was happening in Austrasia. This time, for fear of a second misadventure, he made a long detour and headed north by way of Limousin, Auvergne, and the highway from Lyons to Metz.

Before Duke Erpoald could warn King Guntram and receive his orders concerning the prisoner, Merovech contrived to escape. He took refuge in the basilica erected over the tomb of St. Germain, bishop of Auxerre, and settled down in safety, as he had in Tours, protected by the right of asylum. The news of his flight reached King Guntram almost as soon as that of his arrest. It was more than enough to displease in the highest degree this timorous and peace-loving king, whose principal care was to keep out of any quarrel which might break out around him. He was afraid that Merovech's stay in his kingdom might stir up a host of troubles for him, and he could have wished for one of two things: either that Chilperic's son had been allowed to go peacefully on his way, or that he had been properly guarded. Accusing Erpoald at one and the same time of excessive zeal and of blundering, he at once summoned him to his presence, and when the duke wanted to reply and justify his conduct, the king interrupted him, saying: "You arrested the man my brother calls his enemy, but if your intentions were serious, you should have brought the prisoner to me without wasting any time; otherwise you ought not to have laid hands on someone you didn't want to keep in safe custody."

The ambiguous wording of these reproaches proved, on King Guntram's part, as much reluctance to take sides against the son as fear of falling out with the father. He vented his spleen on Duke Erpoald and, not satisfied with dismissing him from office, sentenced him to a fine of seven hundred gold pieces into the bargain. It appears that in spite of Chilperic's messages and solicitations, Guntram took no steps to harass the fugitive in his new sanctuary and that, quite the contrary, successfully saving the appearances without compromising himself, he arranged matters so that Merovech might promptly find an opportunity to escape and continue his journey. And in fact after a two-month stay in the basilica of Auxerre, the young prince left, accompanied by his faithful Gaïlen, and this time the roads were open. He at last set foot on Austrasian soil, where he hoped to find repose, friends, the joys of marriage, and all the honors associated with the rank of a queen's consort; but all that awaited him were fresh reverses and misfortunes which were to end only with his death.

The kingdom of Austrasia, ruled in the name of a child by a council of lords and bishops, was at that time the scene of continual disorders and violent dissensions. The absence of all legal restraint and the unleashing of individual wills made themselves felt more strongly there than in any other part of Gaul. In this respect there was no distinction of race or social condition: Barbarians and Romans, prelates and military leaders, every man who thought himself strong by virtue of power or wealth, vied with the others in turbulence and ambition. Divided into rival factions, they agreed only on one point, their relentless hatred for Brunhild, whom they wanted to deprive of all influence over the governance of her son. The principal leaders of this formidable aristocracy were Aegidius, bishop of Rheims, who was notoriously in the pay of the king of Neustria, and Duke Raukhing, the richest of the Austrasians, a wonderfully depraved man who did evil because he liked it, whereas the other Barbarians did it out of passion or self-interest.

Tales were told of his almost legendary cruelty, which resembled that attributed by popular tradition to some feudal castellans, whose memory lingers around the ruins of their castle keeps. When he supped, light was provided by a slave holding a wax torch, and one of his favorite amusements was to force the poor slave to extinguish his light against his bare legs, then to light it and put it out again several times in the same way. The deeper the burn, the more Duke Raukhing enjoyed himself and laughed at the contortions of the unfortunate man subjected to this kind of torture. He had two of his tenant-farmers, a young man and a girl guilty of having married without his consent, buried alive in the same grave. At the entreaty of a priest, he had sworn not to separate them. "I have kept my word," he said with a ferocious sneer, "they are together for eternity."

The usual confederates of this terrible man, whose insolence to the queen passed all bounds and whose conduct was a permanent rebellion, were Bertefred and Ursio, the former of Teutonic descent, the latter, although the son of a Gallo-Roman, thoroughly steeped in the crude and violent Germanic mores. In their savage opposition they attacked not only the queen, but anyone who tried to come to an agreement with her for the sake of preserving public order and peace. They had a special grudge against the Roman Lupus, duke of Champagne (or of the Rheims district), an austere and vigilant administrator, brought up in the old traditions of the imperial government. Almost every day his estates were laid waste, his houses sacked, and his life threatened by Duke Raukhing's faction. On one occasion, Ursio and Bertefred, with a troop of horsemen at their heels, swooped down upon him and his retinue at the very gates of the palace where the young king was living with his mother. Drawn by the uproar, Brunhild ran up and courageously threw herself into the midst of the armed horsemen, crying to their leaders: "Why attack an innocent man in this way? Don't do this wicked thing, don't start a conflict which could ruin the country." "Woman," replied Ursio in accents of brutal pride, "get back; let it be enough that you ruled during your husband's lifetime: your son is reigning now, and it is our guardianship and not yours which keeps the kingdom safe. So get back, or we will crush you beneath our horses' hooves."

The state of affairs in Austrasia was little in keeping with the hopes which Merovech had been entertaining; his illusions were not long-lived. Scarcely had he reached Metz, the capital, when the regency council ordered him to leave again immediately, if indeed he was even allowed to enter the city. The ambitious chieftains who treated Brunhild like a foreigner with no rights and with no power were not the kind of men to tolerate the presence of the husband of a queen whom they feared (while pretending to despise her.) The more she begged and pleaded that Merovech be received hospitably and allowed to live in peace at her side, the harsher and more intractable those ruling in the young king's name proved to be. Their excuse was the danger of a breach with the king of Neustria; they did not fail to make capital out of this; and the only concession made to the queen's affections consisted in merely sending Merovech packing, without either doing him violence or handing him over to his father.

Deprived of his last hope of refuge, Merovech went back the way he had come, but, before crossing the frontier of Guntram's kingdom, he left the main highway and began wandering from village to village across the countryside around Rheims. He traveled aimlessly, moving by night and hiding by day, taking care above all not to show himself to persons of high rank (who might have recognized him), afraid of betrayal, exposed to all sorts of miseries, and having no prospects for the future but to go back in disguise to the sanctuary of St. Martin of Tours. As soon as his trail had been lost, it was believed that he had opted for the latter course, and this was reported as far away as Neustria.

On hearing the rumor, King Chilperic immediately sent his army to occupy the city of Tours and to guard St. Martin's abbey. Once in Touraine, the army began to plunder, to wreak havoc, and to burn, without even sparing church property. All kinds of rapine went on in the abbey buildings, where a garrison was quartered. Military posts were bivouacked at every exit from the basilica. The doors remained closed day and night, with the solitary exception of one through which a few clerics had permission to enter in order to sing the services. The people were barred from the church and deprived of hearing mass. At the same time as these steps were being taken to cut off the fugitive's retreat, King Chilperic, probably with the consent of the Austrasian lords, crossed the border in force and searched every inch of the territory where Merovech might possibly be hiding. Tracked down like a wild beast pursued by hunters, the youth nevertheless succeeded in eluding his father's searches, thanks to the commiseration of the lowly of both Frankish and Roman descent, who were the only people he could trust. Having fruitlessly scoured the countryside and skirted the forest of the Ardennes, Chilperic returned to his kingdom without a single hostile act against the inhabitants having been committed by the troops that he was leading on his constabulary expedition.

While Merovech was reduced to leading the life of a wandering exile, his former chance companion, Guntram-Bose, returned from Poitiers to Austrasia. He was the only man of some importance in that kingdom whom Chilperic's son could call upon for help; and he was probably not long in learning the unfortunate fugitive's hiding place and all his secrets. So utterly desperate a case offered Guntram only two prospects, of a kind between which he was not wont to hesitate: a burdensome devotion and the rewards of treachery. He decided in favor of treachery. Such at least was the general belief, for, as was his custom, he avoided committing himself openly, working under cover and playing an ambiguous enough role so that he would be able to deny everything with effrontery if the plot did not succeed. Queen Fredegund, who never failed to take matters into her own hands whenever her husband's cunning was deficient—which was not uncommon—saw the scant success obtained by his hunting down of Merovech, and resolved to turn to other means, less noisy, but more certain. She made known her scheme to Aegidius, bishop of Rheims, who was on friendly terms with her, as well as being her associate in political intrigue. With this man acting as go-between, Guntram-Bose once again received dazzling promises and the queen's instructions. From the cooperation of these two men with Merovech's implacable foe, there resulted a cleverly planned scheme to lure him to his destruction through his greatest weakness, his crazy young man's ambition and his eagerness to be king.

Some men from the Térouanne region, whose people were devoted to Fredegund,[13] journeyed to Austrasia secretly to have an interview with Chilperic's son. When they had found him in his retreat, they gave him the following message in the name of their fellow-countrymen: "Since your hair has grown long again, we desire to be your subjects, and are ready to desert your father if you will come among us." Merovech eagerly grasped at this hope; on the word of strangers, questionable representatives of a mere canton of Neustria, he believed himself certain to unthrone his father. He set out forthwith for Térouanne, accompanied by the few men who were blindly devoted to his fortune; Gaïlen, his bosom friend in good and bad times alike; Gaukil, count of the palace of Austrasia under King Sigibert, but now in disgrace; finally, Grind and several others whom the chronicler does not name, but whom he calls brave men.

They ventured into Neustrian territory without considering that the further they advanced the more difficult it was to withdraw. At the boundaries of the wild district which extended from north of Arras to the Atlantic coast, they found what had been promised them, bands of men who greeted them by hailing Merovech as king. Invited to take their ease in one of the farmhouses lived in by the Franks, they went in unsuspectingly; but the doors were immediately shut behind them, all the exits were guarded, and armed pickets were set up all around as if the house were a besieged city. At the same time, couriers mounted their horses and sped towards Soissons to announce to King Chilperic that his enemies had fallen into the trap and he could come and dispose of them.

At the sound of the doors' being barricaded and the sight of the military dispositions which made a sortie impossible, Merovech, all at once aware of the danger, became pensive and downcast. The dreamy, melancholy Nordic imagination which was his most outstanding trait gradually grew excited to the point of frenzy. He was obsessed with thoughts of violent death and horrible images of torture. A great terror of his impending fate filled him with such anguish that, in utter despair, he saw no hope save in suicide. But he lacked the courage to kill himself, he needed another arm than his own; and, addressing his brother-in-arms, he said: "Gaïlen, until now we have had but one soul and one mind; do not, I beseech you, leave me at the mercy of my enemies: draw your sword and kill me." Gaïlen, with a vassal's blind obedience, drew the knife which he wore at his belt and dealt the young prince a mortal blow. King Chilperic, arriving posthaste to lay hands on his son, found nothing but a corpse. Gaïlen was taken prisoner, together with Merovech's other companions; he had clung to life through a last glimmer of hope, or out of unaccountable weakness. There were those who questioned the truth of some of these facts and believed that Fredegund, going straight to her objective, had had her stepson stabbed and invented the suicide story to spare the king's paternal scruples. What is more, the fearful treatment meted out to Merovech's companions seemed to justify his forebodings for himself and his anticipated terrors. Gaïlen perished mutilated in the most barbarous fashion, with his hands, feet, nose, and ears cut off. Grind's limbs were broken on a wheel, which was raised up into the air and on which he died; Gaukil, the eldest of the three, was the least unfortunate—they merely cut off his head.

Thus did Merovech pay the penalty for his deplorable intimacy with his brother's murderer, and Guntram-Bose became for the second time the instrument of that fatal destiny hanging over Chilperic's sons. He felt no more burden on his conscience than before, and, like a bird of prey returning to its nest when the chase is done, became worried about his two daughters whom he had left in Poitiers. And as a matter of fact, this city had again just fallen to the king of Neustria; the plan of conquest deferred by Mummolus's victory had been resumed after a year's suspension, and Desiderius, at the head of a large army, was once more threatening all of Aquitaine. Those who had been the most conspicuously loyal to King Childebert, or against whom King Chilperic was nursing some private grudge, were arrested in their homes and sent off under escort towards the palace at Braine. Among others, the Roman Ennodius, count of Poitiers, guilty of having wanted to defend the city, and the Frank Dak, son of Dagarik, who had attempted to take the field as a guerilla leader, had been seen passing by on the road from Tours to Soissons. In such circumstances, a return to Poitiers was a singularly perilous undertaking for Guntram-Bose, but this time he did not weigh the consequences, and determined at all costs to remove his daughters from the danger of abduction from sanctuary. Accompanied by a few friends (for he always found some, in spite of his repeated betrayals) he headed south by the safest route, reached Poitiers without mishap, and succeeded with no less good fortune in taking his daughters out of St. Hilary's basilica. This was not all, however; they had to get away as quickly as possible to a place where pursuit was no longer to be feared. Guntram and his friends, losing no time, remounted and left Poitiers by the gate opening onto the road to Tours.

Armed with daggers and short lances, the usual attire of even the most peaceful travelers, they rode along beside the covered cart carrying the two girls. Scarcely had they traveled more than a few hundred yards along the highway when they saw horsemen coming towards them. The two parties halted to make themselves known to each other, and Guntram-Bose's got ready to defend itself, for the men facing it were hostile. These people were led by a certain Drakolen (a very active supporter of the king of Neustria), who was, as it happened, returning from the palace of Braine where he had taken Dagarik's son and other captives with their hands tied behind their backs. Guntram sensed that he would have to fight, but before coming to blows he tried to parley. He detailed one of his friends to go to Drakolen, giving him the following instructions: "Go and tell him this from me: you know that we were once allies, so I beg you to let me pass freely; take all that you want from me, I give you everything, to the point of nakedness, but let me go where I want to with my daughters."

When he heard this, Drakolen, who believed himself to be the stronger, burst out laughing and, pointing to a bundle of cords hanging from his saddle-bow, told the messenger: "Here is the rope with which I bound the other culprits whom I have just taken to the king; it will serve for him, too." And he at once clapped spurs to his horse, charged at Guntram-Bose, and thrust at him with his spear: but his aim was bad, the shaft snapped, and the spearhead fell to the ground. Guntram resolutely seized his opportunity and, striking Drakolen in the face, made him reel in the saddle; another man knocked him down and finished him off with a lance through the ribs. The Neustrians, seeing their leader dead, turned back, and Guntram-Bose set off again, but not before he had carefully stripped the body of his foe.

After this adventure, Duke Guntram journeyed quietly towards Austrasia. Once in Metz, he resumed the life of a great Frankish lord, a life of fierce and unruly independence, with none of the dignity of the Roman aristocracy and none of the chivalric ways of the feudal courts. History has little to tell of him for a period of three years; then all at once we see him in Constantinople, where he seems to have been taken by his restless and nomadic spirit. It was during this journey that Guntram was instrumental in weaving the greatest intrigue of the century, an intrigue which shook the whole of Gaul, and in which the rivalry the Austrasian Franks felt for their brothers of the west forged an alliance with the nationalistic hatred of the southern Gauls, for the destruction of the two kingdoms whose capitals were Soissons and Chalon-sur-Saône.

FOURTH EPISODE
History of Praetextatus,
Bishop of Rouen (577–586)

hile Merovech, with no safe place to go to in either his father's kingdom or his wife's, was wandering over the moors and through the forests of Champagne, there was only one man in Neustria with the courage to proclaim himself his friend. This was Praetextatus, bishop of Rouen, who, since the day he had stood godfather at the young prince's baptism, had been bound to him in one of those devoted, absolute, unreflecting attachments of which only a child's mother or nurse seems capable. The sheer blind sympathy which had led him to favor Merovech's passion for his uncle's widow in the teeth of canon law only increased with the misfortunes which resulted from this ill-considered passion. It was to the zeal of Praetextatus that, in all likelihood, Brunhild's husband owed the financial assistance thanks to which he contrived to escape from the basilica of St. Martin of Tours and to reach the Austrasian frontier.

When he learned of the unfavorable issue of this escape, the bishop was not discouraged; on the contrary, he redoubled his efforts to obtain friends and asylum for the fugitive whose father in religion he was and whose own father was persecuting him. He took small pains to hide his feelings and the actions which he thought were incumbent upon him. Not a single Frank of any eminence living in his diocese came to pay him a visit without his holding forth to the visitor at some length about Merovech's misfortunes, and earnestly soliciting affection and support for his godson (for his dear son, as he himself used to say). These words formed a kind of refrain which, in his simpleheartedness, he would constantly repeat and bring into his every utterance. If he happened to receive a present from some powerful or wealthy man, he hastened to return it twofold, getting his promise to come to Merovech's aid and to remain faithful to him in his distress.

As the bishop of Rouen flung aside all restraint in his talk and would imprudently confide in all sorts of people, it was not long before King Chilperic knew everything through either public report or officious friends, and heard false, or at least exaggerated, denunciations. Praetextatus was accused of strewing presents among the people to incite them to treason, and of weaving a conspiracy against the king's power and his very person. Chilperic had, at this news, one of those fits of anger mingled with fear during which, uncertain what decision he should take, he would leave it up to Fredegund to counsel and direct him. Since the day he had succeeded in separating Merovech and Brunhild, he had almost forgiven Bishop Praetextatus for having solemnized their marriage; but Fredegund, who was less disposed to forget and less confined by her passions to the advantage of the moment, had conceived a deep hatred for the bishop, one of those hatreds which, so far as she was concerned, could end only with the life of the one who had had the misfortune to arouse it. Seizing the opportunity, therefore, she persuaded the king to arraign Praetextatus before a council of bishops on a charge of high treason under Roman law, and to demand at the very least that his breach of canon law be punished if he could not be found guilty of another crime.

Praetextatus was arrested at his home and taken to the royal residence, there to undergo an interrogation concerning the deeds with which he was charged and his dealings with Queen Brunhild since the day she had left Rouen to return to Austrasia. The bishop's replies disclosed that he had not returned all the valuables the queen had left in his care on her departure, that he still had two bales of cloth and jewels valued at three thousand gold *solidi*, besides a sack of about two thousand gold coins. More overjoyed at such a discovery than at any other information, Chilperic promptly had this sacred trust seized and confiscated for himself; then he banished Praetextatus under strict guard far from his diocese until the meeting of the synod which was to try him.

Letters of convocation addressed to all the bishops of Chilperic's kingdom enjoined them to make their way to Paris in the last days of spring, in the year 577. Since Sigibert's death, the king of Neustria regarded this city as his property, and no longer took any account of the oath which forbade him entry. Whether he really was afraid of some enterprise on the part of secret supporters of Brunhild and Merovech, or whether he wished to make more of an impression on Praetextatus's judges, he made the trip from Soissons to Paris accompanied by so large a retinue that it could pass for an army. This body of men bivouacked at the gates of the king's lodging, which was in all likelihood the old imperial palace whose buildings stood on the banks of the Seine to the south of the city. Its eastern facade parallelled the Roman road which, beginning at the little bridge from the Ile de la Cité, headed south. In front of the main gate, another Roman road, starting out due east but soon changing to a southeasterly direction, led across the fields of vines to the highest plateau of the southern hill, on which there was a church dedicated to the apostles St. Peter and St. Paul. This was chosen as the chamber for the

synod hearings, probably because of its proximity to the royal residence
and the billets of the troops.

The church, built half a century earlier, contained the tombs of King
Clovis, Queen Clotilde, and St. Genovefe or Genevieve. Clovis had
ordered its construction at Clotilde's request as he was setting out for the
war against the Visigoths; having reached the designated site, he had
hurled his battle-axe straight in front of him so that one day the strength
and reach of his arm might be measured by the length of the edifice. It
was one of those basilicas of the fifth and sixth centuries, more remarkable for the opulence of their ornamentation than for their architectural
scale, decorated on the inside with marble columns, mosaics, and
painted and gilded ceilings, and on the outside with a copper roof and a
portico. The portico of St. Peter's church consisted of three galleries, one
applied to the facade of the building, the other two to its lateral walls.
These galleries were decorated from end to end with frescoes portraying
the four hosts of saints under the Old Law and the New: the patriarchs,
prophets, martyrs, and confessors.

Such are the details supplied by contemporary documents concerning
the place where this council—the fifth to be held in Paris—convened. On
the day appointed by the letters of convocation, forty-five bishops
gathered in St. Peter's basilica. The king, for his part, made his entrance
accompanied by some of his leuds armed only with swords; and the main
body of Franks in full war gear halted beneath the portico, filling all its
avenues. The choir of the basilica most probably formed the precinct
reserved for the judges, the plaintiff, and the defendant. The two bales
and the sack of gold pieces seized in Praetextatus's house figured conspicuously as exhibits. On his arrival, the king drew the bishops' attention to them, announcing that these objects were to play an important
part in the case which was to be argued. Of the members of the synod,
who had come either from the cities originally belonging to Chilperic's
kingdom or from those which he had conquered since his brother
Sigibert's death, some were of Gallic and some of Frankish descent.
Among the former, who were by far the more numerous, were Gregory,
bishop of Tours, Felix of Nantes, Domnolus of Le Mans, Honoratus of
Amiens, Aetherius of Lisieux, and Pappolus of Chartres. Among the
others were to be seen Raghenemod, bishop of Paris, Leudowald of
Bayeux, Romahaire of Coutances, Marovech of Poitiers, Malulf of Senlis,
and Bertram of Bordeaux. The last-named was, it would appear, honored
by his colleagues with the dignity and functions of president.[1]

He was a man of high birth, a close relative of kings through his mother
Ingheltrude, and owing his immense credit and great wealth to this
kinship. He affected a Roman urbanity and elegance, and was fond of
appearing in public in a four-horse chariot, escorted by the young clerics
of his church just like a Roman patron surrounded by his clients. To this

liking for luxury and senatorial pomp, Bishop Bertram added a taste for poetry, and composed Latin epigrams which he would confidently hold up for the admiration of connoisseurs (although they were full of stolen lines and faults of scansion). More ingratiating and cleverer than Germans usually were, he had retained their characteristic penchant for shameless and unrestrained debauchery. Following the example of the kings his relatives, he would take maidservants as concubines and, not content with that, would look for mistresses among married women also. He was commonly believed to be carrying on an adulterous relationship with Fredegund and, either for this or some other reason, had espoused the queen's resentment of the bishop of Rouen in the most lively fashion. In general, the Frankish prelates, possibly through being accustomed to a vassal's obedience, were disposed to decide in favor of the king by sacrificing their colleague. The Roman bishops had more sympathy for the accused, more sense of justice, and more respect for the dignity of their order; but they were frightened by the military array surrounding King Chilperic and, above all, by the presence of Fredegund, who, mistrustful as ever of her husband's ability, had come in person to work for the accomplishment of her vengeance.

When the defendant had been brought in and the court had come to order, the king stood up and, instead of addressing the judges, abruptly apostrophized his adversary thus: "Bishop, how dared you join in wedlock Merovech, my enemy, who should have simply been my son, with his aunt, by which I mean with his uncle's wife? Were you unaware of the canonical enactments in this respect? And not only do you stand convicted of having failed in this, but you have also conspired with the man I speak of, and distributed presents to have me assassinated. You have turned the son into his own father's enemy; you have suborned the people with money, so that none might keep the allegiance which is my due; you have desired to deliver my kingdom into another's hands . . ." These last words, pronounced emphatically in the general silence, reached the ears of the Frankish warriors, who, stationed outside the church, were thronging curiously around the doors, which had been shut since the beginning of the session. At the sound of the king's voice saying that he had been betrayed, this armed multitude at once responded with a rumble of indignation and yells of "Death to the traitor!" Then, becoming frenzied, it set about smashing the doors in order to burst into the church and drag out the bishop to stone him. The members of the council, appalled by this unexpected tumult, left their places, and the king himself was obliged to go and head off the attackers so as to placate them and reduce them to order.

The assembly having calmed down sufficiently for the hearing to continue, the bishop of Rouen was called upon to clear himself. He could not exonerate himself of having infringed canon law by solemnizing the marriage, but he categorically denied the acts of conspiracy and treason of which the king had just accused him. Chilperic then announced that he had witnesses to be heard, and commanded that they be brought in. Several Franks then appeared in court, holding sundry valuable articles which they set before the accused, saying: "Do you recognize this? This is what you gave us to promise allegiance to Merovech." The bishop, not in the least abashed, replied: "You are telling the truth; I have more than once given you presents, but not so that the king might be driven from his kingdom. When you came to give me a fine horse or something of the kind, could I fail to appear as generous as yourselves, and give you back gift for gift?" There was to be sure a little misrepresentation concealed in this reply, however sincere it might otherwise be, but the reality of the alleged conspiracy could not be established by valid testimony. The continuation of the trial did not bring any proofs sufficient for a conviction, and the king, dissatisfied with the scant success of this first attempt, adjourned the session and left the church to return to his quarters. His leuds followed him, and all the bishops went off together to take a break in the sacristy.

While they were sitting in groups, chatting familiarly but somewhat guardedly (for they did not trust one another), a man whom most of them knew only by name came forward unexpectedly. This was the Gaul Aëtius, archdeacon of Paris. When he had bowed to the bishops, he tackled the very thorny topic of conversation with extreme precipitancy and said: "Listen to me, priests of the Lord here assembled, the present occasion is of great importance to you. Either you are about to gain distinction through the luster of a fair name, or else you are about to lose the title of God's ministers in everyone's opinion. It is a matter of choosing; show yourselves to be judicious and steadfast, therefore, and do not let your brother perish." This short address was followed by a deep silence: the bishops, not knowing whether or not they had before them an agent provocateur sent by Fredegund, replied only by putting their fingers to their lips as a sign of discretion. They recalled with dread the fierce cries of the Frankish warriors and the thuds of their battle-axes on the church doors. Nearly all of them, and the Gauls in particular, trembled at the thought of being pointed out as suspicious persons to the easily offended loyalty of these hotblooded vassals of the king; they remained in their seats, motionless and as though aghast.

But Gregory of Tours, of stouter conscience than the others and indignant at their faintheartedness, took up archdeacon Aëtius's harangue and admonishments on his own account. "I beseech you," he said, "pay attention to my words, most holy priests of God, and especially those of you who are intimates of the king. Give him godly counsel worthy of the priesthood, or it is to be feared that his relentlessness against a minister of the Lord may bring down upon him the divine wrath and cause him to lose both his kingdom and his fame." The Frankish bishops, for whom this speech was more particularly intended, remained silent like the others, and Gregory added firmly: "Remember, my lords and colleagues, the words of the prophet, who says 'But if the watchman see the sword come, and blow not the trumpet; if the sword come, and take any person from among them; his blood will I require at the watchman's hand.[2] Do not keep silent therefore, but speak up and lay the king's injustice before him, for fear that misfortune befall him and you be responsible for it." The bishop stopped, to wait for a response, but not a word did any of those present answer. They hurried to leave the place, some to decline any share of complicity in such talk, and to take cover from the tempest which they thought they could already see rushing upon their colleague's head; the others, like Bertram and Raghenemod, to go and pay court to the king and carry him tales.

It was not long before Chilperic was informed in detail of all that had just occurred. His flatterers told him (and these were their own words) that he had no greater enemy in this affair than the bishop of Tours. The king, beside himself with anger, immediately dispatched one of his courtiers to go with all possible speed to fetch the bishop. Gregory obeyed and followed his guide serenely and confidently. He found the king outside the palace, in a hut made of boughs, in the midst of the tents and hutments of his soldiers. Chilperic was standing with Bertram, bishop of Bordeaux, on his right, and Raghenemod, bishop of Paris, on his left. They had both just played the part of informer against their colleague. In front of them was a broad bench covered with loaves of bread, cooked meats, and sundry dishes intended for each new arrival; for custom (and etiquette of a kind) decreed that nobody should leave the king's presence after a visit without taking something at his table.

On seeing the man whom he had sent for in his anger, and knowing that he did not yield to threats, Chilperic composed himself, the better to attain his ends, and affecting—instead of rancor—a mild and facetious tone, he said: "Bishop, it is your duty to dispense justice to all, and here am I unable to obtain it from you; instead, I see plainly that you are in connivance with iniquity and bear out the proverb: The crow does not pluck out the crow's eye." The bishop did not think it seemly to lend himself to the jest, but with the traditional respect of the former subjects of the Roman Empire for the sovereign, a respect which in his case at least was not incompatible with either personal dignity or a sense of independence, he gravely replied: "If one of us, Sire, strays from the paths of justice, he can be chastised by you; but if *you* are at fault, who will reprove you? We speak to you, and if you wish it, you listen to us; but if you do not so wish, who will pass judgment on you? Only He who has declared that He is justice itself." The king interrupted and retorted: "I have found justice with all men and cannot find it with you; but I know very well what I shall do so that the people may take note of you and know that you are not a just man. I will summon the inhabitants of Tours and tell them 'Raise your voices against Gregory and cry out that he is unjust and dispenses justice to none': and while they are shouting, I shall add: 'I, who am king, cannot obtain justice from him; how shall *you*, who are beneath me, obtain it?' "

This kind of glib hypocrisy, by which the man who could do anything he liked was trying to pass himself off as the persecuted one, stirred up such a feeling of contempt in Gregory that he found it hard to keep it in check; it caused him to express himself more curtly and more haughtily. "If I am unjust," he went on, "it is not you who knows it, but He who knows my conscience and who looks deep within our hearts; and as for the outcries of the people aroused by you, they will amount to nothing, for everyone will know that they came from you. But enough of this; you have the laws, civil and ecclesiastical: consult them carefully, and if you do not observe what they command, know that God's judgment is on your head."

The king felt the effect of this austere language, and as though to blot out from Gregory's mind the unfortunate impression which had brought it down upon him, he assumed a coaxing manner and, pointing to a bowl of broth which happened to be there among the loaves of bread, the dishes of meat, and the drinking-cups, he said: "Here is a soup which I have had prepared especially for you; there is nothing in it but fowl and a few chick peas." These last words were calculated to flatter the bishop's self-esteem; for the holy men of the day—and in general those who aspired to Christian perfection—abstained from red meat as being too substantial, and lived only on vegetables, fish, and poultry. Gregory was not taken in by this latest trick, but, shaking his head, replied: "Our sustenance must consist in doing the will of God, and not in the enjoyment of dainty fare. You who tax others with injustice, begin by promising that you will not set aside the law and the canons, and we will believe that you are indeed pursuing justice." The king, who was anxious not to fall out with the bishop of Tours and who (if need be) was not averse to pledging his word—if only to find some means of evading it later—raised his hand and swore by Almighty God not to transgress the law and the canons in any way. Gregory then took some bread and drank a little wine, in a kind of communion of hospitality, which could not be declined under another man's roof without gravely offending against good manners and consideration for others. Outwardly reconciled with the king, he left him to go to his lodging in St. Julian's basilica, hard by the imperial palace.

That night, while the bishop of Tours, having sung the office of nocturns, was resting in his apartment, he heard a thunderous knocking at the door. Astonished at this din, he sent down one of his servants, who reported that messengers from Queen Fredegund were asking to see him. When these people had been ushered in, they greeted Gregory in the queen's name and told him that they had come to beg him not to oppose her desires in the matter before the council. They added, in confidence, that they were authorized to promise him two hundred pounds of silver if he caused Praetextatus's downfall by declaring against him. The bishop of Tours, with his usual prudence and self-control, calmly objected that he was not the sole judge of the case and that his voice, no matter which side it was on, would decide nothing. "Indeed it would," retorted the envoys, "for we already have everybody else's word; what is essential is that you do not run counter to them." The bishop went on without changing his tone: "Even though you were to give me a thousand pounds of gold and silver, I would be unable to do anything except what the Lord commands; all that I can promise is to join the other bishops in whatever decision they reach in conformity with canon law." The envoys mistook the meaning of these words, either because they had not the faintest idea what canon law was, or because they imagined that the word "lord" applied to the king, who in ordinary parlance was often referred to by this simple title. Thanking the bishop effusively, they went off, delighted to be able to tell the queen the good news which they thought they had just received. Their mistake relieved Bishop Gregory from further intrusions and allowed him to rest until the next morning.

The council members convened early for the second session, and the king, already quite recovered from his disappointments, made his way there with great punctuality. In order to find a means of reconciling the previous day's oath with the plan of vengeance which the queen was set on, he had brought all his literary and theological learning to bear. He had leafed through the collected canons and had stopped at the first article which assigned the heaviest possible penalty—namely, deposition—against a bishop. Nothing now mattered to him but to start afresh and accuse the bishop of Rouen of a crime covered by this article, which scarcely perplexed him in the least; assured, as he believed himself to be, of all the synod's votes, he gave himself free play in the matter of imputations and lies. When the judges and the defendant had taken their places as before, Chilperic took the floor and said with all the gravity of a doctor of divinity commenting on ecclesiastical law: "The bishop convicted of theft must be dismissed from episcopal office; such is the decision of canonical authority." The members of the synod, astonished at this opening, of which they understood nothing, all asked at once who was this bishop charged with the crime of theft. "There he is," replied the king, turning, with singular impudence, to Praetextatus, "there is the very man; did you not see what he has stolen from us!"

They remembered indeed the two bales of cloth and the sack of money that the king had shown them without explaining where they came from or what he thought they had to do with the charges. No matter how insulted by his adversary's latest attack, Praetextatus patiently answered, "I think you will recall that after Queen Brunhild had left the city of Rouen, I came to see you and informed you that I had the queen's effects in safekeeping, to wit, five bales of considerable size and weight; I informed you that her servants frequently came and asked me to return them, but that I would not do this without your consent. You then told me 'Get rid of these things and let them return to the woman who owns them, for fear that they may cause enmity between me and my nephew Childebert.' When I had returned to my diocese, I handed over one of the bales to the queen's servants, for they could not carry any more. They came back later and asked me for the rest, and once again I went to consult Your Magnificence. The command that you gave me was the same as the first: 'Out with all these things! bishop, out with them, for fear that they may give birth to dissensions.' I accordingly handed over two more bales, and the last two were left with me. Now why do you slander me and accuse me of theft when there is no question here of stolen property, but of articles entrusted to my safekeeping?"

"If this trust had been turned over to you," replied the king unabashed, giving yet another twist to the accusation and dropping the role of complainant for that of indicter, "if you were the depositary, why did you open one of the bales, take out the fringe of a robe of cloth of gold and cut it into pieces to distribute it to men conspiring to drive me from my kingdom?"

The accused replied as calmly as before: "I have already told you once that these men had given me presents. Having nothing of my own, for the time being, that I could give them in return, I took something from the bale, nor did I believe that I was doing wrong; I considered what belonged to my son Merovech, to whom I stood godfather, as my own property." The king did not know how to answer these words so artlessly revelatory of the paternal feelings which were a kind of obsessive passion for the old bishop. Chilperic felt himself at the end of his resources; the self-confidence he had displayed at first was followed by an air of embarrassment and almost of confusion; he abruptly adjourned the hearing and withdrew, even more disconcerted and annoyed than the day before.

What preoccupied him above all else was the welcome which, after such a setback, he would certainly receive from the imperious Fredegund; and it seems that his return to the palace was in fact followed by a domestic storm whose violence dismayed him. No longer knowing how to crush, to his wife's satisfaction, the harmless old priest whom she had sworn to destroy, he called to his side those members of the council who were the most devoted to him, Bertram and Raghenemod among others. "I admit it," he told them. "I am defeated by the bishop's words, and I know that he is telling the truth. So what action shall I take that the queen's will may be done?" The embarrassed prelates did not know how to answer; they remained glumly silent: then all at once the king, stimulated and as though inspired by the mixture of love and fear which constituted his conjugal passion, continued warmly: "Go and find him and pretend to advise him yourselves. Tell him 'You know that King Chilperic is kind and easily touched, that he readily lets himself be won over to mercy; humble yourself before him and humor him; say that you did what he accuses you of: we will then all throw ourselves at his feet and obtain your pardon.' "

The bishops may have persuaded their weak and gullible colleague that the king, repenting of his prosecution, simply desired not to be given the lie, or they may have frightened him by pointing out that his innocence before the council would not save him from the royal vengeance if he persisted in defying it. At any rate, Praetextatus, intimidated into the bargain by what he knew of the servile or venal predispositions of most of his judges, did not spurn such strange advice. He kept the disgraceful expedient which was offered him at the back of his mind, as a last chance of safety, thus giving a sorry example of the moral laxity which was then winning over even those responsible for maintaining the rule of duty and the scruples of honor in that half-disintegrated society. Thanked as though they had done him a good turn by the very man they were betraying, the bishops went to take King Chilperic the news that their mission had succeeded. They promised that the defendant, falling headlong into the trap, would admit to everything at the first peremptory question; and Chilperic, freed from the worry of inventing some new device to revive the proceedings, resolved to let them take their ordinary course. The third hearing accordingly took matters up at the exact point reached at the end of the first, and the witnesses who had already appeared were once again subpoenaed to confirm their previous allegations.

The next day, when the court was in session, the king, as if he were merely continuing his closing remarks of two days before, said to the defendant, while pointing to the witnesses (who were standing): "If you only wanted to give these men gift for gift, why did you ask them to swear to remain loyal to Merovech?" Praetextatus, through an instinctive sense of shame stronger than all his apprehensions, shrank from the lie he was supposed to tell against himself. "I admit it," he replied, "I asked for their friendship in his behalf, and I would have called to his aid not only men, but the heavenly angels, if I had had the power to do so, for he was, as I have already said, my spiritual son through baptism."

At these words, which seemed to indicate a willingness on the prisoner's part to continue to defend himself, the king, beside himself with disappointment, gave way to a terrifying explosion of rage. His anger, as brutal at that moment as his stratagems had been patient, gave the feeble old man a nervous shock which immediately annihilated what remained of his moral powers. He fell on his knees and said, prostrating himself: "Most merciful king, I have sinned against heaven and you; I am a detestable murderer, I wanted to kill you and put your son on the throne . . ." As soon as the king saw his adversary at his feet, his anger abated and hypocrisy once again came to the fore. Pretending to be overcome by excessive emotion, he himself knelt down before the assembly and cried: "Do you hear, most godly bishops, do you hear the criminal confess his abominable offense?" The members of the council all sprang from their seats and ran to set the king on his feet again as they surrounded him, some of them moved to the point of tears, others perhaps laughing to themselves at the bizarre scene which their previous day's treachery had helped to prepare. As soon as Chilperic was on his feet, as though he could no longer stand the sight of so great an offender, he ordered Praetextatus to leave the basilica. He himself withdrew almost immediately to let the council deliberate, as was the practice, before a verdict was handed down.

On his return to the palace the king, without wasting a second, had a copy of the collected canons taken from his library and carried to the assembled bishops. Over and above the complete code of canon law acknowledged beyond all question by the Gallican Church, this volume contained a supplementary section of canons ascribed to the Apostles, but not widely accepted or studied in Gaul at that time, and little known to even the most learned theologians. It was this supplement which contained the disciplinary clause cited so grandiloquently by the king at the second hearing, when he took it into his head to alter the charge of conspiracy to one of theft. This article, which assigned the penalty of deposition, was very much to his liking for that reason; but since his text no longer tallied with the defendant's admission of guilt, Chilperic, carrying double-dealing effrontery to the limit, made no bones about falsifying it, either by his own hand or by one of his secretaries. In the copy thus retouched could be read: "The bishop convicted of homicide, adultery, or perjury will be dismissed from episcopal office." The word "theft" had disappeared, to be replaced by the word "homicide"; and, even stranger, not one of the council members, not even the bishop of Tours, suspected the fraud. However, it does appear that the upright and conscientious Gregory, the man of justice and faith, endeavored, though in vain, to induce his colleagues to abide by the ordinary code and to reject the authority of the so-called apostolic canons.

When the deliberations were concluded, the contending parties were summoned once more to hear sentence passed. The fatal clause (from the twenty-first apostolic canon) having been read aloud, the bishop of

Bordeaux, as president of the council, addressed the accused as follows: "Listen to me, brother and co-bishop, you may no longer remain in communion with us and enjoy our charity until the king, with whom you are in disgrace, shall pardon you." At this verdict delivered by a man who had so unworthily trifled with his simplicity the day before, Praetextatus remained silent and as though stupefied. As for the king, so total a victory was already inadequate, and he was still racking his brains to find some additional means of augmenting the sentence. Immediately taking the floor, he asked that before the condemned man was allowed to leave, his tunic should be torn asunder on his back, or else that the 108th Psalm be recited over him. This contains the maledictions applied by the Acts of the Apostles to Judas Iscariot: "Let his days be few; and let another take his office. Let his children be fatherless and his wife a widow. Let his children be continually vagabonds, and beg; let them seek their bread also out of their desolate places. Let the extortioner catch all that he hath; and let the strangers spoil his labor. Let there be none to extend mercy unto him: neither let there be any to favor his fatherless children. Let his posterity be cut off; and in the generation following let their name be blotted out."[3]

The first of these ceremonies was a symbol of ignominious degradation; the other applied only in cases of sacrilege. Gregory of Tours spoke out calmly and reasonably (yet firmly) against allowing such an increase in the penalty, and the council did not in fact allow it. Chilperic, still in a pettifogging mood, then wanted the sentence suspending his opponent from his episcopal duties to be set down in writing with a clause declaring this deposition to be perpetual. Gregory opposed this request too, reminding the king of his express promise to restrict the proceedings to the limits appointed by the tenor of canon law. This discussion, which was prolonging the hearing, was suddenly interrupted by a denouement recognizably due to the hand and determination of Fredegund, for she was weary of the law's delays and her husband's subtleties. Armed men entered the church and carried off Praetextatus before the assembly's very eyes, and nothing remained but to disperse. The bishop was marched off to prison within the walls of Paris, in a jail whose ruins long survived on the left bank of the great arm of the Seine. The following night he attempted to escape, and was cruelly beaten by the soldiers guarding him. After a day or two of imprisonment he left for his place of exile at the uttermost ends of the kingdom, on an island near the shores of the Cotentin Peninsula, probably Jersey, settled a century earlier—like the coast itself as far as Bayeux—by Saxon pirates.

The bishop of Rouen should on the face of it have spent the rest of his life among this population of fishermen and corsairs, but after seven years of exile a great event suddenly restored him to freedom and to his church. In the year 584, King Chilperic was assassinated under circumstances which will be related elsewhere, and his death, which rumor imputed to Fredegund, became the signal for a kind of revolution throughout the kingdom of Neustria. All the malcontents of the late reign, all those who had cause to complain about harassments and injuries, took the law into their own hands. They fell upon those royal officials who had abused their power or exercised it harshly and without consideration for anyone; their property was overrun, their houses ransacked and burned; everybody jumped at the chance of engaging in reprisals against his oppressors or his enemies. Between family and family, between city and city, and between district and district, feuds were revived and brought forth private wars, murders, and other acts of lawlessness. Convicts came out of the prisons, and exiles returned home as if their sentence of banishment had been quashed by the death of the prince in whose name it had been delivered. In this manner did Praetexatus return from exile, recalled by a deputation sent him by the citizens of Rouen. He made his entrance into the city escorted by an immense throng, amid the acclamations of the people, who, of their own authority, reinstated him on the archdiocesan throne and turned out the Gaul Melantius whom the king had put in his place.

Meanwhile, Queen Fredegund, who carried the blame for all the evil done during her husband's reign, had been compelled to take refuge in the principal church of Paris, leaving her only son, aged four months, in the hands of the Frankish lords, who proclaimed him king and took over the government in his name. When the disorders had become less violent she left this asylum and was obliged to go off and let herself be forgotten in a retreat far away from the young king's residence. Renouncing her accustomed pomp and autocratic ways with the utmost chagrin, she went to the domain of Rotoïalum (nowadays known as the Val de Reuil), near the confluence of the Eure and the Seine. Thus did circumstances bring her to within a few miles of that city of Rouen where the bishop whom she had had deposed and banished had just been reinstated in spite of her. Although there was no room in her heart for either forgiving or forgetting, and although the old man's seven years of exile had not made him any less odious to her than on the first day, she had, to begin with, no leisure to think about him; her thoughts and all her hatred were directed elsewhere.

Sorrowful at seeing herself brought down to the condition almost of an ordinary citizen, she had unceasingly before her eyes the good fortune of Brunhild, now sole and undisputed guardian of a fifteen-year-old son. She used to say bitterly: "That woman is going to think herself above me." Such thoughts made Fredegund think of murder; as soon as her mind had settled on it, she had no time for anything but dark and terrible studies: how to perfect the murder weapons, how to indoctrinate men of fanatical bent in crime and dauntlessness. The individuals who appeared the best suited to her purposes were young Barbarian clerics, poorly schooled in the spirit of their new state of life and still retaining the ways and customs of vassalage. There were several of these among the habitual guests of her house; she sustained their devotion by a kind of familiarity and by giving them handsome presents; from time to time she would try out on them intoxicating liquors and cordials whose mysterious ingredients were known only to herself. The first of these young men who seemed sufficiently prepared received from her own lips the command to go to Austrasia, to present himself to Queen Brunhild as a deserter, to win her trust, and at the first opportunity, to kill her. He set off and in fact succeeded in making his way into the queen's presence; he even entered her service, but after a few days aroused suspicion. They put him to the question; and when he had confessed everything, they sent him on his way otherwise unharmed, telling him "Go back to your mistress." Fredegund, beside herself with rage at such clemency, which seemed both an insult and a challenge, avenged herself on her blundering emissary by having his hands and feet cut off.

Some months later, when she believed the time was ripe for a second attempt, collecting all her genius for evil, she had some daggers of a new type made to her own specifications. They were long sheath knives (in shape similar to those habitually worn by the Franks) whose engraved blades were covered from end to end with incised figures. Innocent to look at, this decoration had a truly diabolical purpose: it enabled the steel to be poisoned more thoroughly, and in such a way that the toxic substance, instead of sliding off the polished surface, might become encrusted in the tooling. Two of these weapons, rubbed with a pervasive poison, were given by the queen to two young clerics whose devotion had not been cooled by the sorry fate of their companion. They were commanded to go to King Childebert's residence, dressed as poor people, to lie in wait for him when he went walking, and, at a favorable opportunity, to approach him for alms and both at once to stab him with their knives. "Take these daggers," Fredegund told them, "and leave quickly, so that at last I may see Brunhild, whose arrogance springs from that child, lose all power through his death and become my inferior. If the boy is too well guarded for you to approach him, kill my enemy Brunhild instead; if you perish in the attempt, I will shower your families with riches. I will make them wealthy through my gifts and raise them to the highest rank in the kingdom. Be fearless, therefore, and give no thought to death."

At this speech, which bluntly put before them the prospect of inescapable danger, some signs of anxiety and hesitation appeared on the young clerics' faces. Fredegund became aware of it and immediately sent for a drink compounded with every possible art to fire the spirit while gratifying the senses. Each of the young men drained a cup of this brew, the effects of which did not take long to show themselves in their expression and their bearing. Satisfied with the test, the queen then continued: "When the day comes to carry out my commands, before you set to work I want you to take a drink of this liquor, so as to be resolute and alert." The two clerics set out for Austrasia, equipped with their poisoned daggers and a flask containing the precious cordial; but the young king and his mother were well guarded. On their arrival, Fredegund's emissaries were seized as suspects, and this time no mercy was shown them—both of them were tortured to death.

These events took place during the final months of the year 585; about the beginning of the following year, it happened that Fredegund, bored perhaps with her solitude, left the Val de Reuil to go and spend a few days in Rouen. She thus found herself on more than one occasion at public gatherings and ceremonies where she was confronted by the bishop whose return gave, as it were, the lie to her authority. According to her experience of this man's character, she expected at least to see him before her with a humble and uncertain countenance and apprehensive behavior, like an exile who had received mere *de facto* amnesty through simple tolerance; but instead of displaying that obsequious respect which she craved even more since she felt herself fallen from her former rank, Praetextatus, it would appear, showed himself to be both dignified and disdainful: his soul, once so feeble and so unmanly, had in a way acquired new strength through suffering and misfortune.

In one of the encounters that civic or religious solemnities brought about between the bishop and the queen, the latter, unable to contain her anger and spite, said, loudly enough to be heard by all those present: "This man should know that the time may come for him to take the road for exile again." Praetextatus did not let the remark pass, and, braving the wrath of his terrible foe, replied to her face: "In exile and out of it, I have never ceased to be a bishop: I am a bishop, and I shall always be one, but can you say that you will always enjoy royal power? From the depths of my exile (if I return there), God will call me to the kingdom of heaven; and you, from your kingdom of this world, will be cast into the pit of hell. It is time to give up your folly and wickedness, to renounce this vainglory which puffs you up unceasingly, and to take a better road, so that you may deserve life everlasting and bring to manhood the child you have brought into the world." These words, in which the bitterest irony was mingled with the lofty gravity of a priestly reprimand, aroused all the passion in Fredegund's soul; but, far from giving way to furious utterance and making an exhibition of her shame and anger, she left without a word and went away to swallow the insult and prepare her vengeance in the privacy of her house.

Melantius, who for seven years had unlawfully occupied the bishop's throne, had, as the queen's former protégé and client, made his way to her when she arrived at the estate of Reuil, and since that time had never left her. He was the first to be let into the secret of her baleful designs. This man, so tortured by his regrets at no longer being bishop that he was capable of venturing anything to become bishop again, did not hesitate to make himself a party to a scheme which could lead him to the goal of his ambition. His seven years as bishop had not been without influence on the staff of the archdiocesan church. Several of the dignitaries promoted during that period considered themselves his creatures and looked with displeasure upon the restored bishop, to whom they owed nothing and from whom they expected few favors. Praetextatus, guileless and trustful by nature, had not been made uneasy, on his return, by the new faces he encountered in the episcopal palace; he had given no thought to those whom such a change could not fail to alarm, and since he was benevolent to all, he did not believe himself to be hated by anybody. However, despite the deep and lively affection in which he was held by the people of Rouen, most members of the clergy had little zeal or liking for him.

In some of them, especially among the higher ranks, there was utter aversion to him; one of the archdeacons or vicars metropolitan carried it to the point of fury, either out of devotion to Melantius or because he himself aspired to the episcopal dignity. Whatever the motives for the deadly hatred he bore his bishop, Fredegund and Melantius believed that they could not do without him, and admitted him as third party to the plot. They and the archdeacon conferred together and discussed ways and means of putting it into effect. It was decided that they would look among the serfs attached to the lands of the church of Rouen for a man capable of letting himself be suborned by the promise of liberty for himself, his wife, and his children. A serf was found who, intoxicated by this dubious hope of freedom, was prepared to commit the double crime of murder and sacrilege. By way of encouragement, this wretch received two hundred gold pieces, one hundred from Fredegund, fifty from Melantius, and the rest from the archdeacon; all the arrangements were made, and the following Sunday, which was February 24, was appointed for the deed.

On that day, the bishop of Rouen, for whom the murderer had been lying in wait since sunrise, made his way to church early. He sat down in his usual place, a few paces from the high altar, on an isolated seat in front of which was a prayer-stool. The rest of the clergy occupied the choir-stalls, and the bishop, as was the custom, intoned the first verse of the morning service. While the psalm-singing, taken up by the cantors, was continuing in choir, Praetextatus knelt down, bowing his head on his hands which were resting on the prayer-stool in front of him. This posture, in which he remained for a long while, gave the assassin—who had stolen in from behind—the opportunity he had been looking for since the beginning of the day. Taking advantage of the fact that the bishop, bowed down in prayer, could see nothing of what was going on around him, he drew nearer little by little until he was within arm's reach, then, drawing his knife, stabbed him under the armpit. Praetextatus, feeling himself wounded, cried out; but either through ill-will or cowardice, not one of the clerics present ran to help him, and the murderer had time to slip away. Thus forsaken, the old man got up unaided and, pressing both hands against his wound, turned towards the altar, whose steps he still had strength enough to climb. Once there, he stretched out his bloody hands to reach the golden vessel suspended above the altar by chains, in which was kept the Eucharist reserved for the communion of the dying. He took a piece of the consecrated bread and took communion; then, giving thanks to God that he had had time to fortify himself with the last sacrament, he collapsed fainting into the arms of his faithful servants, who carried him to his apartment.

Informed of the occurrence either by public report or the murderer himself, Fredegund wanted to indulge in the abominable pleasure of seeing her enemy in his death agony. She hurried to the bishop's house, accompanied by Dukes Ansowald and Beppolen, neither of whom knew what part she had played in this crime, nor what strange scene they were about to witness. Praetextatus was in bed, with every sign of imminent death written on his face, but still conscious and still able to understand what was happening. The queen disguised her feelings of joy and, assuming a tone of royal dignity and a sympathetic manner, she said: "We are grieved, holy bishop, as are the rest of your people, that such harm should have befallen your venerable person. Would to God that someone might tell us who has dared to commit this horrible deed, so that he might be punished with torments befitting his crime."

The old man, whose suspicions were all confirmed by the very fact of this visit, raised himself up on his bed of pain and, fastening his gaze on Fredegund, replied: "And who struck the blow if not the hand which has slaughtered kings, which has often shed innocent blood and done so much evil in the kingdom?" Not a trace of agitation appeared on the queen's face; and, as though these words were meaningless to her and the mere product of a fevered brain, she continued in the calmest and most affectionate way: "There are in our service highly skilled physicians capable of healing that wound; permit them to call on you." The long-suffering bishop could not hold out against such impudence, and in a transport of indignation which drained the rest of his strength, he said: "I feel that God wishes to summon me from this world; but as for you, who have come in order to conceive and direct the crime which has taken my life, you will be an object of loathing for evermore, and divine justice will avenge my blood on your head." Fredegund withdrew without a word, and, a few moments later, Praetextatus breathed his last.

The entire city of Rouen was aghast at this news; the citizens, without distinction of race, Romans and Franks alike, were united in the same sadness and horror. The former, having no political existence beyond their city limits, could only give vent to impotent grief at the sight of the crime whose chief instigator was a queen; but among the latter a certain number at least, those endowed by wealth or hereditary nobility with the title of lords, were able to speak out to any man in accordance with the ancient privileges of Germanic liberty, and to take legal action against any culprit whatsoever. There were, around Rouen, several of these heads of families, independent landowners who sat as judges in the most important cases and who proved themselves to be as proud of their personal rights as they were jealous of the upholding of ancient customs and national institutions. Numbered among them there was a great-hearted and impulsive man blessed in the highest degree with that courageous sincerity which the conquerors of Gaul considered to be the dominant virtue of their race, an opinion which, when popularized, eventually gave birth to a new word, *frankness.* This man got together some of his friends and neighbors and persuaded them to do something to create a stir: namely, to go with him and inform Fredegund that they were about to institute legal proceedings against her.

They all mounted their horses and, setting off from an estate situated a short distance from Rouen, went to the queen's lodging in the city. On their arrival, only one of them (the man who had counselled the visit) was admitted to Fredegund's presence, for, redoubling her precautions since her latest crime, she was careful to be on her guard; all the others remained in the entrance hall or in the porch. When the queen asked what he wanted, the leader of the deputation said to her in deeply outraged tones: "You have committed many heinous crimes in your lifetime, but the most monstrous of all is what you have just done in ordering the murder of a priest of God. May God soon make Himself known as the avenger of guiltless blood! But in the meantime, we will all investigate the crime and will prosecute the culprit so that you will no longer find it possible to perpetrate such acts of cruelty." After uttering this threat, the Frank went out, leaving the queen troubled to the depths of her being by a statement whose probable consequences were not without danger for her in her widowed and isolated condition.

Fredegund soon recovered her audacity, however, and made a quick decision; she sent one of her servants running after the Frankish nobleman to tell him that the queen invited him to dinner. This invitation was received by the Frank, who had just rejoined his companions, as one would expect of a man of honor: he declined it. The servant delivered his reply and came running back again to beg him, if he did not wish to stay for the meal, at least to accept something to drink, and not to insult a royal dwelling by leaving it without taking some nourishment. Such requests were always granted: custom and good manners as they were then practiced got the better of indignation, and the Frank, who was about to mount his horse, waited in the vestibule with his friends.

A moment later the servants came down carrying big cups filled with the drink that Barbarians most readily took between meals, wine mixed with honey and wormwood. The Frank to whom the queen's message had been sent was the first to be served. He rashly drained the cup of spiced liquor at one draught; but scarcely had he drunk the last drop when an agonizing pain and a griping in his vitals told him that he had just swallowed the most deadly poison. He remained silent for an instant in the grip of this shattering sensation, but when he saw his companions preparing to follow his example and do justice to the absinth wine, he cried, "Do not touch that drink; get away from here, unhappy men, get away from here lest you perish with me!" These words filled the Franks with a kind of panic; the idea of poisoning, then inseparable from sorcery and black magic, the presence of a mysterious danger impossible to beat off with their swords, caused these warriors who would not have fallen back in battle to take to flight. They all ran to their horses; the one who had drunk the poision did the same and managed to mount, but his sight was growing dim and his hands were losing the strength to grasp the reins. No longer able to control his horse, which was galloping after the others, he was carried a few hundred yards and then fell dead. The report of this affair spread superstitious terror far and wide; among the landowners of the diocese of Rouen, no one spoke any more of summoning Fredegund to appear before the great judicial assembly which, under the name of mâl, met at least twice a year.

While the see was vacant, the administration of the metropolitan church fell to Leudowald, bishop of Bayeux, in his capacity as first suffragan bishop of the archdiocese of Rouen. He made his way to the city and from there addressed an official report of the violent death of Praetextatus to all the bishops of the province; then, having convened the city clergy in municipal synod, he gave orders, following that assembly's recommendation, that all the churches of Rouen should be closed and that no services should be held until a public inquest had put him on the track of the authors of the crime and their accomplices. A few Gauls of low degree were arrested as suspects and put to the question; more of them had known of the plot against the archbishop's life and had even received overtures and offers in that connection; their revelations bore out the general suspicion hanging over Fredegund. But they named neither of her two accomplices, Melantius and the archdeacon. The queen, feeling that she could make short work of these ecclesiastical proceedings, took all of the accused under her protection and openly procured them the means of evading the preliminary investigations, either by flight or by offering armed resistance.

Far from letting himself be discouraged by the obstacles of every kind which he encountered, Bishop Leudowald, a conscientious man devoted to his priestly duties, became more zealous than ever to discover the perpetrator of the murder and to get to the bottom of this shocking and mysterious conspiracy. Then Fredegund put into effect the measures she kept in reserve for extreme circumstances: assassins were seen prowling around the bishop's house, trying to get in; Leudowald was obliged to have himself guarded day and night by his servants and his clergy. His constancy was not up to such alarms: the proceedings, undertaken at first with a certain ostentation, slowed down, and the inquest under Roman law was soon abandoned, just like the legal action before the Frankish judges assembled under Salic law.

The report of these events, which spread by degrees throughout Gaul, reached King Guntram in his residence at Chalon-sur-Saône. The emotion it caused him was keen enough to jolt him—for a short time—out of the kind of political listlessness in which he took pleasure. His character was, as we have already seen, an odd mixture of contrasting elements: a basically gentle piety and rigid impartiality, beneath which the poorly extinguished remains of a savage and sanguinary nature bubbled up, so to speak, and now and then broke through. This old leaven of Germanic ferocity revealed its presence in the soul of the mildest of the Merovingian kings now by outbursts of brutal fury, now by acts of cold-blooded cruelty. Guntram's second wife, Austrehild, attacked in the year 580 by a sickness which she felt must be fatal, had the barbarous whim not to want to die alone, and to ask that both her physicians be beheaded on the day of her funeral. The king promised this as if it were the most ordinary of requests, and had both the doctors' heads cut off. After this act of conjugal complaisance worthy of the most atrocious tyrant, Guntram returned, with inexplicable ease, to his habitual fatherly rule and his customary good nature. On learning of the double crime of murder and sacrilege of which the general outcry accused his brother's widow, he was genuinely indignant and, as head of the Merovingian house, believed that a great deed of patriarchal justice was called for on his part. He dispatched, as ambassadors to the nobles exercising the regency in the name of Chilperic's son, three bishops: Artemius of Sens, Agroecius of Troyes, and Veranus of Cavaillon in the province of Arles. These envoys were ordered to obtain authorization from the Neustrian lords to seek out, by means of a formal investigation, the person guilty of the crime, and to bring him (or her) before King Guntram by fair means or foul.

The three bishops proceeded to Paris, where the child in whose name the kingdom of Neustria had been governed for the past two years was being brought up. Admitted to the presence of the regency council, they stated their business, stressing the enormity of the crime for which King Guntram was requesting punishment. When they had finished speaking, the Neustrian chief who was the highest-ranking of the young king's guardians, and who was called his foster-father, stood up and said: "We too most strongly dislike such misdeeds, and are ever more desirous that they be punished; but if the guilty party is here in Neustria, he is not to be taken before *your* king, for with the royal assent we ourselves have the means of repressing all crimes committed among us."

This ostensibly resolute and dignified language concealed an evasive answer, for the regents of Neustria were less concerned with the independence of the kingdom than with handling Fredegund with kid gloves. The ambassadors were not taken in, and one of them replied sharply: "Know that if the criminal is not discovered and brought out into the open our king will come with an army to devastate this whole land with fire and sword; for it is manifest that she who murdered the Frank with her baleful magic is the same who slew the bishop with the sword." The Neustrians were not much alarmed by such threats; they knew that King Guntram's will always failed him when the time came to act. They repeated their previous replies, and the bishops put an end to this fruitless interview by protesting beforehand against the reinstatement of Melantius in the see of Rouen. But scarcely had they returned to King Guntram when Melantius was restored, thanks to the queen's influence and to the ascendancy that she had just regained through intrigue and terror. This man, a creature worthy of Fredegund, went every day for more than fifteen years to sit and pray in the same seat where the blood of Praetextatus had flowed.

Proud of such successes, the queen crowned her work by a final stroke of insolence, a mark of the most incredible contempt for all who had dared to attack her. She ordered to be publicly seized and brought before her that same land-serf whom she herself had paid to commit the crime and whom she had helped thus far to elude all investigations. "So it is you," she said, feigning the warmest indignation, "you who stabbed Praetextatus, bishop of Rouen, and who are responsible for the slanders against me?" Then she had him beaten before her eyes and turned him over to the bishop's relatives with no more concern for the consequences than if the man had known nothing of the plot whose instrument he had been. Praetextatus's nephew—one of those hot-tempered Gauls who, following Teutonic example, lived only for private vengeance and always went abroad armed, like the Franks—laid hands on the wretched man and had him tortured in his own house. The assassin did not make him wait long for his answers and admissions. "I did the deed," he said, "and for doing it I received one hundred gold *solidi* from Queen Fredegund, fifty from Bishop Melantius, and fifty from the archdeacon of Rouen; they also promised to free my wife and me."

However factual this information might be, it was obvious that nothing could come of it. Every power in the society of the day had tried in vain to exert its influence in this appalling affair: the aristocracy, the priesthood, the crown itself had remained impotent to get at the true culprit. Convinced that he would find no justice beyond the reach of his own arm, Praetextatus's nephew settled everything with an act worthy of a savage, but in which despair perhaps played as great a part as ferocity: he drew his sword and hacked to pieces the slave who had been thrown to him. As was nearly always the case in that disorderly age, the sole redress for brutal murder was another murder. Only the people did not fail the cause of their murdered bishop; they conferred the title of martyr on him, and, while the official church was enthroning one of the assassins and the bishops were calling him brother, the citizens of Rouen were invoking the victim's name in their prayers and were kneeling at his tomb. It is with this halo of popular veneration that the memory of St. Prétextat (an object of pious homage for the faithful who hardly knew anything of him but his name) has come down through the centuries. If the details of a life which was thoroughly human in its misfortunes and weaknesses may diminish the glory of the saint, they will at least evoke a feeling of sympathy for the man; for is there not something touching about the character of this old priest who died because he loved his godson too well, thus fulfilling the Christian ideal of spiritual fatherhood?

FIFTH EPISODE
History of Leudast, Count of Tours—
The Poet Venantius Fortunatus—
The Convent of Radegund at Poitiers
(579–581)

During the reign of Lothar I, the Ile de Ré, seven miles off the Saintonge coast, was a royal domain. Its vines, the sparse product of a soil ceaselessly battered by the ocean winds, were at that time tended by a Gaul named Leocadius. This man had a son whom he called by the Teutonic name Leudast—which was probably that of some wealthy Frankish lord, a local celebrity—doubtless chosen by the Gallic vine-grower in preference to any other either to obtain a useful patronage for the newborn child or to place, as it were, the augury of a great fortune over his head, and to cherish his own illusions and paternal ambitions. Born a serf of the royal household, Leocadius's son was included, on emerging from childhood, in a group of young men conscripted for the kitchen staff by the chief steward of King Charibert's estates. This kind of impressment of the families peopling their vast lands was practiced on numerous occasions by order of the Frankish kings, and persons of every age and profession (and even those of gentle birth) found themselves obliged to submit to it.

Taken in this manner far from the little island where he had been born, young Leudast was at first conspicuous among all his fellow-serfs by his lack of zeal for work and his unruly spirit. He had weak eyes, and the acrid smoke bothered him a great deal, a circumstance of which he took—more or less understandably—the maximum advantage in his negligence and his refusals to obey. After vain attempts to train him in the duties required of him, there was nothing for it but to let him go or to give him a different occupation. The latter course was taken, and the vine-grower's son went from the kitchens to the bakery, or, as his earliest biographer puts it, from the pestle to the kneading-trough. Deprived of the excuse which had been valid against his former work, Leudast from then on tried to dissemble, and appeared to be extremely content with his new duties. He carried them out for some time with an ardor thanks to which he succeeded in lulling the vigilance of his superiors and keepers; then, seizing the first favorable opportunity, he ran away. They ran after him and brought him back, and he ran away again, no less than three times. The disciplinary punishments of the whip and the prison cell (to which, as a runaway, he was successively subjected) being judged inadequate against such stubbornness, the last and most effective penalty, that of slitting one of his ears, was imposed on him.

Although this mutilation made escape both more difficult and less safe, he escaped again, at the risk of not knowing where to find a refuge. After wandering in different directions, always trembling at the thought of being detected because the mark of his servile condition was so plainly visible, weary of this life of alarms and miseries, he determined to take a very bold course of action. It was the time when King Charibert had just married Markovefa, a palace maidservant and daughter of a wool-carder. Perhaps Leudast had had some dealings with this woman's family; perhaps he merely relied on her kindheartedness and her sympathy for a former fellow-slave. At all events, instead of going straight on, to get as far away as possible from the royal residence, he retraced his steps and, hiding in some nearby forest, waited for the moment he could appear before the new queen without fear of being seen and apprehended by one of the household servants. He was successful, and Markovefa, much affected by his entreaties, took him under her protection. She entrusted him with the care of her finest horses and gave him the title, among her retainers, of *mariskalk*[1] (to use the Teutonic term).

Leudast, encouraged by this success and this unlooked-for favor, soon stopped limiting his desires to his present position and, aiming higher, coveted the chief stewardship of his patroness's stud farm and the title of count of the stable,[2] a dignity which the Barbarian kings had borrowed from the Imperial court. He soon achieved his ambition, in which he was well served by his lucky star, for he had more audacity and braggadocio than shrewdness and genuine ability. In this post, which placed him at the level not merely of free men but of Frankish nobles, he completely forgot his origins and the old days of slavery and distress. He became callous and scornful towards all those beneath him, arrogant with his peers, hungry for money and every luxury, unbridled and immoderate in his ambitions. Raised by the queen's fondness to a kind of favorite's position, he acted as go-between in all her dealings and derived immense profits therefrom, unrestrainedly imposing upon her easy-going and trustful nature. When she died some years later, he was already rich enough from his depredations to be able—by means of intrigue and presents—to solicit the same employment in King Charibert's service that he had exercised in the household of the queen. He triumphed over all his rivals, became count of the royal stables and, far from being ruined by the death of his patroness, found in it the beginning of a new career of honors. After enjoying his exalted rank in the palace staff for a year or two, the fortunate serf's son from the Ile de Ré was promoted to a political dignity and made count of Tours, one of the most considerable cities in

Charibert's kingdom.

The office of count, as it had existed in Gaul since the Conquest, corresponded, according to Frankish political conceptions, to that of the magistrate they called the *graf*, who, in each district of Germany, administered criminal justice, assisted by the householders or notables of his district. The naturally unfriendly relations between the conquerors and the populations of the conquered cities had resulted in the addition of military functions to these judicial ones, and a dictatorial power which was almost always abused, either because of the personal inclination to violence or the selfish motives of the men who exercised them in the name of the Frankish kings. It was a kind of Barbarian proconsulate superimposed on the old municipal institutions in each important town, without any care being taken to adjust it in such a way that it could harmonize with them. Despite their enfeeblement, these institutions still sufficed to maintain law and order within the cities of Gaul, and their inhabitants felt more terror than joy when a royal letter came to notify them of the arrival of a count, sent to govern them in accordance with their own customs and to do justice to all. Such was doubtless the impression created in Tours by the coming of Leudast, and the citizens' repugnance could hardly fail to grow from day to day. He was unlettered, had no knowledge of the laws he was to administer, and even lacked that uprightness and natural impartiality which was at least found beneath a rough exterior in the *grafs* from beyond the Rhine.

Schooled originally in the ways of slavery and then in the turbulent life of the vassals of the royal household, he had not a trace of that ancient Roman civilization with which he was about to find himself in contact, except for the love of luxury, display, and sensual pleasures. He behaved in his new employment as if he had received it simply for his own benefit and for the gratification of his immoderate instincts. Instead of instituting the rule of order in the city of Tours, he spread mischief by his lack of self-control and his dissolute ways; his marriage to the daughter of a local magnate made him neither more temperate nor more cautious. He was violent and haughty towards men, his licentiousness respected no woman, and his rapacity far exceeded all that he had revealed hitherto. He used every trick he could think of to instigate unjust lawsuits against wealthy persons and then to arbitrate them himself, or else to bring false charges against them and make a profit out of the fines which he shared with the Treasury. By means of his extortions and pillaging, he rapidly increased his wealth and accumulated much gold and many valuables in his house. His good fortune and impunity lasted until King Charibert's death in 567. Sigibert, who then inherited the city of Tours, did not share his elder brother's fondness for the former slave. Quite the contrary—his ill-will was so great that to escape it, Leudast hurriedly left the city, abandoning his estates and the greater part of his treasure, which were seized or pillaged by the king of Austrasia's men. He sought asylum in Chilperic's kingdom and swore allegiance to that king, who took him in among his leuds. During his years of misfortune, the ex-count of Tours lived in Neustria on the hospitality of the palace, following the court from estate to estate and taking his place at the immense table where the king's vassals and dining-companions were seated in order of age and rank.

Five years after Count Leudast's flight, Georgius Florentius (who took the name of Gregory on his accession) was appointed bishop of Tours by King Sigibert at the request of the citizens, whose affection and esteem he had won during a pilgrimage from Auvergne (his native province) to St. Martin's tomb. This man, whose character has already been made known in earlier episodes, was, through his religious fervor, his taste for sacred literature, and the seriousness of his principles, one of the most perfect types of the high Christian aristocracy of Gaul, to which his ancestors had added luster. From the time of his installation in the metropolitan see of Tours, Gregory, by virtue of the political prerogatives then attached to the rank of bishop (and also because of the personal esteem he enjoyed) found himself invested with supreme influence over the affairs of the city and the deliberations of the senate which governed it. The brilliance of this lofty position was to be amply offset by countless fatigues, anxieties, and perils; Gregory was not long in finding this out for himself. During the first year of his episcopate, the city of Tours was invaded by King Chilperic's troops and recaptured in rapid succession by those of Sigibert. The next year, Theodebert, Chilperic's eldest son, waged a campaign of devastation along the banks of the Loire which struck terror into the hearts of the citizens of Tours, and compelled them to submit to the king of Neustria for the second time. It appears that Leudast, in order to make his fortune anew, had enlisted in this expedition, either as a troop leader or among the picked vassals who formed the entourage of the king's youthful son.

When he entered the city he had just forced to submit to his father, Theodebert presented the former count to the bishop and the municipal senate, saying that it would be well for Tours to be governed once more by the man who had ruled it so wisely and firmly in the days of the former partition of Gaul. Quite independently of the memories Leudast had left behind in Tours, which were well calculated to disgust the pious, decent Gregory, this descendant of the most illustrious senatorial families of Berry and Auvergne could not, without aversion, see a man of naught, who bore on his body the indelible mark of his servile parentage, rise to a position so near his own. However, the recommendations of the young chief of the Neustrian army were commands, no matter how deferentially they seemed to have been made. In the present interests of the city, threatened with sacking and burning, it was necessary to give a willing response to the conqueror's whims, and this the bishop of Tours did, with that prudence exemplified by his entire life. The leading citizens seemed thus to be in agreement with Theodebert's plans for reinstating Leudast in his duties and his honors. This restoration was not long in coming, and, a few days later, Leocadius's son received from the palace of Neustria his letter of appointment, a document whose tenor (as revealed in the official phraseology of the period) was strangely at odds with his character and his behavior.

"If there are occasions on which the perfection of the royal clemency is made to shine forth with more especial brightness, it is above all in the choice which it is able to make, out of all the people, of upright and watchful persons. It would not indeed be seemly for the dignity of magistrate to be bestowed upon someone whose integrity and steadfastness had not previously been tested. Now, being well informed as to your fidelity and merit, we have appointed you to the office of count in the district of Tours, to possess it and exercise all its prerogatives in such a way as to maintain an entire and inviolable fealty towards our rule, that those dwelling within the bounds of your jurisdiction, whether Franks or Romans, or of any other nation whatsoever, may live in peace and good order under your authority and power; that you may guide them on the right paths in accordance with their laws and customs; that you may show yourself to be the special defender of widows and orphans; that the crimes of thieves and other evildoers may be sternly repressed, and lastly that the people, finding life good under your government, may rejoice thereat and remain at peace, and that the amount due the Exchequer from the receipts of your office may through your care be paid each year punctually into our Treasury."

The new count of Tours, who did not yet feel the ground quite steady beneath his feet and who was afraid that the fortunes of war might cause the city to fall into the hands of the king of Austrasia once again, made a point of living on good terms not only with the municipal senators, but above all with the bishop, whose powerful patronage he might need. In Gregory's presence, his manner and speech were modest and even humble, and he observed the distance separating him from a man of such high nobility, being careful to gratify the aristocratic vanity with which the sterling qualities of that steadfast and serious spirit were slightly leavened. He promised to take care not to exceed his powers and to adopt justice and reason as his rules of conduct. Finally, to make his promises and protestations more worthy of belief, he accompanied them with numerous oaths on St. Martin's tomb. He would often swear to Gregory, like a client to his patron, always and in every circumstance to remain faithful to him, never to fail him in anything, either in matters concerning him personally or in those where the interests of his church were at stake.

This was how matters stood, and the city of Tours was enjoying a calm that nobody had at first dared hope for, when Theodebert's army was destroyed near Angoulême, and Chilperic, believing his cause to be desperate, took refuge behind the walls of Tournai (events which have been narrated in detail in one of the foregoing Episodes[3]). The citizens of Tours, who were obedient to the king of Neustria only under duress, again acknowledged the authority of Sigibert, and Leudast fled once more as he had done seven years earlier; but this time, thanks possibly to the intervention of Bishop Gregory, his property was respected and he left the city without suffering any loss. He withdrew to Western Brittany, a region which at that time enjoyed complete independence from the Frankish kingdoms and which often served as a place of refuge for their exiles and malcontents.

The murder which, in the year 575, so abruptly ended Sigibert's life brought about a double restoration: that of Chilperic as king of Neustria and of Leudast as count of Tours. He returned after one year of exile and reinstated himself in his office. From then on, certain of what the future held in store, he no longer took the trouble to restrain himself, but threw off the mask and began once more to follow the wicked ways of his first administration. Giving way at one and the same time to all the evil passions which may tempt a man in power, he exhibited the spectacle of the most arrant frauds and the most sickening acts of brutality. When he held his public hearings, his assessors were the leading men of the city, Frankish lords, Romans of senatorial family, and dignitaries of the metropolitan church. If some litigant whom he wished to ruin or some defendant whom he wished to destroy came confidently before him, maintaining his rights and asking for justice, the count would cut him short and fidget about like a madman in his seat. If the crowd encircling the judges' bench then happened to show sympathy for the oppressed by its gestures or its murmuring, Leudast would turn on it angrily and would upbraid the citizens in coarse and insulting language. As impartial in his violent outbursts as he should have been in his administration of justice, he took no account of anybody's rights, rank, or social condition; he had priests brought before him with manacles on their wrists and Frankish warriors cudgelled with rods. One might had said that this upstart slave took pleasure in muddling every distinction, in defying every convention of the social order from which the accident of birth had at first excluded him, and within which other strokes of luck had afterwards raised him so high.

However despotic Count Leudast's ways, and however much he desired to reduce everything and everybody to the same level to suit his own advantage, there was a power in the city rivalling his own and a man against whom it was forbidden to venture all, on pain of destroying himself. He sensed this, and resorted to cunning rather than to overt violence to compel the bishop to yield, or at least to keep silent before him. Gregory's reputation, widely known throughout Gaul, was high at the court of Neustria; but his well-known affection for Sigibert's family sometimes alarmed Chilperic, who was always uneasy about his possession of Tours—the spoils of war—which was the key to the territory he wished to conquer south of the Loire. It was on King Chilperic's touchiness in this regard that Leudast based his hopes of destroying the bishop's credit by making him appear ever more suspect, and by having himself considered indispensable to the holding of the city, just like a front-line sentinel always on the alert and exposed, on account of his vigilance, to hate-filled prejudice and veiled or overt hostility. This was the surest means of securing complete impunity for himself and of finding opportunities for molesting his most redoubtable opponent without appearing to go beyond his rights.

In this war of intrigue and petty scheming, he occasionally resorted to the oddest expedients. When obliged to go to the bishop's house on business, he would make his way there fully armed, wearing a helmet and breastplate, with his quiver slung across his back and a long pike in his hand, either to make himself look terrible or to give the impression that there was a danger of snares and ambushes in that house of peace and prayer. In the year 576 when Merovech, on his way through Tours, carried off all Leudast's money and valuables, the latter claimed that the young prince had only indulged in this plundering as a result of Gregory's advice and at his instigation.[4] Then, through native volatility (or because this unsubstantiated charge was quite ineffective), he all at once attempted a reconciliation with the bishop and swore by the most sacred oaths, while clutching a handful of the silk cloth which covered St. Martin's tomb, that he would never again commit a hostile act against him so long as he lived. But Leudast's inordinate desire to make good as quickly as possible the enormous losses he had just suffered caused him to multiply his exactions and depredations. Among the wealthy citizens who were his favorite prey, several were close friends of Gregory, and they were shown no more consideration than the others. Thus, despite his most recent promises and his resolve to be prudent, the count of Tours found himself once more indirectly at war with his rival in authority. Before long, increasingly carried away by the desire to amass riches, he began to encroach upon church property, and the difference between the two adversaries became a personal one. Gregory, with a forbearance which was due both to priestly long-suffering and the traditionally circumspect policy of the aristocracy, at first offered only a moral resistance to acts of physical violence. He took the blows without returning any himself until the precise moment when it seemed to him that the time was ripe for action; and then, after two years of waiting calmly and, as one might have thought, resignedly, he energetically took the offensive.

Towards the end of the year 579, a deputation sent secretly to King Chilperic denounced, on unimpeachable evidence, Count Leudast's embezzlements and the innumerable wrongs he had done the churches and the whole population of Tours. We do not know under what circumstances this deputation made its way to the palace of Neustria, nor the various causes which contributed to the success of its representations: but they were fully successful; and, in spite of the king's favor which Leudast had for so long enjoyed, in spite of the many friends he had among the vassals and confidential servants of the palace, it was decided to remove him from office. When the envoys took their leave of him, Chilperic sent Ansowald, his closest advisor, with them to take the necessary steps and to effect the changeover requested in their petition. Ansowald arrived in Tours in November and, not content with declaring Leudast dismissed from office, left the appointment of a new count to the bishop and the entire citizenry. The unanimous choice fell upon a Gaul named Eunomius, who was installed in his functions amid the acclamations and hopes of the people.

Taken unawares by this blow, Leudast, who in his unshakeable self-confidence had never given a single thought to the possibility of such a setback, became violently angry and put all the blame on his friends at the palace, who to his way of thinking should have supported him. He was especially bitter in accusing Queen Fredegund, whom he had served devotedly regardless of right or wrong, and who now requited him with ingratitude by withdrawing her protection,[5] although (as he believed) she was all-powerful to save him from this peril. These grievances, whether well-founded or not, made so strong an impression on the dispossessed count that from that time onwards his hatred for his former patroness was equal to that he bore the bishop of Tours, the instigator of his removal. No longer making any distinction between them in his desire for revenge, seething with resentment, he began to formulate the most reckless schemes, concocting plans for making his fortune and for rising all over again, plans in which he included—this being one of his ardent wishes—the bishop's ruin and, even more astonishingly, the ruin of Fredegund herself, her repudiation by her husband and her fall from the queenly estate.

There was at that time in Tours a priest called Rikulf, who may well have been of Gallic origin despite his Teutonic name, like Leudast, whom he much resembled in character. Born in the city, of poor parents, he had received advancement in holy orders as a protégé of Bishop Euphronius, Gregory's predecessor. His self-importance and ambition were boundless; he believed himself to be out of his rightful place so long as he was not bishop. In order to achieve his goal more surely some day, he had some years before put himself under the protection of Clovis, youngest son of King Chilperic by Queen Audovera. Although repudiated and banished, this queen, who was freeborn and probably of distinguished parentage, had in her misfortune retained numerous supporters, who hoped that she would return to favor and believed in the prospects of her sons (who were already grown men) rather than in those of her rival's young children. Fredegund, despite her power and her brilliant triumphs, had not been entirely successful in making those around her forget her baseborn origins and in inspiring complete confidence in the solidity of her present good fortune. There were doubts as to how long the kind of spell she cast over the king's mind could last; many people only reluctantly paid her the honors due a queen. Her own daughter Rigonthe, the oldest of her four children, blushed for her and, with a precocious instinct of feminine vanity, was bitterly ashamed of having a former palace serving-maid for her mother. Thus King Chilperic's beloved wife did not lack grounds for mental anguish, and the greatest of all—together with the ineffacable stigma of her lowly birth—was the dread occasioned by the rivalry for the crown between her children and those of the king's first marriage.

Violent death had rid her of Audovera's two elder sons, but she still saw the third one, Clovis, holding in check the fortunes of her own two sons Chlodobert and Dagobert, the older of whom was not yet fifteen.[6] Opinions, desires and ambitious hopes were divided, in the palace of Neustria, between the future of the one and that of the others; there were two opposing factions which had ramifications outside the palace and were met with in every part of the kingdom. Both of them included men who had long been staunchly devoted to the cause, as well as transient recruits who attached themselves or broke away on the spur of the moment. Thus it was that Rikulf and Leudast, the former a longstanding supporter of Clovis's fortunes, the latter until recently hostile to the young prince, as he had been to his brother Merovech, suddenly found their political sentiments to be in perfect conformity. They soon became bosom friends, confided all their secrets to one another, and cooperated in their projects and hopes. During the final months of the year 579 and the first months of the following year, these two men, equally experienced in intrigue, frequently conferred together in the presence of a third party, a subdeacon named—like the priest—Rikulf, the same Rikulf we saw acting as an emissary of the cleverest schemer of the age, the Austrasian Guntram-Bose.[7]

The first point agreed upon by the three associates was to avail themselves of the widespread rumors of Fredegund's marital infidelities and licentiousness by bringing them to the ears of King Chilperic. They thought that the blinder and more trusting the king's love in the face of evidence which was plain to everyone else, the more terrible his anger must be when he was undeceived. Fredegund turned out of the king-dom, her children the objects of the king's aversion, banished with her and disinherited, Clovis succeeding to his father's kingship without question and with no need to share with his half-brothers: such were the results (certain, according to them) which they promised themselves from their officious proceedings. As quite a subtle device to rid them-selves of the responsibility of formally denouncing the queen, and at the same time to compromise their second enemy, the bishop of Tours, they resolved to accuse him of having made before witnesses the scandalous remarks which were then being spread by word of mouth, and which they themselves dared not repeat.

In this intrigue there was a double chance that the bishop would be deposed; either immediately, owing to an outburst of King Chilperic's wrath, or a little later, when Clovis came into the kingship; and the priest Rikulf was already putting himself forward as his replacement on the episcopal throne. Leudast, who guaranteed his new friend the absolute certainty of this advancement, was himself staking out a place by King Clovis's side, as the second most important person in the kingdom, whose supreme administrator he (with the title of duke) would be. So that Rikulf the subdeacon should similarly find a post which suited him, it was decided that Plato, the archdeacon of Tours and Bishop Gregory's bosom friend, should be compromised with him and involved in the same ruin.

It would seem that the three conspirators, having settled things thus in their secret meetings, sent messages to Clovis to inform him of the enterprise framed in his behalf, to convey their plans to him, and to name their terms. The young prince, unthinking by nature and imprudently ambitious, promised everything they asked for, and much more besides, in the event of a successful outcome. It was now time for action, and a role was assigned to each man. Rikulf the priest was to prepare the way for Gregory's future dismissal by stirring up agitators against him in the city, as well as those who, in a spirit of local patriotism, disliked him because he was an outsider[8] and wanted a native bishop in his stead. Rikulf the subdeacon, until recently one of the humblest guests of the episcopal household, and who had deliberately fallen out with his patron so as to be more at liberty to see Leudast regularly, returned to make his apologies to the bishop and to feign repentance; he attempted, by regain-ing his confidence, to lure him into some suspicious action which might serve as evidence against him. Last of all, the ex-count of Tours un-hesitatingly took upon himself the really dangerous mission of going to the palace at Soissons and speaking to King Chilperic.

He left Tours in or about April, 580, and as soon as he arrived, having been granted a private interview with the king, he said, attempting to sound both grave and thoughtful: "Hitherto, most pious king, I watched over your city of Tours, but now that I have been set aside from my office, give heed to how it will be guarded in future; for you must know that Bishop Gregory intends to deliver it to Sigibert's son." Like a man rebelling against a disagreeable piece of news and playing the skeptic so as not to appear frightened, Chilperic replied brusquely: "That isn't true." Then, watching closely for the slightest trace of uneasiness and hesitancy to appear on Leudast's features, he added: "It is because you have been dismissed from office that you have come here to make such statements." But the ex-count, without losing any of his self-assurance, went on: "That's not all the bishop is up to; he says things which are insulting to you; he says that your queen has an adulterous relationship with Bishop Bertram." Struck in his most sensitive and touchy spot, Chilperic was overcome by such an attack of fury that, losing all sense of royal dignity, he fell with all his might, kicking and punching, upon the unlucky author of this unexpected revelation.

Having vented his anger in complete silence and somewhat recovered his senses, he found his tongue and said to Leudast: "What! you declare that the bishop has said such things about Queen Fredegund?" "I do so declare," he replied, not at all disconcerted by the brutal reception his secret had just been given, "and if you would have Gallienus, the bishop's friend, and Plato, his archdeacon, put to the torture, they would convict him in your hearing. "But are you yourself appearing as a witness?" asked the king, with keen anxiety. Leudast answered that he had an earwitness, and he named the subdeacon Rikulf, without mentioning torture for him, as he had done a moment before in connection with Bishop Gregory's two friends. But the distinction he was trying to make in his accomplice's behalf was lost on the king, who, equally enraged with all those who had had a share in this scandal wounding his honor, had Leudast himself clapped in irons and immediately dispatched orders to Tours for Rikulf's arrest.

Rikulf, a consummate rogue, had been completely successful a month before in reingratiating himself with Bishop Gregory, and as a faithful client was once more welcome in his house and at his board. When he judged by the number of days which had elapsed since Leudast's departure that the denunciation must have been made and his own name mentioned before the king, he set about drawing the bishop into some suspicious action, by taking advantage of his kindheartedness and compassion. He came before him looking woebegone and deeply anxious, and as soon as Gregory began to ask what was the matter, he threw himself down at his feet, crying: "I am lost if you do not swiftly come to my aid. Egged on by Leudast, I have said things that I ought not to have said. Grant me leave of absence to go to another land forthwith, for if I stay here the king's officers will seize me and I shall be put to the torture." A cleric could in fact move away from the church to which he was attached only with his bishop's permission, nor could he be received in another bishop's diocese without a letter from his own as a passport. By soliciting this leave of absence under cover of the so-called danger of death which he claimed was threatening him, the subdeacon was playing a double game: he was trying to provoke an incident capable of substantiating what Leudast had told the king, and in addition was procuring a means of disappearing from the scene and awaiting the outcome of this great intrigue in perfect safety.

Gregory in no way suspected the reasons for Leudast's departure, nor what was then going on in Soissons; but the subdeacon's request, wrapped up as it was in obscure language and accompanied by a kind of tragic pantomime, surprised and alarmed him instead of moving him. The violence of the age, the sudden catastrophes which every day put paid, before his very eyes, to the most exalted fortunes, the prevailing sense of instability in every man's position and life, had led him to practice the most watchful circumspection. He was accordingly on his guard, and to the great disappointment of Rikulf, who was hoping to lure him into the trap by means of his sham despair, replied: "If you have said things contrary to reason and your duty, on your own head be it; I will not let you leave for another kingdom, for fear of making myself look suspicious in the king's eyes."

Rikulf stood up, mortified over the failure of this first attempt, and was doubtless preparing to try some fresh trick, when he was arrested without any fuss by order of the king and taken away to Soissons. As soon as he arrived, he was made to undergo, alone, an interrogation during which, despite his critical situation, he fulfilled in every particular the commitments he had made to his two accomplices. Passing himself off as a witness to the fact, he testified that on the day Bishop Gregory had spoken ill of the queen, Archdeacon Plato and Gallienus were present, and that both of them had talked in the same way as the bishop. This formal testimony resulted in the freeing of Leudast, whose veracity no longer seemed doubtful and who in any case promised no new information. Released while his companion in falsehood took his place in prison, he was entitled to believe from then on that he was the object of a kind of royal favor; for he it was that, by an odd choice, King Chilperic sent to Tours to apprehend Gallienus and Archdeacon Plato. No doubt this commission was given him because, with his customary vainglory, he boasted that he alone was capable of successfully accomplishing it, and also because—to make himself indispensable—the accounts which he gave of the state of the city and the mood of its citizens were most apt to alarm the king's suspicious mind.

Leudast, proud of his new role as confidential agent and of the fortune which he believed was already his, set off during Easter week. On Good Friday, in the halls serving as annexes to Tours cathedral, there was a great uproar occasioned by the unruliness of Rikulf the priest. Far from conceiving the slightest apprehension at the arrest of the subdeacon, his namesake and accomplice, this fellow, unshakeable in his hopes, had merely seen it as a step towards the conclusion of the intrigue which was to carry him to the episcopate. In the expectation of a favorable outcome (which he no longer doubted), he got so excited that he became as one intoxicated, unable to control his actions or his language. During one of the rest periods taken by the clergy between services, he walked back and forth in front of the bishop several times in a defiant manner, and finally said out loud that all Auvergnats should be swept out of the city of Tours. Gregory was only indifferently affected by this unseemly outburst, the reason for which was beyond him. Accustomed—especially on the part of his plebeian clergy—to the uncouth tones and utterance which were becoming more and more prevalent in Gaul through imitation of Barbarian manners, he replied without anger and with just a hint of aristocratic dignity: "It is not true that the natives of Auvergne are strangers here; for with only five exceptions, every bishop of Tours has come from a family related to our own; you ought not to be unaware of that." Nothing could have been better calculated than this retort to provoke the ambitious priest's jealousy to the utmost degree. It so increased that, unable to contain himself any longer, he began to aim direct insults and threatening gestures at the bishop. From threats he would have progressed to blows, if the other clerics had not forestalled the ultimate effects of his frenzy by coming between him and Gregory.

The day after this disorderly scene, Leudast arrived in Tours, entering the city without either display or armed retinue, as though he had simply come on private business. This untypical discretion had in all likelihood been stipulated by the king's express command, as a means of more surely carrying out the arrests he was supposed to make. During part of the day, he pretended to be busy with other matters; then suddenly, swooping down on his prey, he broke into the homes of Gallienus and Archdeacon Plato with a troop of soldiers. The two unfortunates were seized in the most brutal manner, stripped of their clothes, and chained together. By leading them through the city like this, Leudast was mysteriously proclaiming that short work was about to be made of all the queen's enemies and that no time would be lost in laying hands on a more important offender. Perhaps he wanted to impress people with the importance of his confidential mission and his capture, or perhaps he was genuinely afraid of some ambush or riot; in any case, he took extraordinary precautions over his departure. On leaving the city, instead of crossing the Loire by the bridge, he took it into his head to ferry it, with the two prisoners and their guards, on a kind of mobile bridge consisting of two boats joined together by planking and towed by other craft.

When the news of these events reached Gregory's ears, he was in the episcopal residence seeing to the numerous matters which took up every hour left free by the exercise of his sacred ministry. The misfortune of his two friends, which was only too certain, and the threat to himself implicit in the vague but ominous rumors which were beginning to circulate, added to his still vivid impression of the previous day's trying scenes, caused him the profoundest agitation. Overcome with heartfelt melancholy, perturbation, and despondency, he broke off his routine business and went alone to his private chapel. He fell to his knees and began to pray; but his prayer, no matter how fervent, did not calm him. "What is going to happen?" he wondered in his distress, and he kept turning this totally unanswerable question over and over in his mind, without being able to find the solution. To escape from the torture of uncertainty, he went so far as to do something which he had himself more than once censured, in conformity with the Councils and the Fathers of the Church: he took the book of Psalms and opened it at random, to see if he might not come across—as he puts it himself—some verse of consolation. The passage on which his eye lighted was the following: "He made them to go out full of hope, and they were not afraid, and their enemies were swallowed up in the depths of the sea." [9] The fortuitous relationship between these words and the ideas which obsessed him had an effect which neither reason nor unaided faith had been able to produce. He believed he saw in them an answer from on high, a promise of divine protection for his two friends and whoever might be involved with them in the kind of proscription which public rumor was foretelling, and whose first victims they were.

Meanwhile, the ex-count of Tours, trying to look like a prudent leader accustomed to surprise attacks and stratagems, was carrying out his Loire crossing in a kind of military formation. The better both to direct the maneuver and to carry out a reconnaissance, he had taken his place up front, on the prow of the raft; the prisoners were in the stern, the detachment of guards took up the rest of the planking, and this clumsy craft was heavily laden with people. They had already passed midstream, the most dangerous place because of the strong current, when a command abruptly and thoughtlessly given by Leudast suddenly brought a larger number of people onto the forward section of the deck. The boat supporting it, sinking beneath the weight, filled with water; the planking tilted sharply, and most of those who were on that side lost their balance and were hurled into the river. Leudast was one of the first to fall in, and he swam to the bank while the raft, half submerged, half supported by the second boat, above which the chained prisoners happened to be, made its way with great difficulty towards the landing stage. Aside from this mishap, which very nearly gave the force of a literal prediction to the verse from the Psalms, the journey from Tours to

Soissons took place without hindrance and with all possible speed.

As soon as the two captives had been brought before the king, Leudast did his best to stir up his anger against them and to extract a sentence of death and a warrant of execution from him before he had given the matter any thought. He sensed that such a blow struck right at the beginning would make the bishop of Tours's position extremely critical, and that once he was committed to such deeds of monstrous violence, the king would no longer be able to draw back: but he was disappointed in his hopes and calculations. Blinded anew by the charms under whose sway he spent his life, Chilperic had recovered from his first misgivings over Fredegund's fidelity, and no longer displayed the same heated testiness. He was taking a calmer view of the whole affair, and wanted from now on to pursue matters with due deliberation, and even to bring to bear in the investigation of the facts and the legal proceedings all the regularity of a jurist (a pretension which he joined to those of being a skilled versifier, a connoisseur of the fine arts, and a profound theologian).

Fredegund herself was putting all her forcefulness and discretion into governing her behavior. She shrewdly judged that her best method of allaying any shadow of suspicion in her husband's mind was to appear dignified and serene, to assume a matronly attitude, and not to seem in any hurry to see the end of the judicial inquiry. The respective states of mind of Chilperic and Fredegund, which Leudast had not foreseen in either case, saved the prisoners' lives. Not only was no harm done them, but, by a capricious act of courtesy which is hard to explain, the king, treating them much better than he did their accuser the subdeacon, left them in semi-liberty, guarded by his law-officers.

King Chilperic now had to get hold of the principal defendant; but that was where his troubles and perplexities began. He had, not long before, shown himself full of determination and even of tenacity in his prosecution of Bishop Praetextatus.[10] But Gregory was not an ordinary man; his reputation and influence extended throughout Gaul: he was, so to speak, the epitome and personification of the moral force of the episcopate. Against such an adversary violence would have been dangerous; it would have caused a widespread scandal, of which Chilperic at the height of his anger would perhaps have taken no account, but which he dared not face in cold blood. Relinquishing the use of force, therefore, he thought only of resorting to one of those rather crudely cunning schemes in which he delighted. While reasoning with himself, it occurred to him that the bishop, whose popularity frightened him, might well for his part be afraid of the royal power, and might attempt to avoid the redoubtable risks of a treason charge by taking flight. This idea, which struck him as brilliant, became the foundation for his plan of attack and the text of the secret orders which he dispatched with all speed to Duke Berulf, who, vested by virtue of his title with the government of a province, was commander-in-chief at Tours, Poitiers, and several other cities recently conquered south of the Loire by Neustrian generals. Berulf, according to these instructions, was to proceed to Tours without any ostensible objective but to inspect the city's defenses. Staying on guard and keeping his intentions totally hidden, he was to await the moment when Gregory, by some attempt to escape, would publicly compromise himself and lay himself open to arrest.

The news of the great trial which was about to begin had reached Tours, officially confirmed and magnified (as never fails to happen) by a host of popular exaggerations. King Chilperic's confidant mainly relied for the success of his mission on the probable effect of these ominous rumors. He flattered himself that this type of bogey would serve, as in a hunt, to run the bishop to earth and drive him to take some false step, leading him straight into the trap. Berulf entered the city of Tours and visited the ramparts, as was his customary practice on his periodic tours of inspection. The new count, Eunomius, accompanied him to receive his comments and his orders. Whether or not the Frankish duke let the Roman count into his secret, or whether he wanted to trick him also, he told him that King Guntram was planning to take the city, either by surprise attack or by naked force, and added: "The time for ceaseless vigilance has come; the city must be garrisoned so that no oversight need be feared." Under cover of this piece of fiction and of the terror—which spread immediately—of an imaginary peril, troups were brought in without arousing any suspicions; guardhouses were set up and sentries posted at all the city gates. Their orders were not to keep their eyes on the surrounding countryside to see if the enemy was coming, but to be on the lookout for the bishop leaving town, and to arrest him if he passed by wearing any sort of disguise or dressed for traveling.

These strategic dispositions were fruitless, and days passed in waiting for them to take effect. The bishop of Tours seemed to be giving no thought to running away, and Berulf found himself reduced to underhand maneuvering to induce him to do so. He bribed several of Gregory's close acquaintances to go, one after another, with an air of lively sympathy, and speak to him of the danger he was in and of the fears of all his friends. Probably, while they were making these treacherous insinuations, King Chilperic's character was not spared, and the names of the Herod and the Nero of the age—which many people applied to him sotto voce—were pronounced, this time with impunity, by these agents of betrayal. Reminding the bishop of the words of Holy Scripture, "Flee from city to city before them that persecute you," they advised him to carry off in secret his church's most valuable possessions and to withdraw to one of the cities of Auvergne, there to wait for better days. But either because he suspected the true motivation for this strange proposal or because such advice, even if sincere, appeared unworthy to him, he remained unmoved and declared that he would not leave.

There was accordingly no way of bodily securing this man whom they dared not touch unless he gave himself up of his own free will. The king had to resign himself to waiting for the accused, whom he wished to prosecute legally, to make a voluntary appearance. For the preliminary investigation of this important trial, letters of convocation were sent to all the bishops of Neustria, as they had been during the case against Praetextatus; they were enjoined to be in Soissons at the beginning of August, in the year 580. To all appearances, this synod was to be even larger than that of Paris in 577, for the bishops of several of the cities of southern Gaul recently conquered from Austrasia (the bishop of Albi among others) were invited to attend. The bishop of Tours received the invitation in the same form as did all his colleagues; by a kind of point of honor, he hastened to obey immediately, and was one of the first to arrive in Soissons.

Public expectation was at that time strongly aroused in the city, and the defendant, of so exalted a rank, of such virtue and renown, excited universal interest. His unfeignedly calm and dignified manner, his serenity, as unruffled as though he had come to sit on the judge's bench at another man's trial, his regular vigils in the churches of Soissons, by the tombs of the martyrs and confessors, changed the respect and curiosity of the common people into genuine enthusiasm. Before any trial, all the Gallo-Romans, that is to say the great mass of the inhabitants, sided with the bishop of Tours against his accusers, whoever they might be. The common people, especially, less guarded and less timid in the face of authority, gave free play to their feelings, and expressed them publicly with impassioned boldness. Pending the arrival of the members of the synod and the opening of the hearing, the preliminary examination of the case was still being pursued with no other foundation than the testimony of a single man. Rikulf the subdeacon, who never wearied of making new statements and multiplying the lies he told against Gregory and his friends, was frequently taken from prison to the king's palace, where he was questioned with all the secrecy observed in matters of the utmost importance. During his journey to and from the palace, a crowd of artisans, leaving their workshops, would assemble along the way and harry him with their murmuring, which was barely kept in check by the grim appearance of the Frankish vassals escorting him.

Once, when he was returning with his head in the air, looking triumphant and pleased with himself, a woodworker named Modestus said to him: "You scoundrel, plotting so eagerly against your bishop, wouldn't you do better to beg his pardon and try and obtain mercy?" At these words, Rikulf, pointing to the man, called out in the Teutonic language to his guards, who either had not clearly understood the Roman's reprimand or else paid little mind to it, "There is someone who is advising me to keep quiet so that I shan't uncover the truth; there is an enemy of the queen who wants to prevent anyone from informing against her accusers." The Roman craftsman was plucked from the midst of the throng and taken away by the soldiers, who immediately went to make Queen Fredegund a report of what had just occurred and to ask her what was to be done with this man.

Fredegund, no doubt troubled by the news brought her every day about what was being said in town, had a fit of impatience which revealed her true character and caused her to cast off the mildness she had till then assumed. On her orders, the luckless workman was flogged, tortured in other ways, and finally put in prison with his hands and feet in irons. Modestus was one of those men, not uncommon in those days, who possessed not only boundless faith but an ecstatic imagination; convinced that he was suffering for the cause of justice, not for one instant did he doubt that the divine omnipotence would intervene to set him free. Towards midnight the two soldiers guarding him fell asleep, and he at once began to pray with all his might, asking God to assist him in his misfortune and to set him at liberty through the agency of the holy bishops St. Martin and St. Médard. His prayer was followed by one of those facts, strange, but vouched for, in which the faith of the old days saw miracles and which the science of our own time has attempted to re-examine by attributing them to ecstatic phenomena. Perhaps the rooted conviction that his prayer had been heard provided the prisoner with a sudden and extraordinary increase in strength and dexterity; perhaps his deliverance was merely the result of a series of lucky chances: at any rate, according to a witness, he managed to break his chains, open the door, and escape. Bishop Gregory, who was spending the night keeping vigil in St. Médard's basilica, was greatly astonished to see him come in and ask, weeping, for his blessing.

The report of this adventure, quickly spread by word of mouth, was all it took to heighten the restlessness of the people of Soissons. No matter how inferior the station of Romans in the society of the period, there was in the voices of an entire city raised in opposition to the prosecution of the bishop of Tours something which could not fail in the highest degree to thwart his adversaries and even to put pressure on the judges in his behalf. Either to shield the members of the synod from this influence, or himself to get away from the scene of a popularity which displeased him, Chilperic decided that the bishops should foregather at the royal estate of Braine, where the case would be judged. He went there himself with his family, followed by all the bishops who had already met in Soissons. As there was no church at Braine, only private chapels, the council members were commanded to conduct their hearings in one of the estate buildings, possibly in the great timber-roofed enclosure which was used twice a year, when the king was in residence, for the national assemblies of the Frankish chieftains and free men.

The first event signalling the opening of the synod was a literary one: it was the arrival of a lengthy piece of verse composed by Venantius Fortunatus and addressed at one and the same time to King Chilperic and all the assembled bishops. At this point a digression is called for to tell of the singular existence that this Italian, the last poet of Gallo-Roman high society, had made for himself thanks to his wit and knowledge of the world. Born in the neighborhood of Treviso and brought up in Ravenna, Fortunatus had come to Gaul to fulfill a vow of devotion at St. Martin's tomb, but as the journey turned out to be a thoroughly delightful one, he was in no hurry to end it. After making his pilgrimage to Tours, he continued his progress from city to city, warmly welcomed, feted and sought after by those wealthy and eminent men who still prided themselves on their urbanity and refinement. From Mainz to Bordeaux and from Toulouse to Cologne, he toured Gaul, visiting as he went the bishops, counts, and dukes, both Franks and Gauls, and finding in most of them attentive hosts and, before long, true friends.

Those whom he had just left after a more or less lengthy stay in their episcopal palace, their country house, or their castle from then on kept up a regular correspondence with him, and he would answer their letters with pieces of elegiac poetry, in which he recalled the memories and incidents of his journey. He would speak to each man of the natural beauties or monuments of his locality; he would describe the picturesque sites, rivers, forests, cultivated fields, the wealth of the churches, and the amenities of the country seats. These descriptions, sometimes fairly lifelike and sometimes vaguely grandiloquent, were sprinkled with compliments and flatteries. The witty poet praised the Frankish lords for their good-natured air, their hospitality, the ease with which they conversed in Latin; the Gallo-Roman nobles he hailed for their political ability, their shrewdness, their knowledge of affairs and of the law. To his eulogies on the piety of the bishops and their zeal in building and consecrating new churches, he added those of their administrative labors for the prosperity, embellishment, or security of the cities. He praised one for having restored ancient buildings, a praetorium, a portico, public baths; another for having altered the course of a river and dug irrigation canals; a third for having erected a citadel fortified with towers and engines of war. All of this, it must be confessed, bears the stamp of extreme literary decadence, written in a style which is at once showy and slipshod, full of incorrect and awkward expressions and puerile puns; but, these reservations once made, it is interesting to see how the appearance of Fortunatus in Gaul revives one last glimmer of intellectual life there, and how this foreigner becomes the common bond between those individualists who, in a world inclining towards barbarism, retained a taste for letters and the pleasures of the mind. Of all his friendships, the warmest and most lasting was that which he struck up with a woman, Radegund (one of the wives of King Lothar I), who was then living in seclusion at Poitiers, in a convent which she herself had founded and where she had taken the veil as an ordinary nun.

In the year 529, Lothar, king of Neustria, had joined with his brother Theoderic who was marching against the Thorings or Thuringians, a tribe of the Saxon Confederation and the neighbors and enemies of the Austrasian Franks. The Thuringians lost several battles; the bravest of their warriors were cut to pieces on the banks of the Unstrudt: their land, ravaged by fire and sword, became a Frankish tributary, and the victorious kings divided up the booty and prisoners equally. To the king of Neustria's lot fell two children of royal blood, the son and daughter of Berther, last king but one of the Thuringians. The girl (Radegund) was barely eight years old, but her grace and precocious beauty made such an impression on the sensual soul of the Frankish prince that he resolved to have her brought up to suit himself, so that she might one day become one of his wives.

Radegund was carefully guarded in one of the Neustrian royal houses, at the domain of Aties, on the Somme. There, by a laudable whim on the part of her master and future husband, she received not the plain education of German girls, who learned hardly anything except spinning and galloping after the hunt, but the refined upbringing of wealthy Gallic girls. In addition to all the elegant occupations of a civilized woman, she was made to study Greek and Latin literature, to read the profane poets as well as ecclesiastical authors. Her intelligence was naturally open to every delicate impression—perhaps the downfall of her country and family and the scenes of Barbarian life which she had witnessed had filled her with melancholy and disgust—and she began to love books as though they had opened an ideal world to her, better than the one around her. When reading the Scriptures and Lives of the Saints, she would weep and wish for martyrdom; and less somber dreams too, dreams of peace and freedom, probably accompanied her secular readings. But religious enthusiasm, which in those days monopolized everything that was noble and exalted in humanity, soon became dominant in her, and this young Barbarian, attaching herself to the ideas and manners of civilization, embraced them in their purest form, the Christian life.

Averting her thoughts more and more from the men and affairs of that violent and brutal century, she saw with terror the approach of the marriageable age, when she would be wife to the king whose captive she was. When the command was given for her to be brought to the royal residence for the marriage, carried away by an invincible instinct of revulsion, she took to flight, but was overtaken and brought back; and, married in Soissons against her will, she became queen, or rather one of the queens, of the Neustrian Franks—for Lothar, faithful to the ways of old Germany, was not content with a single wife, although he also had concubines.[11] Unutterable loathing, which, for a soul like Radegund's, could not be attenuated by the allurements of power and wealth, followed this forced union of the Barbarian king with the woman irretrievably alienated from him by all the moral perfections that he had rejoiced to find in her, and had himself given her.

In order to escape (at least in part) from the duties of her estate, which weighed on her like a chain, Radegund set herself others, even harsher in appearance: she devoted all her leisure time to works of Christian charity or asceticism; she dedicated herself personally to serving the poor and the sick. The royal residence of Aties, where she had been brought up and which she had received as a wedding gift, became a home for destitute women. One of the queen's pastimes was to go there, not merely to visit, but to carry out the duties of a nurse down to their most repulsive details. The festivities of the Neustrian court, boisterous banquets, dangerous hunts, military reviews, jousting, the society of uncultured and rough-spoken vassals, wearied and saddened her. But the unexpected arrival of a bishop or some pious and lettered cleric, a man of peace and gentle conversation, would at once cause her to forsake all other company for his; she would stay close to him for hours together, and when the time came for him to depart, would load him with gifts as a token of remembrance, say farewell a thousand times, and then fall back into her melancholy.

At mealtimes, when she was supposed to be eating with her husband, she was invariably late, either through forgetfulness or on purpose, and absorbed in her reading or her devotions. She would have to be told several times, and the king, tired of waiting, would quarrel violently with her, without managing to make her either more attentive or more punctual. At night she would get up from beside Lothar on some pretext or other and lie down on the floor on a plain straw mat or a hair shirt, only coming back to bed when she was chilled to the bone, thus making a curious association between Christian mortification and the insuperable aversion she felt for her husband. So many signs of revulsion did not, however, weary the king of Neustria's love. Lothar was not the kind of man to have qualms on that score; so long as the woman whose beauty pleased him remained in his possession, he cared little for the moral violence he did her. Radegund's loathing provoked him without actually hurting him, and at moments of matrimonial annoyance he would merely say, testily, "I have a nun here, not a queen."

And indeed there was but one refuge for that soul, bruised by all its worldly ties, and that was the life of the cloister. Radegund longed for it with all her heart, but the obstacles were great and six years passed before she dared defy them. A final misfortune in her family gave her the necessary courage. Her brother, who had grown up at the court of Neustria as a Thuringian hostage, was put to death on the king's orders, perhaps because of his homesickness or some ill-considered threat he had made. As soon as the queen heard this horrible news, her mind was made up: but she concealed her intentions. Pretending that she was going away merely to seek spiritual consolation, while in fact looking for a man capable of becoming her deliverer, she went to Noyon, to Bishop Médard, the son of a Frankish father and a Roman mother and famous throughout Gaul on account of his saintliness. Lothar was not in the least suspicious of this devout proceeding, and not only did he not oppose it, but himself ordered the queen to set out, for her tears annoyed him and he was eager to see her in a calmer and less somber frame of mind.

Radegund found the bishop of Noyon in his church, saying mass. When she was before him, the feelings which troubled her and which she had hitherto kept under control burst out, and her first words were a cry of distress: "Most holy priest, I want to leave the world and take the veil! I entreat you, most holy priest, consecrate me to the Lord!" Despite the dauntlessness of his faith and his proselytizing zeal, the bishop, taken aback by this sudden request, hesitated and asked for time to think. What in fact was at stake was a dangerous decision: the breaking of a royal marriage contracted under both the Salic law and Germanic custom—a custom which the Church, though abhorring it, tolerated for fear of alienating the Barbarians. There was more: added to this inner struggle between prudence and zeal was a combat of quite another sort for St. Médard. The Frankish lords and warriors of the queen's retinue surrounded him, shouting, with threatening gestures: "Don't take it upon yourself to give the veil to a woman who is married to the king! Priest, beware of robbing the prince of a queen solemnly wedded to him!" The most infuriated among them, laying hands on him, dragged him violently from the altar steps as far as the nave, while the queen, frightened by the commotion, sought refuge with her ladies in the sacristy. Once there, however, pulling herself together instead of giving way to despair, she conceived an expedient in which womanly shrewdness played as big a part as strength of will. So as to put the bishop's zeal to the strongest and severest test possible, she flung a religious habit over her royal robes and walked in this disguise towards the sanctuary where, sad, pensive, and irresolute, St. Médard was sitting. "If you put off consecrating me," she told him firmly, "and if you fear man more than God, you will have to answer for it, and the shepherd will ask you to give him back the soul of his ewe lamb." This unforeseen spectacle and mystical language struck the old bishop's imagination and all at once revived his faltering will. Elevating his priestly conscience above human fears and political circumspection, he hesitated no longer, but on his own authority annulled Radegund's marriage, ordaining her deaconess by the laying on of hands. For their part, the Frankish lords and vassals were also swept off their feet, for they did not dare force Radegund—a woman who for them thereafter possessed the two-fold character of queen and one consecrated to God—to return to the royal residence.

The first thought of the new convert (which was the term then used to denote a person renouncing the world) was to strip herself of all the jewels and precious objects she was wearing. She covered the altar with the ornaments from her head, her bracelets, her jewelled clasps, the fringes of her robe which were of purple and cloth of gold: with her own hand she broke her rich girdle of solid gold, saying: "I give it to the poor." Then she gave thought to sheltering herself from any possible danger by taking hasty flight. At liberty to choose her route, she made for the south, moving away from the center of Frankish sovereignty by an instinct for safety, and perhaps too by a more delicate instinct which was drawing her towards those parts of Gaul which had been least ravaged by barbarism. She reached the city of Orléans and there took a boat down the Loire as far as Tours. Then, under the protection of the numerous sanctuaries near St. Martin's tomb, she halted to await whatever action her husband might decide to take. Accordingly, she led for some time the uneasy and troubled life of the exiles who had taken refuge in the shadow of the basilicas, sending the king petitions, now proud, now imploring, adjuring him (with the most saintly people acting as go-betweens) to give up the hope of seeing her again, and to allow her to fulfill her religious vows.

At first, Lothar was deaf to prayers and entreaties; he claimed his rights as a husband, calling the law of his ancestors to witness and threatening to come and drag the fugitive back by force. Terror-stricken when rumor or letters from her friends brought her news of this sort, Radegund would devote herself to redoubled austerities, fasting, vigils, mortifying her flesh with the hair shirt, in the hope of obtaining help from on high and at the same time of losing her charm for the man persecuting her with his love. In order to put more distance between herself and Lothar, from Tours she went to Poitiers, and from the sanctuary of St. Martin to the no less revered sanctuary of St. Hilary. The king, however, did not lose heart, and on one occasion came as far as Tours on a trumped-up excuse of piety; but a bishop's strenuous remonstrances prevented him from going any further.[12] Encircled, so to speak, by that moral force against which the impetuous wills of the Barbarian kings had broken, he consented that the Thuringian princess might found a convent at Poitiers, following the example given in the city of Arles by Caesaria, an illustrious Gallo-Roman lady, sister to Bishop Caesarius, or St. Césaire.

Everything Radegund had received from her husband as marriage portion and morrow-gift, in accordance with Teutonic usage, was devoted to the establishment of the congregation which was to give her a family of her own choosing, to replace the one she had lost through the disasters of conquest and the distrustful tyranny of her country's conquerors. She had the foundations of the new abbey laid on a plot of land at the gates of Poitiers. It was a place or refuge open to those women desirous of escaping from the allurements of the world and the encroachments of barbarism. Despite the queen's eagerness and the assistance given her by Pientius, bishop of Poitiers, it would appear that several years elapsed before the building was finished. It was a house in the Roman style, complete with all its outbuildings, gardens, porticos, baths, and a chapel. By a peculiar arrangement, the abbey grounds were laid out partly inside the city and partly outside; a section of the city wall with several towers was included and, serving as the claustral buildings' facade towards the garden and countryside, gave a martial appearance to that peaceful convent. People were deeply impressed by these preparations for retiring from the world which were being made by a royal personage, and the announcement of their progress traveled far afield like important news: "See," they said, in the mystical language of the age, "see the ark being built near us against the Flood of the passions and the storms of the world."

The day all was ready and the queen entered this place of refuge which, as stipulated by her vows, she could never leave again during her lifetime, was a day of popular rejoicing. The streets and squares of the city she was to pass through were filled with an immense throng; the roofs of the houses were covered with spectators agog to see her go by or to watch the convent gates close behind her. She crossed the city on foot, escorted by a large number of girls—drawn to her by the renown of her Christian virtues, and also perhaps by the glamor of her rank—who were going to share her cloistered life. Most of them were Gallo-Romans and senators' daughters; it was they who, through their customary self-control and domestic tranquillity, would best respond to their superior's maternal cares and pious intentions; for Frankish women took something of the inherent vices of barbarism with them right into the convent. Their zeal was ardent but short-lived, and, incapable of obeying any rule or keeping within any bounds, they would go abruptly from uncompromising rigidity to the most thoroughgoing forgetfulness of all sense of duty or subordination.

It was about the year 555 that Radegund actually began the life of seclusion which she had for so long desired. This life she had dreamed of was the peace of the cloister, the austerity of the convent combined with some of the pleasures of civilized society. Literary studies figured in the front rank of the occupations prescribed for the entire community; two hours of each day were to be devoted to them, and the remaining time was given up to spiritual exercises, the reading of pious books, and needlework. One of the sisters would read aloud during the tasks performed in common, and the most intelligent among them, instead of spinning, sewing, or embroidering, busied themselves in another room transcribing books so as to multiply the copies available. Although strict in some respects, such as abstinence from meat and wine, the rule tolerated some of the comforts and diversions of secular life; frequent bathing in vast heated pools and sundry amusements, dice-throwing among them, were permitted. The foundress and dignitaries of the convent entertained not only the bishops and members of the clergy, but also distinguished laymen. A table was frequently set for visitors and friends, who were served dainty collations and, sometimes, downright feasts. The queen would courteously do the honors, while not herself actually taking part.

Such was the order established by Radegund in her abbey at Poitiers, blending her personal inclinations with the traditions preserved for half a century in the famous convent of Arles. Having set the course and given the impetus, through Christian humility (or political shrewdness) she abdicated all official supremacy. Then she had the congregation elect an abbess whom she herself took good care to nominate, and put herself, with the other sisters, under her absolute authority. For elevation to this dignity she chose a woman much younger than herself, Agnes, a Gaul, of whom she had been fond since her childhood and who was devoted to her. Having stepped down voluntarily to the rank of ordinary nun, Radegund would do her week's stint in the kitchen, sweep the house when it was her turn to do so, and carry water and wood like the others; but despite this semblance of equality, she remained queen in the convent by virtue of the prestige of her royal birth, by her title of foundress, by the ascendancy of her wit, her scholarship, and her goodness.[13] She it was who maintained the rule or modified it as she saw fit, she who steadied wavering souls by daily exhortations, she who explained and who commented upon the text of Holy Scripture for her young companions, interspersing her grave homilies with little sayings marked throughout with womanly grace and tenderheartedness: "You, whom I have chosen to be my daughters; you, young plants, object of all my cares; you, my eyes, my life, my repose, and all my happiness . . ."

The abbey of Poitiers had already been attracting the attention of the Christian world for more than ten years when Venantius Fortunatus, on his excursion of piety and pleasure across Gaul, visited it as one of the most noteworthy places his trip had to offer. He received a distinguished welcome: the marked attentions which the queen paid devout and cultivated men were lavished upon him, as upon the most illustrious and agreeable of guests. He found himself overwhelmed by her, and by the abbess too, with special attentions, consideration, and, above all, praise. This admiration, revived every day in every shape and form and, so to speak, distilled into the poet's ears by two women, one older, the other younger than himself, by the very novelty of its charm kept him in Poitiers much longer than he had anticipated. The weeks and months passed by, all extensions of time were used up; and when the traveler spoke of setting out again, Radegund said to him "Why leave? Why not stay with us?" This expression of friendship was like the decree of destiny for Fortunatus; he no longer thought of going back across the Alps, but settled in Poitiers, took holy orders, and became a priest of the metropolitan church.

His relationship with his two friends, whom he called by the names of mother and sister, was made easier by this change of state, and became more assiduous and more intimate. In addition to the usual womanly need of the foundress and the abbess of Poitiers to be directed by a man, there were circumstances urgently calling for characteristically masculine attention and firmness. The abbey owned considerable property which had not only to be administered, but vigilantly guarded every day against underhand or violent depredations and armed encroachments. This could only be achieved by dint of royal charters, excommunication threats hurled by the bishops, and endless negotiations with dukes, counts, and judges, who, displaying little readiness to act out of a sense of duty, would do a great deal through self-interest or private affection. Such a task called for skill and, at the same time, energy, frequent journeys, visits to the courts of kings, a gift for being agreeable to the mighty and for negotiating with all sorts of people. To this end, Fortunatus used his resourcefulness and knowledge of the world with equal success and zeal; he became the advisor, confidential agent, ambassador, steward, and secretary to the queen and the abbess. His influence, which was absolute with regard to external affairs, was scarcely less so over the internal ordering and administration of the abbey; he was the arbitrator of petty quarrels, the moderator of rival passions and outbursts of female tempers. Mitigations of the rule, acts of forgiveness, exceptions to the regulations governing meals, were all obtained through his intervention and at his request. He was even, up to a point, spiritual director, and his decisions—sometimes given in the form of verse—always inclined to the more lenient point of view.

What is more, Fortunatus combined great mental agility with considerable moral pliancy. A Christian above all by imagination (as has often been said of the Italians), his orthodoxy was above reproach, but in actual practice, his habits were soft and sensuous. He would gladly indulge in the pleasures of the table, and not only was he always a merry table companion, a great drinker, and an inspired improvisor at banquets given by his wealthy patrons, whether Roman or Barbarian, but he also loved to depict in verse the abundance—and the very drunkenness—of a meal which he had been served. Skilled (like all women) at keeping and holding a friend through his characteristic weaknesses, Radegund and Agnes vied with one another in accommodating the poet's gourmandise, just as they made much of a nobler failing in him—literary vanity. Every day they would send to Fortunatus's lodging the first fruits of the convent's meals, and, not content with that, would have dishes that they themselves were forbidden to eat prepared for him with every possible refinement. There were meats of all kinds, dressed in countless ways, and vegetables moistened with juice or honey, served in dishes of silver, jasper, and crystal. At other times he was invited to dine at the abbey, and on those occasions not only was the fare dainty, but the embellishments of the dining room exuded a stylish voluptuousness. Garlands of fragrant blossoms mantled the walls, and a layer of rose petals covered the table in lieu of a cloth. For the guest, to whom it was forbidden by no vow, the wine flowed in fine goblets. There was a hint of the elegance of Antiquity in this meal offered a Christian poet by two recluses who had renounced the world.

No less curiously, the three persons united in this manner addressed one another in affectionate language whose meaning a pagan would certainly have misinterpreted. The names of mother and sister were accompanied on the Italian's lips by terms such as these: my life, my light, joy of my soul. All of this was basically only exalted friendship, quite chaste: a kind of intellectual love. As to the abbess, who was scarcely more than thirty when their relationship began, her intimacy with the poet might well have appeared questionable and have become the subject of malicious talk. Fortunatus sensed this and became concerned for Agnes's honor, as well as his own. Whether his fears were well-founded or not, it was to the abbess herself that he dared to confide them, and he did it with dignity. He sent her a poem in which, protesting that he loved her only as a brother, he calls Christ and the Virgin to witness his blamelessness of heart.

This cheerful, frivolous man, whose maxim was to enjoy the present moment and always to look on the bright side of life, was in his conversations with the daughter of the Thuringian kings the confidant of a deep-seated suffering, of a melancholy recollection of which he himself must have felt incapable. Radegund had reached the age when the hair turns grey without forgetting any of the impressions of her early childhood, and at fifty, the remembrance of days spent in her own country and among her own people came back to her as fresh and as painful as at the time she was captured. She would often say: "I am a poor woman who has been abducted," and she took pleasure in recalling, down to the smallest detail, the scenes of desolation, murder, and violence which she had witnessed and of which she had been in part a victim. After so many years of exile, and despite the fact that her tastes and habits were totally changed, the memory of her father's house and of old family affections remained the object of her passionate devotion; it was a remnant, the only one she had kept, of the Teutonic character and its customs. The image of her dead or banished kinsmen was ever present to her, in spite of her new friendships and the peace she had made for herself. There was even a touch of wildness, an almost savage ardor, in the way she poured out her soul towards all that remained of her line: her uncle's son who had taken refuge in Constantinople, cousins born in exile and known to her only by name. This woman, who on foreign soil had been able to love only that which bore at once the impress of Christianity and of civilization, colored her homesickness with a tinge of untutored poetry, an echo of her people's songs, which she had listened to long ago in the wooden palace of her ancestors or on her native moors. A trace of it may be found here and there, still visible—though certainly watered down—in several pieces where the Italian poet, speaking for the Barbarian queen, attempts to convey, just as he had heard them, her melancholy confidences:

"I have seen women dragged away into slavery, with bound hands and dishevelled hair, one of them walking barefoot in her husband's blood, another stepping over her brother's corpse. —Each had her own reason for tears, and I wept for all of them. —I wept for my dead kinsmen, and I must weep too for those who are still alive. —When my tears cease to flow, when my sighing is hushed, my grief is not stilled. —When the wind sighs, I listen to hear if it brings me any news, but of those near and dear to me I can see nothing. —An entire world keeps me from those I love the most. Where are they? I ask the whistling wind; I ask the passing clouds; I would like a bird to come and give me news of them. —Ah! were I not restrained by this sacred cloister, they would see me coming when they least expected me. I would take ship in foul weather; I would joyfully sail into the storm. The sailors would tremble, but I would have no fear. If the ship were wrecked, I would cling to a plank and go on my way: and if I could not seize any wreckage, I would swim all the way."

Such was the life that Fortunatus had been leading since the year 567, a life made up of religion without gloom, and affection without uneasiness, of grave responsibilities and of leisure hours filled with pleasant futilities. This latest and most curious example of an attempt to fuse Christian perfection and the social refinements of the old civilization would have gone unremembered had not the friend of Agnes and Radegund himself recorded it in his poetry, right down to the smallest phases of the destiny which he had so felicitously picked out for himself. Written there is the almost day-to-day history of that society of three persons linked together by warm friendship, religious fellow-feeling, a taste for the things of the intellect, and the need for instructive or playful conversation. There are verses for the small happenings which are the stuff of that simultaneously sweet and monotonous life: on the pain of separation, the tedium of absence, and the joy of returning; on the little presents given and received, flowers, fruit, all kinds of tidbits, wicker baskets that the poet amused himself weaving for his two friends with his own hands. There are verses written about suppers for three given in the convent and enlivened by "delightful chats," and about solitary meals when Fortunatus regretted having only one pleasure and lamented the absence of the delights of his eyes and ears. Lastly, there are verses for the sad or happy days which returned regularly each year, such as Agnes's birthday and the first day of Lent, when Radegund, keeping a vow made in perpetuity, would shut herself up in her cell, there to spend the time of the great fast. "Where is my light hiding? Why does she steal away from my eyes?" the poet would cry, in passionate tones which one might well have believed profane; and, when Easter came, and with it the end of that long absence, clothing the grave thoughts of the Christian faith in the garb of a madrigal, he would say to Radegund: "You took my joy away: and here it is, coming back to me with you; you make me celebrate this solemn day twice over."

Over and above the good fortune of a tranquillity unique in that century, the Italian expatriate possessed a reputation which was no less unique, and was even able to delude himself about how long that dying literature, of which he was the last and most frivolous representative, would endure. The Barbarians admired him and did their best to enjoy his witticisms; his slightest works—notes written as he stood while the messenger waited, mere distichs extemporized at table—would go quickly from hand to hand, and were read, copied, and learned by heart; his religious poems and works addressed to kings were the object of public expectation. On his arrival in Gaul, he had celebrated the nuptials of Sigibert and Brunhild in the pagan manner, and in the Christian, the conversion of the Arian Brunhild to the Catholic faith.[14] The warlike character of Sigibert, conqueror of the nations beyond the Rhine, was the earliest theme of his poetic flatteries; later on, having settled in Poitiers, which was in Charibert's kingdom, he sang the praises of the peace-loving king, in honor of this prince who was not in the least bellicose. Charibert died in the year 567, and the precarious situation of the city of Poitiers, taken and retaken turn and turn about by the kings of Neustria and Austrasia, caused the poet to maintain a discreet silence for a long while. He did not find his tongue again until the day the city in which he lived seemed to have fallen once for all into the hands of King Chilperic. He then composed his first panegyric (in elegiacs) for that monarch: this is the piece mentioned above, whose sending to the Council of Braine gave rise to this lengthy digression.

The opportunity offered by the council was adroitly seized upon by Fortunatus in the interest of his literary success, for the bishops convened at Braine were the elite of the learned men and wits of Gaul: in a word, a veritable academy. Furthermore, while placing his work under their patronage, he carefully avoided making the slightest allusion to the thorny case they were called upon to judge. Not a word about the painful ordeal that Gregory of Tours, the first of his literary confidants, his friend and benefactor, was about to undergo. Nothing, in this work of one hundred and fifty lines, touching on the occasion, giving a reflection of local color or some trait of an individual character. Nothing but beautiful generalities which could as well apply to any period or any place: an assembly of venerable prelates; a king, the very pattern of justice, enlightenment, and courage; a queen admirable for her virtues, her grace, her goodness: all figures of fantasy, pure abstractions as far removed from contemporary reality as was the peaceful retreat at the abbey of Poitiers from the actual political condition of Gaul.

After the bishops, with the warped judgment and complacent taste of periods of literary decadence, had admired the poetic tours de force, hyperboles, and subtle conceits of the panegyrist, they were obliged to return from the vain imaginings of this meretricious ideal to the impressions of real life. The synod was called to order, and all the judges sat down on benches arranged around the courtroom. As in the trial of Praetextatus, Frankish vassals and warriors clustered around the doors, but in an entirely different frame of mind as regards the accused.[15] Far from quivering with impatience and anger at the sight of him, they showed nothing but respect, and even shared in the enthusiastic sympathies which the Gallo-Roman populace displayed in his favor. King Chilperic wore an expression of strained gravity which was foreign to him. He seemed either to be afraid to come face to face with the adversary he himself had challenged, or to feel embarrassed by the scandal of a public investigation into his queen's morals.

When he entered, he greeted all the council members and, having received their blessing, sat down. Then Bertram, bishop of Bordeaux—allegedly Fredegund's partner in adultery—took the floor as complainant; he set forth the facts of the case and, calling upon Gregory to answer, demanded that he declare whether it was true that he had made such charges against the queen and himself. "Indeed, I have never spoken of it," replied the bishop of Tours. "But this wicked gossip is rife," Bertram at once went on with a hastiness which might well seem suspicious, "you must know something about it?" The defendant replied calmly, "Others have spoken of it; I may have heard it, but I have never thought it."

The low murmur of satisfaction evoked in the assembly by these words found expression outside the courtroom in the form of stamping and hubbub. Despite the presence of the king, the Frankish vassals, unacquainted with Roman notions of royal majesty and the sanctity of judicial proceedings, abruptly intervened in the debate with rough and outspoken exclamations. "Why are they bringing such charges against a priest of God?" "How comes it that the king is pursuing such an affair? Is the bishop really capable of saying things of that kind, even about a slave?" "Ah! Lord God, come and help your servant." At these cries of opposition, the king stood up, not in anger, but rather as one long accustomed to the brutal frankness of his leuds. Raising his voice so that the crowd outside could hear his apologia, he said to the assembly: "The charge aimed at my wife is an outrage against me; I have perforce been affected by it. If you deem it proper that witnesses for the prosecution be produced, there they are; but if it appears to you that this should not be done, say so, and I will gladly comply with your instructions."

The bishops, delighted and somewhat astonished at King Chilperic's restraint and tractability, immediately gave him permission to bring in the prosecution witnesses whom he said were present, but he was able to produce only one, Rikulf the subdeacon. Plato and Gallienus persisted in saying that they had no statement to make. As for Leudast, taking advantage of his freedom and the confusion reigning at the preliminary investigation, not only had he not come to the hearing, but he had taken the additional precaution of removing himself from the scene. Rikulf, brazen to the bitter end, made ready to speak, but the members of the synod stopped him, shouting from all sides: "The word of a cleric of lower rank cannot be accepted in a court of law against that of a bishop." Oral evidence having thus been ruled out, nothing remained but to abide by the sworn word of the defendant; the king, true to his promise, made no objections to the substance, but cavilled at the form. Either by a quirk of imagination or because vague memories of some old Germanic superstition came back to him in Christianized form, he wanted Bishop Gregory's vindication to be accompanied by strange rites that would make it resemble a kind of ordeal by magic. He insisted that the bishop say three consecutive masses at three different altars, and that at the conclusion of each mass he should swear, standing on the altar steps, that he had not made the remarks attributed to him.

The saying of mass in conjunction with the swearing of an oath was already scarcely consonant with orthodox ideas and practices; but the accumulation of several oaths for one and the same fact was expressly forbidden by canon law. The members of the synod acknowledged this, but were nonetheless of the opinion that they should make this concession to the king's bizarre whim. Gregory himself consented to infringe the rule which he had so often promulgated. Perhaps, being himself the accused party, he made it a point of honor not to shrink from any kind of ordeal; perhaps too, in that house where everything had a Teutonic flavor, where the appearance of men was barbaric, and manners were still half pagan, he did not find the same energy, the same liberty of conscience as within the walls of the Gallic cities or beneath the roofs of the basilicas.

While this was going on, Fredegund, keeping in the background, was waiting for the judges' ruling, affecting an impassive calm but deep in her heart contemplating cruel reprisals against those convicted, whoever they might be. Her daughter Rigonthe, out of dislike for her mother rather than from a truly sincere affection for the bishop of Tours, seemed deeply moved by the tribulations of this man whom she hardly knew except by name, and whose merit she was in any case incapable of comprehending. That day, shut up in her quarters, she fasted, and made all her women fast with her, until a servant stationed for that very purpose came to tell her that the bishop had been found not guilty. It appears that the king, so as to give the council members a mark of his full and utter confidence, refrained from personally attending the ordeals which he had requested, but let the bishops accompany the accused by themselves to the chapel of the palace at Braine, where the three masses were said and the three oaths sworn on three different altars. Immediately afterwards, the council session resumed. Chilperic had already taken his place; the president of the assembly remained standing and said, with stately gravity, "Sire, the bishop has performed everything required of him; his innocence is proven; and what must we do now? It remains for us to cut you off from Christian communion, you and Bertram, the accuser of one of his brethren." Shaken by this unexpected sentence, the king was taken aback and, looking like an embarrassed schoolboy throwing the blame on his accomplices, he answered, "But I only told you what I heard." "Who told you first?" replied the president of the council, even more authoritatively. "I heard it all from Leudast," said the king, still nervous at hearing the terrible word "excommunication" ringing in his ears.

The order was at once given for Leudast to be brought to the bar of the assembly, but he could not be found either in the palace or anywhere else nearby, for he had prudently made himself scarce. The bishops resolved to proceed against him *in absentia* and to declare him excommunicated. When the debate was ended, the president of the synod stood up and pronounced the anathema in the time-honored form of words:

"By the judgment of the Father, and of the Son, and of the Holy Spirit, by virtue of the power granted the Apostles and their successors to bind and to loose both in heaven and on earth, we unanimously decree that Leudast, the sower of scandal, false denouncer of a bishop, having absconded from this court so as to escape judgment, shall henceforth be excluded from all Christian communion, both in this life and in the life to come. Let no Christian give him greeting nor the kiss of peace. Let no priest celebrate mass for him, nor administer to him the Holy Communion of the body and blood of Jesus Christ. Let no man keep him company, nor receive him into his house, nor have any dealings with him, nor drink, nor eat, nor converse with him, unless it be to urge him to repent.

May he be accursed of God the Father who created man; may he be
accursed of God the Son who suffered for man's sake; may he be accursed
of the Holy Spirit who comes down upon us at baptism; may he be
accursed of all the saints who since the beginning of the world have
found favor in the sight of God. May he be accursed wherever he may be,
in the house or in the fields, on the highway or in the footpath. May he be
accursed living and dying, waking and sleeping, at work and at rest. May
he be accursed in every power and in every organ of his body. May he be
accursed in all the frame of his members, and from the top of his head to
the soles of his feet may there not be the smallest part of him remaining
healthy. May he be given up to everlasting punishment with Dathan and
Abiram, and those who said to the Lord: 'Depart from us.' And just as
fire is quenched in water, so may his light be extinguished forever,
except he repent and make amends." At these final words, all the members of the assembly, who had listened thus far in meditative silence,
raised their voices together and cried several times "Amen, so be it, so be
it, let him be anathema; amen, amen."

This decree, whose threats were truly terrifying from the religious
point of view and whose civil effects were equivalent, for the condemned
man, to being outlawed throughout the kingdom, was conveyed by
circular letter to all the Neustrian bishops who had not attended the
council. The next order of business was to pass judgment upon Rikulf the
subdeacon, whom the bishop of Tours's vindication had, ipso facto,
convicted of perjury. Roman law, which was that of all ecclesiastics
regardless of race, punished with death those who brought slanderous
charges in respect of a capital crime, such as high treason; this law was
applied in all its rigor, and the synod brought in against Rikulf a verdict
which turned him over to the secular arm. This was the final act of the
assembly, which dispersed forthwith, and each of the bishops, having
taken leave of the king, made arrangements to return to his diocese.
Before giving thought to his departure, Gregory begged that the man
who had so perversely and so impudently harried him with his impos-
tures be pardoned. Chilperic was then in the mood for clemency, either
because of the joy he felt at the end of the embarrassments that concern
for his conjugal honor had got him into, or because he was bent on
mollifying the bishop of Tours's resentment by being obliging. At Gregory's request, he remitted the death penalty, keeping only that of torture,
which, under Roman law, was inflicted not by way of punishment, but
as an additional form of questioning.

Fredegund herself deemed it politic to ratify this act of clemency and to
spare the life of the man whom a solemn verdict had just delivered into
her hands. But it would seem that, while sparing him, she wanted to
experiment on him to see how much pain a man might endure without
actually dying of it; and in this ferocious sport she was seconded only too

well by the over-obliging zeal of her household vassals and retainers, who competed with one another to become the condemned man's torturers. "I do not believe," says the contemporary narrator (who is none other than the bishop of Tours), "I do not believe that any inanimate object, any metal could have withstood all the blows with which that poor wretch was bruised. From the third hour of the day until the ninth, he was left hanging from a tree by his hands, which were tied behind his back. At the ninth hour he was cut down and stretched on a rack, where he was beaten with cudgels, rods, and doubled straps, and that not by one or two men only, but as many as could get close to his miserable limbs set to work striking him."

His sufferings, added to his resentment against Leudast, whose foil he had been, made him reveal the as yet unknown background of this mysterious intrigue. He confessed that the aim of his two accomplices and himself in accusing the queen of adultery had been to have her expelled from the kingdom with both her sons, so that Audovera's son Clovis would be the only one left to succeed his father. He added that their expectations in the event of success were that Leudast would be made duke, the priest Rikulf bishop, and himself archdeacon of Tours. These revelations did not directly implicate young Clovis in the conspiracy, but he was found to have had common interests with the three conspirators. Fredegund did not forget this, and from that moment on he was marked down in her mind—as she was wont to mark down her mortal enemies—for the first convenient opportunity.

News traveled slowly in those days unless it was carried by express messenger, and so several weeks elapsed before those in Tours learned the results of the trial which had opened in Soissons and been tried in Braine. During those days of uncertainty, the citizens concerned for the fate of their bishop suffered also from the disorder caused by the unruliness and boasting of Gregory's enemies. Their leader, Rikulf the priest, had, on his own authority, moved into the bishop's house; and there, as though he already possessed episcopal rank (the object of his insane ambition), he was trying his hand at exercising the absolute power that went with it. Disposing in a lordly way of the property of the metropolitan church, he drew up an inventory of all the silver, and in order to win devoted followers began to distribute handsome presents to the principal members of the clergy, giving valuable pieces of furniture to one, meadows or vineyards to others. As for the lower clergy, whom he did not think he needed, he treated them quite differently, and the authority that he had arrogated to himself was made known to them only through his harshness and violence. For the smallest fault, he had them beaten with rods or struck them with his own hand, saying "Acknowledge your master!" He would repeat at every turn, with bombastic vanity: "It is I who, by my wit, have purged the city of Tours of that brood of Auvergnats." If his familiar friends occasionally displayed some doubts over the success of this usurpation and the sincerity of those drawn to him by his extravagant bounties, he would say, with a superior smile: "Leave it to me; the sagacious man is never caught napping; he can only be deceived by the perjurer."

This braggart, so full of himself, was all of a sudden dragged down from his ambitious dreams by the arrival of Gregory, who reentered Tours to universal rejoicing. Compelled to return the episcopal palace to its legitimate possessor, Rikulf, unlike the clergy and every other citizen, did not come to greet the bishop. At first he affected a contemptuous manner and a kind of taciturn bravado; then his impotent spite turned to frenzy, he raved and uttered nothing but threats of death. Gregory, always careful to observe due process, was in no hurry to use force against this dangerous enemy, but, acting coolly rather than arbitrarily, convened the suffragan bishops of the archdiocese of Tours in provincial synod.

His letters of convocation were addressed individually to the bishops of every city of the third province of Lyons, with the probable exception of those possessed by the Bretons, a nation equally jealous of its independence in religious and political matters, and whose national church had no fixed and regular relations with the church of Gaul. The bishops of Angers, Le Mans, and Rennes took keenly to heart the peace of the church of Tours and the cause of their archbishop. But Felix, bishop of Nantes, either by his absence from the synod or by his attitude during its deliberations, displayed unmistakable signs of ill-will towards Gregory and partiality for his enemies. He was a high-born Gaul, who claimed descent from the ancient paramount chiefs of Touraine, and numbered praetorian prefects, patricians, and consuls among his ancestors. In addition to this nobility, of which he was very vain, he possessed qualities uncommon in his day: a quick and enterprising wit, the gift of speaking eloquently and writing fluently, and a spark of that administrative genius which had shone in Gaul under Roman government.

As bishop of a border region continually menaced by the hostile incursions of the Bretons—a region to which the Merovingian kings were unable to afford steady protection—Felix had taken it upon himself to see to everything, to look after both the security and the prosperity of his diocese. For lack of an army, he opposed Breton encroachments by a policy of vigilance and skillful negotiation, and whenever peace returned, would carry out great public works at his own expense. In the course of this active and eventful life, his character had developed a ruthless, imperious quality, vastly different from the moral type of the priest consistent with apostolic tradition. On one occasion he chanced to lay claim to an estate which the church of Tours owned near Nantes and which was perhaps necessary to him for a great undertaking—that of altering the course of the Loire and digging a new riverbed, in the interests of commerce and agriculture. Gregory, in his punctilious and somewhat unbending way, refused to give up the smallest particle of his church's property; and this dispute, gradually becoming acrimonious, stirred up a paper war between the two bishops which must have been a great source of scandal. They would send one another diatribes in the form of letters, which they made a point of communicating to their friends and which circulated publicly like genuine pamphlets.

In this conflict of cutting words and injurious allegations, the bishop of Tours, more artless, less acerbic, and not so witty as his opponent, was far from getting the best of it. To the mordant and angry reproaches which Felix heaped upon him on account of his refusal to hand over the estate in question, he would reply with heavy good nature: "Remember the words of the prophet: 'Woe unto them that join house to house, that lay field to field, till there be no place, that they may be placed alone in the midst of the earth!' " [16] And when the irascible bishop of Nantes, setting aside the object of the controversy, attempted to cast ridicule and odium on his antagonist's person and family, the only retorts that Gregory could think of were sallies of the following kind: "Oh! if Marseilles had you for its bishop, ships would bring no more oil and spices there, nothing but cargoes of papyrus, so that you would have the means of writing at your ease, to slander decent folk. But the paper shortage is putting an end to your verbosity . . ."

Perhaps the disagreement setting the bishops of Tours and Nantes at loggerheads had deeper causes than this chance dispute. The charge of inordinate pride which Gregory levels at Felix leads one to believe that there was some aristocratic rivalry between them. It would seem that the descendant of the former princes of Aquitaine was grieved at finding himself a hierarchical subordinate of a man of lesser nobility than his own; or else that through exaggerated local patriotism, he would have liked ecclesiastical dignities in the western provinces to be the exclusive birthright of the great families of the region. That was probably the origin of his sympathy for and collusion with the faction at Tours which hated Gregory as an outsider, for he had long known about the schemes of the priest Rikulf and had even encouraged them.

This hostile bias on the part of the most powerful and ablest of the suffragan bishops of the diocese of Tours did not prevent the provincial synod from duly convening and administering justice. Rikulf, condemned both as a troublemaker and as being contumacious to his bishop, was sent away to be confined in some unspecified monastery. Scarcely had he been shut up there for a month when trusted servants of the bishop of Nantes cleverly wormed their way in to the abbot in charge of the monastery. They employed all kinds of tricks to outwit him, and with the help of perjury, prevailed upon him to let the prisoner out, on promise of his returning. But no sooner did Rikulf find himself outside than he took to his heels and hurried away to Felix, who took him in with alacrity, thus outrageously defying his archbishop's authority. Such was the final vexation caused the bishop of Tours by this wretched affair, and perhaps it was the sharpest sorrow of all, for it came to him from a man of the same background, rank, and education as himself, a man of whom he could not say, as he could of his other enemies, whether Barbarians or simply those of limited intelligence (who were as much enslaved by their passions as were the Barbarians): "Father, forgive them, for they know not what they do."[17]

Meanwhile Leudast, outlawed by a sentence of excommunication and by a royal edict forbidding any man to give him either resting place or bread or shelter, was leading a vagrant life full of perils and setbacks. He had come from Braine to Paris intending to take refuge in St. Peter's basilica, but the ban of anathema, which formally barred him from the sanctuary open to all other exiles, compelled him to give up this plan and to trust in the loyalty and courage of some friend. While still hesitating over what direction he should take, he learned that his only son had just died: this may have awakened his affection for his family or perhaps merely struck him with serious concern for his affairs and welfare; at any rate, the news inspired him with an irresistible longing to see his home again. Concealing his identity and traveling alone in the meanest of attire, he set out for Tours, and on his arrival crept stealthily into the house occupied by his wife. When he had given vent to his paternal feelings for a brief spell—which is all his unstable nature would have permitted—he hastened to put the money and valuables accumulated by pillaging those he had governed in a safe place.

He had kept up a relationship of mutual hospitality with several people of Germanic descent in the vicinity of Bourges. Among Barbarians, a relationship of this kind imposed such sacred obligations that neither the prohibitions of the law nor even the menaces of religion could prevail against them. He determined, until better days, to entrust his hosts with all his wealth, and he had time to send them the greater part of it before the edict of outlawry issued against him was promulgated in Tours. However, this breathing-space was not of long duration, and king's messengers soon brought the fatal decree. They were escorted by a troop of armed men tracking the proscript by means of clues gathered between one halting-place and the next. They burst into Leudast's house; he was lucky enough to escape, but his wife, less fortunate than he, was captured and taken to Soissons, then banished to the Tournai region by order of the king.

The fugitive, taking the same route previously followed by the wagons transporting his treasure, made for the city of Bourges and entered King Guntram's territory, where Chilperic's men did not dare pursue him. He and his baggage reached his hosts at the same time. Unfortunately for him, the appearance and bulk of his possessions tempted the cupidity of the local inhabitants. Thinking that a stranger's property was fair game, they banded together to seize it, and the district magistrate put himself at their head to be sure of his share of the booty. Leudast did not have with him any force capable of repelling such an attack, and the resistance of his hosts—if they did try to help him—was to no avail. Everything was looted by the attackers, who made off with the sacks of coin, the gold and silver plate, the pieces of furniture, and Leudast's wardrobe, leaving the man who had been robbed with nothing but the clothes on his back, and threatening to kill him if he did not depart with all possible speed. Compelled to run away once again, Leudast turned around in his tracks and boldly set off for Tours, the state of destitution to which he found himself reduced having inspired him with a desperate resolve.

As soon as he had reached the frontier of Chilperic's realm (which was also that of his old bailiwick), he announced in the first village he came to that there was a raid worth making a day's march away in King Guntram's territory, and that any man of action who wanted to try his luck would be generously rewarded. Young peasants and vagabonds of every condition—who, in those days, were not exactly in short supply on the highways—collected at this news and began to follow the ex-count of Tours without asking too many questions about where he was leading them. Leudast made a point of quickly reaching the place where his despoilers lived, and swooped down unexpectedly on the house where he had seen the booty stored. This bold maneuver was completely successful: the men from Touraine attacked bravely, killed one man, wounded several others, and recaptured a considerable portion of the loot, which the men of Berry had not yet divided among themselves.

Proud of his surprise attack and of the protestations of devotion which he received after distributing liberal presents, Leudast thereafter believed himself capable of dealing with any foe whatsoever, and, resuming his presumptuous demeanor, remained in the neighborhood of Tours without taking any pains to conceal his presence. Acting on widespread reports, Duke Berulf sent his officers with a troop of well-armed men to apprehend this outlaw. Leudast all but fell into their hands; just as he was being arrested, he once more contrived to slip away, but only by abandoning all the money and movables still in his possession. While what was left of his fortune was being inventoried and sent off to Soissons, he himself, going in the opposite direction, was attempting to reach Poitiers in order to take refuge—all else having failed—in the basilica of St. Hilary.

It appears that the proximity of Radegund's abbey, and the very nature of so gentle and revered a woman, had shed a spirit of indulgence over the church at Poitiers, distinguishing it from all others. That at least is the only feasible explanation for the charitable welcome found by a man (at once outlawed and excommunicated) in that church after he had seen the doors of the sanctuary of St. Martin of Tours and the basilicas of Paris shut in his face. Great was Leudast's joy at being quite safe at last. This soon passed, however, and before long all he felt was something his vanity could not endure, the humiliation of being one of the poorest of those sharing St. Hilary's sanctuary. In order to escape this feeling, and to satisfy his inveterate taste for sensuality and debauchery, he organized a gang of the most villainous and most resolute of his companions in refuge. Whenever the policing of the city became weaker or less vigilant, the ex-count of Tours, alerted by his spies, would sally forth from St. Hilary's basilica at the head of his band and, hurrying to some house which had been pointed out to him as a rich one, would break in and carry off the money and valuables, or hold the terrified householder to ransom. The heavily laden bandits would immediately return within the precinct of the basilica, where they would share out the booty; then they would eat and drink together, quarrel, or throw dice.

Often the holy sanctuary became the theater of even more disgraceful licentiousness: Leudast enticed loose women there, several of whom (the married ones) were surprised in the act of adultery with him in the very portico of the church square. Either because, at the report of these outrages, an order dispatched from the court of Soissons had demanded the rigorous execution of the sentence passed at Braine, or because Radegund herself, indignant at so many acts of desecration, had requested Leudast's removal, he was driven out of St. Hilary's basilica as being unworthy of any pity. Not knowing where to lay his head, he once again applied to his hosts in Berry. Despite the obstacles put in their way by recent events, his friends cleverly found him a safe retreat, which after a while he abandoned of his own accord, driven by his irrepressible nature and unruly desires. He resumed the nomadic, adventurous life which was to bring him to his ruin: but even had he been blessed with discretion and a sense of how to conduct himself, there would no longer have been any salvation possible for him. Over his head there hung an inevitable destiny: the vengeance of Fredegund, who could sometimes wait, but who never forgot.

SIXTH EPISODE
Chilperic as Theologian—Priscus the Jew—
Continuation and Conclusion of the History of Leudast
(580–583)

*A*fter the happy outcome of the charges levelled against him, the bishop of Tours had resumed the briefly interrupted course of his avocations, both religious and political. Not only did the affairs of his diocese and the municipal government call for daily vigilance on his part, but more general interests too, those of the Gallican church and of the peace between the Frankish kings, which was constantly being broken, caused him much concern. By himself or in the company of other bishops, he made frequent journeys to the various residences successively occupied by the Neustrian court; and in that same palace of Braine where he had appeared as defendant in a treason trial, he now found himself surrounded only by honors and kind attentions. In order to entertain such a guest suitably, King Chilperic was at pains to assume all the outward appearances of Roman civility, and to give tokens of his learning and good taste. He would even give the bishop private readings of pieces he had composed, asking his advice and showing off before him, with a kind of naive vanity, his slightest literary exercises.

These crude attempts, the fruits of a praiseworthy whim to imitate— which was, however, ineffectual, owing to its desultory nature—touched upon every type of study, grammar, poetry, fine arts, jurisprudence, and theology; and in his flights of love for civilization, the Barbarian king would go from one subject to the next like an impetuous and inexperienced schoolboy. Fortunatus, last of the Latin poets, had extolled this royal caprice as being a great cause for hope for the ever more disheartened friends of the old intellectual culture, but Bishop Gregory, being of gloomier disposition and less dazzled by the glamor of power, did not share such illusions. Whatever his countenance and his remarks on receiving the literary confidences of Clovis's grandson, at bottom he felt only bitter contempt for the writer whom, as king, he was obliged to flatter. In the Christian poems composed by Chilperic on the model of those of the priest Sedulius, he saw nothing but a jumble of ill-formed verses "crippled in every foot," and where, for want of the rudiments of prosody, long syllables were put down for short ones and short for long. As for the less ambitious works such as hymns and parts of the Mass, Gregory held them to be "inadmissible," and, among the clumsy gropings of this untaught intelligence making indiscriminate efforts to put itself in order, did not sufficiently discern the genuinely serious attempts and respectable intentions to be found there.

Guided by a flash of real good sense, Chilperic had given some thought to the feasibility of writing the sounds of the Germanic language in the Roman alphabet. With this in mind, he hit on the idea of adding four letters of his own invention, among which there was one assigned to the pronunciation which has since been represented by "W." Proper names of Teutonic origin were thus to be given an exact and fixed spelling in Latin texts. But neither this result (later sought after with great difficulty) nor the steps taken from that time onward to obtain it appear to have found favor in the eyes of the bishop, who was either too hard to please or too prejudiced. He did scarcely more than smile pityingly at the sight of a Barbarian potentate laying claim to rectify the Roman alphabet and giving orders, in letters addressed to the counts of the cities and the municipal senates, that textbooks in every public school should be erased with pumice stone and rewritten in conformity with the new system.

Once, having taken the bishop of Tours aside as though for a matter of the highest importance, King Chilperic had one of his secretaries read him a little treatise he had just written on high theological questions. The principal thesis defended in this singularly reckless book was this: that the Holy Trinity is not to be referred to by distinguishing between its persons, and that one name only, God, must be given it; that it is unworthy for God to be given the appellation of "person" like a man of flesh and blood; that he who is the Father is the same as the Son, and the same as the Holy Spirit; and that he who is the Holy Spirit is the same as the Father, and the same as the Son; that it is thus that he appeared to the patriarchs and prophets, and thus that he was proclaimed by Mosaic Law. At the first words of this new creed, Gregory was inwardly seized with violent agitation, for he recognized with horror the heresy of Sabellius, the most dangerous of all after that of Arius,[1] because, like the latter, it seemed to have a rational foundation. Whether the king had borrowed from his readings the doctrine he was renewing or whether he had arrived at it by his own, unaided, faulty reasoning, he was at that moment as convinced that he held the truth of Christian dogma as he was proud of having learnedly set it forth. The increasingly visible signs of repugnance which escaped the bishop surprised and irritated him in the highest degree. With a mixture of the despotism which brooks no resistance and the vanity of the logician who believes he is absolutely in the right, he spoke first, and said sharply: "I want you and all the other theologians to believe this."

At this imperious declaration, Gregory, recovering his accustomed calm and gravity, replied: "Most pious king, it behooves you to forsake this error, and to follow the doctrine left us by the Apostles, and after them by the Fathers of the Church, which Hilary, bishop of Poitiers, and Eusebius, bishop of Verceil, taught, and which you yourself confessed at baptism." "But I am well aware," replied Chilperic, whose self-assurance was taking on an ill-tempered tone, "I am well aware that in this cause Hilary and Eusebius are powerful enemies to me." However provocative he may have found this outburst of offended pride, Gregory was not put out, but continued as calmly as ever: "You must take care to offend neither God nor his saints"; and, going on to an exposition of orthodox belief such as he might well have uttered *ex cathedra*, he added: "Know that, to consider them in their respective persons, the Father is different, different the Son, and different the Holy Spirit. It was not the Father who was made flesh, any more than the Holy Spirit; it was the Son, so that, for the redemption of mankind, he who was the son of God might also become the son of a virgin. It was not the Father who suffered the Passion, it was not the Holy Spirit; it was the Son, so that he who had been made flesh in this world might be offered up as a sacrifice for the world. As for the persons of whom you speak, they are to be understood not corporeally, but spiritually, and therefore, although in reality they are three, in them there is but one glory, one eternity, one power."

This kind of pastoral letter was interrupted by the king, who, unwilling to hear any more, exclaimed hastily, "I will have this read to better scholars than you, and they will agree with me." Gregory was nettled by this remark, and, becoming in his turn incensed to the point of throwing caution to the winds, retorted: "No man of learning and good sense will ever admit what you propose; only a madman will do that." It is impossible to say what took place at that moment in Chilperic's soul: he left the bishop without a word, but a quiver of wrath revealed that the well-read and theologically minded king had lost none of the violent temper of his ancestors. Some days later, he tried out his book on Salvius, bishop of Albi; and, this second attempt having no better success than the first, he immediately lost heart and forsook his opinions concerning the nature of God as readily as he had originally determined to uphold them.

Not a trace of this deep dissension remained when, in the year 581, King Chilperic selected for his summer residence the domain of Nogent, on the banks of the Marne near its confluence with the Seine. The bishop of Tours, quite reconciled with the king, came to pay his respects, and during his stay an important event took everyone's mind off the usual monotony of the domestic life of the palace. This was the return of an embassy sent to Constantinople to congratulate the emperor Tiberius—who had succeeded Justin the Younger—on his accession to the throne. The ambassadors, laden with presents for King Chilperic from the new emperor, had returned to Gaul by sea, but instead of landing at Marseilles, a city which was at that time being fought over by King Guntram and the protectors of the young King Childebert, they had preferred—as being safer for themselves—a foreign port, Agde, which belonged to the kingdom of the Goths. Beset by a storm in sight of the coast of Septimania, their ship ran around on a reef; and while they themselves swam safely ashore, the entire cargo was pillaged by the local inhabitants. Fortunately, the official governing the city of Agde in the name of the Gothic king believed it to be his duty (or at least believed it to be politic) to intervene, and caused, if not all their baggage, at least the greater part of the costly gifts intended for their king to be given back to the Franks. They accordingly reached the palace of Nogent, to the great delight of Chilperic, who hastened to have all the precious fabrics, gold plate, and ornaments of every kind which had been sent him by the emperor displayed to his leuds and guests.

Among a great quantity of curious or magnificent objects, what the bishop of Tours examined most attentively—perhaps because he took pleasure in seeing therein a symbol of civilized sovereignty—were large gold medallions bearing on one side the emperor's head with the inscription TIBERII CONSTANTINI PERPETUI AUGUSTI and on the other a four-horse chariot driven by a winged figure with the words GLORIA ROMANORUM. Each medallion weighed a pound and had been struck to commemorate the beginning of the new reign. Confronted with these splendid Byzantine works of art, these signs of imperial grandeur, the king of Neustria, as though fearing some comparison unfortunate for himself, took pride in showing proofs of his own magnificence. He had an enormous golden, bejewelled bowl (which had just been made at his command) brought in and placed beside the gifts which his leuds were contemplating, some with artless amazement, others with covetous looks. This bowl, which was intended to appear on the royal table on great and solemn occasions, weighed no less than fifty pounds. At the sight of it, all the bystanders exclaimed in admiration at the cost of the material and the beauty of the workmanship. The king savored a while in silence the pleasure these praises caused him, then, with a look of self-satisfaction and pride, he said: "I have done this to shed luster and renown on the Frankish nation, and if God grants me long life, I shall do much more."

Chilperic's counsellor and agent in his plans for royal display and his purchases of precious objects was a Parisian Jew named Priscus. This man, of whom the king was very fond, whom he frequently summoned to his side, and with whom he even condescended to act with a certain familiarity, happened to be in Nogent then. After devoting some time to overseeing the farm-work and taking stock of the agricultural produce in his great estate on the Marne, Chilperic had a fancy to take up his abode in Paris, in the old imperial palace, whose remains still exist to the south of the Ile de la Cité, on the left bank of the Seine. On the day of his departure, just as the king was giving the order to harness the baggage wagons which he was going to follow on horseback with his leuds, Gregory came to take leave of him; and while the bishop was saying goodbye, Priscus the Jew arrived to make his farewells too. Chilperic, who was in a good-natured mood that day, caught the Jew teasingly by the hair and, pulling him gently to make him bend his head, said to Gregory, "Come, priest of God, and lay your hands on him."

As Priscus was pulling back and shrinking in terror from a blessing which according to his beliefs would have made him guilty of sacrilege, the king said to him: "Oh! stubborn spirit and still unbelieving race which does not comprehend the Son of God promised it by the mouths of its own prophets, which does not comprehend the mysteries of the Church prefigured by its own sacrifices!" While uttering this exclamation, Chilperic let go of the Jew's hair and left him at liberty; the latter, having got over his fright and giving tit for tat, at once replied: "God does not marry, he has no need to, no offspring is born to him, and he tolerates no equal in power, he who has said through the lips of Moses, 'Behold, I am the Lord, there is no other. It is I who give life and death, I who strike and who heal.' "

Far from being indignant at such bold speech, King Chilperic was delighted that what had, to begin with, been only a game provided him with the opportunity to show off, in a formal disputation, his theological learning, untainted this time by any reproach of heresy. Assuming the grave manner and sedate tone of a doctor of divinity instructing catechumens, he retorted, "God from all eternity begat in the spirit a son who is neither younger than himself nor less mighty, and of whom he himself has said: 'Thou art my son, born like dew before the day-star rises.'[2] In the past age, he sent this son born before time began into the world to heal it, according to what your own prophet says: 'He sent his word and healed them.'[3] And when you claim that he does not beget children, listen to your prophet, speaking in the name of the Lord: 'Shall I bring to the birth, and not cause to bring forth?'[4] Now by that he means the people who were to be reborn in him through faith." The Jew, increasingly emboldened by argument, retorted: "Is it possible that God was made man, was born of a woman, submitted to being beaten with rods, and was condemned to death?"

This objection, which was addressed to the most rudimentary and, so to speak, grossest aspects of human reason, touched the king's mind at one of its weaker points; he seemed astonished and, finding nothing to say in reply, remained silent. This was the moment for the bishop of Tours to step in: "If the son of God," he said to Priscus, "if God himself was made man, it was on our account, and in no way through a necessity peculiar to himself; for he could only redeem mankind from the bondage of sin and enslavement by the devil by putting on human form. I will not take my proofs from the apostles and the Gospels, in which you do not believe, but from your own books, so as to pierce you with your own sword, as David is said to have killed Goliath. Learn therefore from one of your prophets that God was to become man: 'God is man,' he says, 'and who does not know it?' And again: 'Such a God is ours; what rival will be compared to him? He it is who has the key to all knowledge, and gave it to his servant Jacob, to the well-loved race of Israel; not till then would he reveal himself on earth, and hold converse with mortal men.'[5] With respect to his being born of a virgin, listen likewise to your prophet when he says: 'Behold, a virgin shall be with child, and shall bring forth a son, and they shall call his name Emmanuel, which being interpreted is, God with us.'[6] And as to the necessity of his being beaten with rods, pierced with nails, and submitting to other ignominious punishments, another prophet has said: 'They pierced my hands and my feet . . . they part my garments among them, and cast lots upon my vesture.'[7] And again: 'They gave me also gall for my meat; and in my thirst they gave me vinegar to drink.' "[8]

"But," retorted the Jew, "who compelled God to endure such things?" The bishop could see by this question that he had not been properly understood, and had doubtless not been listened to attentively; nevertheless, he continued, without displaying any impatience: "I have already told you that: God created man innocent; but, outwitted by the wiles of the serpent, man equivocated with God's command and, expelled from his abode in Paradise for this sin, was subjected to the toils of the world. It is through the death of Christ, God's only son, that man has been reconciled with the Father."

"But," the Jew retorted yet again, "could not God send prophets or apostles to lead mankind back to the way of salvation without humbling himself to the point of being made flesh?" The bishop still calm and serious, answered him thus: "From the beginning, the human race has sinned unceasingly: neither the Flood, nor the burning of Sodom, nor the plagues of Egypt, nor the miracle which opened the waters of the Red Sea and the Jordan, none of this was capable of frightening it. It has always resisted God's law, it has not believed the prophets; and not only has it not believed, but it has put to death those who came to preach repentance. And this is why if God himself had not come down to ransom it, no one else could have accomplished the work of redemption. We have been regenerated by his birth, washed by his baptism, healed by his wounds, raised up by his Resurrection, glorified by his Ascension, and, to give us to understand that he was to come bringing the remedy for our ills, one of your own prophets has said: 'with his stripes we are healed.'[9] And elsewhere he says: 'He bare the sin of many, and made intercession for the transgressors.'[10] And again: 'He is brought as a lamb to the slaughter, and as a sheep before her shearers is dumb, so he openeth not his mouth. He was taken from prison and from judgment: and who shall declare his generation? The Lord of Hosts is his name.'[11] Jacob himself, from whom you boast that you are descended, when blessing his son Judah, said to him as though he were speaking to Christ, the son of God: 'Thy father's children shall bow down before thee. Judah is a lion's whelp: from thy prey, my son, thou art gone up: he stooped down, he couched as a lion; who shall rouse him up?' "[12]

This discourse, logically not very well connected, yet in its very disorder stamped with a certain grandeur, made no impression whatever on Priscus the Jew: he left off arguing, but without appearing in the least shaken in his beliefs. When the king saw that he was keeping quiet with the look of a man unwilling to yield in any way, he turned to the bishop of Tours and said: "Holy priest, let this unhappy man go without your blessing; as for me, I will say to you what Jacob said to the angel with whom he was conversing: 'I will not let thee go except thou bless me.' "[13] After these words, which lacked neither grace nor dignity, Chilperic called for water so that the bishop and he might wash their hands; and when they had both washed, Gregory, placing his right hand on the king's head, pronounced a blessing in the name of the Father, and of the Son, and of the Holy Spirit.

On a table were bread, wine, and probably various other dishes meant to be offered to distinguished persons coming to take leave of the king. Following the rules of Frankish courtesy, Chilperic invited the bishop of Tours not to part company with him before taking something at his table. The bishop took a piece of bread, made the sign of the cross over it, then, breaking it in half, kept one part and gave the other to the king, who ate it, standing beside him. Next, they both poured themselves a little wine and drank together while saying goodbye. The bishop made ready to return to his diocese; the king mounted his horse, surrounded by his leuds and his servants, escorting in their company the covered cart carrying the queen and their daughter Rigonthe. The Neustrian royal family, lately so numerous, was then reduced to these two persons. Both of Chilperic's sons by Fredegund had died the previous year, carried off by an epidemic; the last of Audovera's sons had perished at almost the same time in a bloody calamity, the melancholy details of which will be the subject of the next episode.[14]

This scene of religious controversy, so strangely brought about by a little joke, had, it would appear, left a deep impression on King Chilperic. During his stay in Paris, he could not help pondering intently on the impossibility of convincing the Jews and of drawing them into the bosom of the Church by reasoning. These thoughts went on preoccupying him even in the midst of great political difficulties and concern over the war of conquest that he was waging on his southern frontier; the upshot of all this was a royal decree commanding every Jew domiciled in Paris to be baptized. This order, addressed, in the usual style, to the city count or magistrate, concluded with a formula concocted by the king himself, a truly barbarous form of words which he was in the habit of using, on some occasions as a kind of bugaboo, on others with the serious intention of following it out to the letter: "If any man scorns our edict, let him be punished by having his eyes put out."

The terror-stricken Jews obeyed and went to church to receive instruction in the Christian faith. The king took a childish pride in attending their baptismal ceremonies with great pomp, and even in standing godfather to several of these converts by coercion. One man, however, dared to resist him and refused to abjure his faith; this was that same Priscus who had put up so logical and so dogged a defense. Chilperic proved to be patient; once more he tried persuasive measures on the mind of the reasoner who had faced up to him; but after a fruitless conference, exasperated at seeing his eloquence at fault for the second time, he exclaimed: "If he won't believe willingly, then I'll make him believe unwillingly." Priscus the Jew, who was then thrown in prison, did not lose heart; shrewdly taking advantage of his intimate knowledge of the king's character, he attacked him at his weakest spot and offered him costly presents on condition he obtained a little breathing-space in exchange. His son, he said, was shortly to marry a Jewish girl from Marseilles, all he needed was time to arrange this marriage, after which he would submit like the others and change his religion. Chilperic cared little whether the pretext was genuine and the promise sincere, and, the golden bait all at once calming his proselytizing mania, he had his Jewish merchant set at liberty. And so Priscus alone remained innocent of apostasy and untroubled in his conscience among his co-religionists who, variously swayed by remorse and fear, would foregather in secret to celebrate the Sabbath and, the next day, as Christians, would attend church services.

Among those of the new converts that King Chilperic had honored with the favor of his spiritual paternity there was a certain Phatir, a native of the kingdom of the Burgondes who had recently settled in Paris. This man, of saturnine disposition, had no sooner abjured the faith of his ancestors than he deeply regretted it; the awareness of the infamy into which he had fallen soon became unbearable. The bitterness of his thoughts turned to violent envy of Priscus, who, more fortunate than himself, was able to carry his head high, free from the shame and anguish preying on the mind of an apostate. This hatred, fostered in secret, grew to the point of frenzy, and Phatir resolved to murder the man whose happiness he envied. Each sabbath day, Priscus would go secretly to perform the rites of Judaism in a secluded house south of the city on one of the two Roman roads intersecting not far from the little bridge. Phatir conceived the plan of waylaying him, and, accompanied by his slaves armed with swords and daggers, took up a position in ambush on the square in front of St. Julian's basilica. The unfortunate Priscus, suspecting nothing, was taking his usual route; after the manner of Jews going to the temple, he had no weapons of any kind about him, and wore knotted about his body, by way of a girdle, the shawl with which he was going to cover his head during the prayers and psalm-singing. He was accompanied by some of his friends, but they, like himself, were defenceless. As soon as they were within Phatir's reach, he fell upon them, sword in hand, followed by his slaves who, stirred up by their master's fury, struck indiscriminately and slaughtered Priscus the Jew and his friends alike. The murderers, immediately escaping to the safest and nearest asylum, took refuge together in St. Julian's basilica.

Either because Priscus was highly esteemed by the Parisians or because the sight of the corpses lying on the pavement was enough to arouse public indignation, the populace gathered menacingly on the spot where these murders had just been committed, and a considerable crowd, yelling "Death to the assassins!" closed in around the basilica. So great was the alarm of the clergy looking after the church that they sent posthaste to the king's palace to ask for protection and orders as to what they should do. Chilperic's reply was that he wanted his godson Phatir's life to be spared, but that the slaves should all be turned out of the sanctuary and put to death. Faithful to the end to the master whom they had served in good and ill alike, the slaves uncomplainingly watched him escape alone with the help of the ecclesiastics, while they prepared to die. To avoid both the sufferings with which they were threatened at the hands of the infuriated people and the torture which, according to the law, would precede their execution, they unanimously resolved that one of their number would kill all the others, then stab himself with his own sword; they appointed by voice vote the man who was to perform the office of executioner and carry out the will of the majority. This slave struck his companions one after another, but when he found himself to be the only one still standing, hesitated to turn the steel against his own breast. A vague hope of escape, or perhaps the thought of at least selling his life dearly, impelled him to dash out of the basilica into the thick of the mob. Brandishing his sword, still dripping with blood, he attempted to hack his way through the crowd, but after a brief fight was overwhelmed by numbers and perished, cruelly mutilated. For his own safety, Phatir petitioned the king for leave to return whence he came. He headed for Guntram's realm, but members of Priscus's family set off to track him down, caught up with him, and avenged their kinsman by his death.

While these things were going on in Paris, towards the end of the year

582, an unexpected event set the city of Tours—which had been fairly peaceful for three years under the administration of its new count, Eunomius—in an uproar. Leudast, the ex-count, turned up again, no longer in secret, but publicly, with his usual self-assured and overweening airs. He was the bearer of a royal edict granting him the right to bring his wife back from exile, to recover his landed property, and to live in his former residence. He owed this favor—which looked to him like the first step towards making his fortune anew—to the earnest petitions of the many friends he had at court among the Frankish chieftains, whose unruly natures were in sympathy with his own. For almost two years, they had ceaselessly pestered with their entreaties now King Chilperic, now Fredegund herself, who had become more open to their influence since the death of the two sons on whom her fortunes depended. Yielding to a need for popularity, and making her hatred and desires for revenge bow to the advantage of the moment, she consented, for her part, that the man who had accused her of adultery be released from the sentence of excommunication passed against him. Scarcely had the words forgiving and forgetting been uttered when Leudast's friends took the field to canvass even more earnestly for the indulgence of the bishops. They went from one to another, begging them to sign their names at the foot of a document, in the form of a pastoral letter, to the effect that the man condemened at Braine should thereafter be taken back into the peace of the church and the Christian communion. In this way they managed to get the support and the signatures of quite a large number of bishops; but out of a kind of discretion (or fear of failure) no approaches were made to the man whom Leudast had attempted to ruin by his lying accusations.

And so Gregory was uncommonly surprised to learn that his greatest enemy, excommunicated by a council and outlawed by the king, was returning, with a reprieve, to live in the vicinity of Tours. He was even more surprised when an envoy from Leudast came to present him with the letter signed by the bishops and to beg him to join with them in agreeing to cancel the sentence of excommunication. Suspecting some new piece of trickery devised in order to compromise him, he said to the messenger: "Can you also show me letters from the queen, since it was on her account especially that he was cut off from Christian communion?" The reply was in the negative, and Gregory went on: "When I have seen orders from the queen, I will receive him into my communion without delay." The prudent bishop was not content with these words alone; he sent off an express messenger with instructions to make inquiries in his name concerning the authenticity of the documents which had been submitted to him, and also concerning Queen Fredegund's intentions. She answered his questions in a letter worded as follows: "Under pressure from many people, I have been unable to do other than allow him to return to Tours: now I beseech you not to make peace with him and not to give him eulogias until we have thoroughly looked into what ought to be done."[15]

Bishop Gregory was familiar with Fredegund's style: he clearly saw that for her there was no question of forgiveness, but rather of vengeance and murder. Forgetting his own grounds for complaint, he took pity on the man who had not long since conspired his ruin and who was about to betray himself for lack of good sense and prudence. He sent for Leudast's father-in-law and, showing him this ominously laconic note, adjured him to see to it that his son-in-law exercised caution and remained in hiding once again until he was quite certain that he had mollified the queen. But this advice, inspired as it was by Christian charity, was misinterpreted and badly received. Leudast, judging others by himself, supposed that a man whose enemy he was could think of nothing but setting traps for him or playing nasty tricks on him. Far from becoming more wary, he acted as though he had taken the warning in the opposite way to what was intended, and, leaving security for the most reckless audacity, made up his mind to go of his own accord and present himself before King Chilperic. He left Tours in the middle of the year 583 and made his way towards the city of Melun, which the king in person was then besieging.

This siege was intended to be merely the prelude to an all-out invasion of King Guntram's states, an invasion which had been planned by Chilperic from the moment he had seen his earliest ambitious desires realized by the conquest of practically all the cities of Aquitaine. Having in less than six years—thanks to the military skill of the Gallo-Roman Desiderius—become sole master of the vast territory comprised within the southern limits of Berry, the Loire, the Atlantic, the Pyrenees, the Aude, and the Cévennes, he conceived—doubtless at the instigation of that venturesome warrior—an even bolder hope, that of adding to the Neustrian provinces the entire body of the kingdom of the Burgondes. In order to ensure the execution of this difficult undertaking, he intrigued with the principal Austrasian nobles, won several of them over with bribes, and received an embassy from them charged with concluding, in the name of young King Childebert, an offensive alliance against Guntram. The pact was drawn up and ratified by reciprocal oaths in the first months of the year 583. King Chilperic at once mustered his troops and started the war on his own account, without waiting for the actual cooperation of the Austrasian forces.

His plan of campaign, in which it is probably permissible to see the inspiration of an intelligence superior to his own—a new consequence of the counsels of the clever Gallo-Roman chief—consisted in first of all taking, by means of a two-pronged attack, the two most important fortified places on the eastern borders of the Burgundian kingdom: the city of Bourges and the stronghold of Melun. The king wanted to command the army which was to march to this latter point himself, and entrusted Desiderius, whom he had made duke of Toulouse, with the responsibility of directing (supported by a large body of men levied south of the Loire) the operations against Bourges. The order dispatched from the Neustrian chancellery to the duke of Toulouse and the dukes of Poitiers and Bordeaux for the general arming of the militia of their provinces was of curiously forceful brevity: "Enter the territory of Bourges and, on reaching the city, have the oath of allegiance sworn there in our name."

Berulf, duke of Poitiers, issued his declaration of war in Poitou, Touraine, Anjou, and the Nantes region; Bladaste, duke of Bordeaux, armed the inhabitants of both banks of the Garonne; and the duke of Toulouse, Desiderius, called to his colors the free men of the Toulouse, Albi, Cahors, and Limoges districts. The two last-named chiefs, uniting their forces, entered Berry from the south, while Duke Berulf came in from the west. Both invading armies were composed almost exclusively of Gallo-Romans; that of the southerners, of which Desiderius, the best of the Neustrian generals, was commander-in-chief, made better time than the other, and despite the enormous distance it had to cover, was the first to reach the territory of Bourges. Warned of its approach, the inhabitants of Bourges and its environs were not at all frightened of the danger threatening them. Their city, formerly one of the strongest and most warlike in Gaul, still retained its ancient traditions of glory and courage, and to this civic pride was added that of the splendor with which it had shone, under Roman administration, by virtue of its title of provincial capital, its public monuments, and the nobility of its senatorial families.

Although it had declined considerably since the Barbarians had come to power, such a city was still capable of displaying signs of energy, and it was no easy matter to compel it to do anything it did not wish to do. Now, either because of the ill repute of Chilperic's rule, or to keep themselves from being tossed from one sovereignty to another, the citizens of Bourges clung steadfastly to the one to which they had belonged ever since the old kingdoms of Orléans and the Burgondes had been united into a single state. Determined not only to withstand a siege, but actually to advance against the enemy, they dispatched from their city fifteen thousand men in full battle array.

A few miles south of Bourges, this army encountered that of Desiderius and Bladaste, which was much more numerous, and superior besides by reason of its commander-in-chief's capacities. Despite such drawbacks, the men of Berry did not hesitate to do battle; they held their own so well and fought so stubbornly that, according to public report, more than seven thousand men were killed on both sides. Briefly pushed back, the southerners finally gained the upper hand through numerical superiority. Driving the remnants of the defeated army before them, they continued their march towards Bourges, and engaged, all the way there, in acts of devastation copied from those of the Barbarian hordes: they set fire to the houses, pillaged the churches, uprooted the vines, and cut off the trees level with the ground. In this way they arrived before the walls of Bourges, where Duke Berulf's army joined them. The city had closed its gates, the defeat of its citizens in open country not having made it any less proud or any more disposed to surrender at the behest of the Neustrian chiefs. Desiderius and his two Frankish colleagues invested it on all sides and, following the enfeebled traditions of Roman military science, began tracing their lines and building siege engines.

The rendezvous assigned to the troops who were to take action against Melun was the city of Paris; for several months they poured in from all sides and caused the inhabitants all kinds of annoyances and damages. In this army, recruited in northern and central Neustria, men of Frankish origin were in the majority, and the native Gauls only a minority. When King Chilperic considered that he had collected sufficient men, he gave the command to march, and started off, at the head of his household troops, by way of the Roman road to the southeast. The soldiers followed the left bank of the Seine which, once beyond the Paris region, belonged to Guntram's kingdom. They marched along without order and without discipline, straying to left and right to sack and burn, stealing the furniture from the houses, and carrying off the cattle, the horses, and men, who, tied together two by two, followed the long line of baggage wagons as prisoners of war.

The devastation extended over all the country south of Paris, from Étampes as far as Melun, and continued around the latter town when the Neustrian bands halted in order to besiege it. Under the leadership of so inexperienced a warrior as King Chilperic, this siege could scarcely fail to drag on. The fortress of Melun, situated, like Paris, on an island in the Seine, was in those days considered very strong by reason of its location; it had almost nothing to fear from the spirited but unscientific attacks of a pack of men unskilled at military operations and capable only of coming gallantly to skirmish on small boats at the foot of its walls. Days and months went by in vainly repeated attempts to storm Melun, during which the Frankish warriors no doubt performed numerous doughty deeds, but which ultimately exhausted their patience. Bored with a prolonged encampment, they became more and more unmanageable, were neglectful of their appointed duties, and showed zeal only when engaged in scouring the countryside to amass booty.

Such was the state of mind of the army encamped in front of Melun when the hopeful and self-confident Leudast arrived at King Chilperic's headquarters. He was welcomed by the leuds, who recognized in him an old comrade in arms, brave in battle, merry at table, and a bold gambler; but when he tried to see the king in person, his own requests for an audience, as well as the petitions of his most highly placed and most influential friends, were denied. Chilperic, who was tolerably forgetful of injuries when his anger was appeased and he did not feel that his interests had suffered any material loss, would have given in to the entreaties of his entourage and let Fredegund's accuser see him, if the fear of displeasing the queen and incurring her reproaches had not restrained him. The ex-count of Tours, having vainly employed the mediation of the lords and chieftains, thought of a new expedient, namely, to make himself popular in the lower ranks of the army and to stir up public interest in his behalf.

He was completely successful, thanks to the very defects of his character, the eccentricity of his temperament, and his unruffled boastfulness; and that mass of men, curious and easy to stir up because they were idle, very soon became filled with ardent sympathy for him. When he believed that the time was ripe to put his popularity to the test, he asked for the whole army to implore the king to let him come before him; and one day when Chilperic was passing through the lines, this petition, uttered by thousands of voices, suddenly rang out in his ears. The entreaties of an undisciplined, discontented, and armed multitude were tantamount to orders; the king gave in for fear of seeing his refusal cause a riot, and announced that the man outlawed at Braine might now come before him. Leudast at once appeared and prostrated himself at the king's feet while asking for pardon.Chilperic made him stand up, told him that he sincerely forgave him, and added, in tones of almost paternal benevolence: "Behave discreetly until I have seen the queen and arranged for you to be restored to her good graces, for, as you know, she has just cause to find you very guilty."

Meanwhile, the report of the twofold aggression against Melun and Bourges forced King Guntram out of his lethargy and unsoldierly habits. Ever since the first Neustrian conquests in Aquitaine, the only assistance he had given the cities of his portion had been to send his generals; never had he placed himself at the head of an army. Threatened with seeing his western frontier breached at two different points and the Neustrian invasion penetrate this time to the very heart of his kingdom, he did not hesitate to march in person against the king of Neustria and to provoke a decisive battle which, in conformity with his beliefs—a mixture of Germanic traditions and Christian concepts—must perforce reveal the judgment of God. He prepared himself for this important proceeding by praying, fasting, and alms-giving; and, marshalling his finest troops, took the road to Melun with them.

Having arrived within a short distance of the city and Chilperic's cantonments, he halted, and despite his great confidence in the divine protection, wanted, following his innate instinct for caution, to observe the enemy positions and deployment at leisure. It was not long before he was apprised of the lack of order prevailing in the Neustrian camp and the carelessness with which they kept watch, both by day and by night. Acting on this information, he made arrangements to approach the besieging army as near as possible without alarming it enough to make it more watchful; and one evening when a good part of its troops were scattered over the countryside foraging and pillaging, he grasped the opportunity and aimed a sudden and well-conducted attack against the depleted lines. The Neustrian soldiers, taken unawares in their camp just when they were least thinking of fighting, were unable to withstand the onslaught, and the bands of foragers, returning one by one, were cut to pieces. Within a few hours, King Guntram remained in sole possession of the field, and thus as a general won his first, and last, victory.

King Chilperic's bearing in this bloody affray is not known to us; maybe he performed feats of valor during the action itself; but after the rout, when it was a matter of rallying the survivors of his army and preparing a counterattack, his will failed him. As he was entirely devoid of foresight, the slightest setback would disconcert him and suddenly take away all his courage and presence of mind. Sick of the enterprise for which he had put into effect such extensive troop movements, he thought only of peace, and first thing in the morning following this night of disaster, sent a message to King Guntram proposing a settlement. Guntram, ever a peace-loving man, and not in the least elated with the pride of his triumph, had himself but one desire, to bring the dispute to a speedy conclusion and return to his tranquillity. He for his part delegated envoys who, meeting with Chilperic's, concluded a treaty of reconciliation between the two kings.

Under the terms of this agreement, drawn up in conformity with ancient Germanic custom, the kings negotiated not as independent sovereigns, but as members of the same tribe, and subject, despite their titles, to a higher authority, that of the national law. They agreed to leave it up to the judgment of the bishops and the elders of the people and promised one another that whichever of them was convicted of having overstepped the limits *would come to terms with the other*, and would compensate him *in accordance with the judges' decision*. Suiting his actions to his words, the king of Neustria at once sent orders to the three dukes investing Bourges to raise the siege and to withdraw from the land. He himself headed back to Paris with his army, now much reduced in size, followed by a host of wounded, and less proud-looking, but still the same as regards its lack of discipline and destructive rapacity.

Peace having been made, this return journey took place on friendly territory, but the Neustrian soldiers took no account of that, and once again began looting, wreaking havoc, and taking prisoners all along the

line of march. Through a highly uncharacteristic qualm of conscience—
or through a belated sense of the need to maintain good order—it grieved
Chilperic to see these acts of brigandage, and he resolved to put a stop to
them. The injunction issued in his name to all commanders to keep an
eye on their men and to restrain them rigidly was too unwonted not to
meet with some resistance. The Frankish lords grumbled about it, and
one of them, the count of Rouen, declared that he was not about to
prevent anyone from doing what had always been permitted. As soon as
the effect had followed these words, Chilperic, suddenly finding his
energy again, had the count arrested and put to death as an example to
the others. Moreover, he commanded that all the booty should be returned and all the captives released, measures which, if taken in time,
would no doubt have averted the failure of his campaign. He thus
returned to Paris more in control of his troops and more capable of
keeping them in check than he had been at his departure; unfortunately,
the qualities essential to a commander-in-chief had flowered in him at an
unseasonable moment, for he was entirely taken up with peace just then.
The harsh lesson of the battle of Melun had put an end to his dreams of
conquest, and thereafter he thought only of trying to keep through guile
everything that he had won hitherto by the use of force.

Leudast, having returned safe and sound, followed the king to Paris,
where Fredegund was at that time in residence. Instead of avoiding a city
which was so dangerous for him, or simply passing through it with the
army, he stopped there, calculating that the good graces of the husband
would, if need arose, be his safeguard against the ill-will of the wife.
After a few not-too-cautiously-spent days, seeing that he was neither
pursued nor threatened, he believed himself to be amnestied by the
queen, and judged that the time had come when he could appear before
her. One Sunday when the king and queen were hearing mass together
in the cathedral of Paris, Leudast went to the church, made his way
through the crowd surrounding the royal pair as boldly as may be
imagined, and, prostrating himself at the feet of Fredegund (who was far
from expecting to see him), begged her to pardon him.

At this sudden apparition of a man whom she cordially detested and
who seemed to her to have come less to implore her forgiveness than to
brave her anger, Fredegund was overcome with the most violent attack of
spleen. Her face became flushed, tears poured down her cheeks, and,
glancing with bitter disdain at her husband, sitting motionless beside
her, she cried: "Since I no longer have any son on whom I can rely to
pursue those who have offended me, I leave it up to you, Lord Jesus."
Then, as if to make one last appeal to the conscience of the man whose
duty it was to protect her, she threw herself at the king's feet, saying with
a look of intense pain and wounded dignity: "Woe is me! I see my enemy
before me and am powerless against him!" This strange scene moved all

the bystanders, and King Chilperic more than anyone, who felt the reproach and at the same time suffered the remorse for having too readily pardoned an insult to his wife. To obtain forgiveness for his untimely indulgence, he gave orders for Leudast to be driven out of the church, promising himself that in future he would abandon him pitilessly and without appeal to the vengeance of Fredegund. When the guards had carried out the explusion order that they had just received and the din had subsided, the celebration of mass which had been momentarily interrupted was resumed, and continued without further incident.

Leudast, who had merely been taken outside the church and left at liberty to flee wherever he wished, gave no thought to taking advantage of this stroke of good luck, which he owed simply to the extreme haste with which Chilperic had given his orders. Far from having his eyes opened to the danger he was in by such an omen, he fancied that if he had suffered a setback with the queen it was for lack of finesse, because he had appeared before her abruptly, instead of leading up to his petition with a lavish present. With this insane notion uppermost in his mind, he decided to remain in the city and immediately to visit the shops of the most renowned goldsmiths and dealers in precious fabrics.

Near the cathedral on the way to the king's palace, there was a vast square adjacent to the bridge across the southern[16] arm of the Seine. This square, intended for commercial purposes, was lined with counters and shops where merchandise of all kinds was displayed. The ex-count of Tours began to stroll through it, going from one shop to the next, looking curiously at everything, acting the rich man, speaking of his concerns, and telling those who happened to be there, "I have suffered great losses, but I still have a good deal of gold and silver at home." Then, like an expert buyer communing with himself to make a deliberate and discerning choice, he would handle the materials, try the jewels against himself, feel the weight of the precious plate in his hand, and, when he had made his selection, would continue in loud and conceited tones: "This is fine, put it to one side; I intend to take all of this."

While he was thus buying articles of great value, without worrying whether he could afford them or not, mass ended and the faithful came crowding out of the cathedral. The king and queen, walking along together, took the street leading to the palace and crossed the Place du Commerce. The retinue following behind them and the people standing aside to let them pass warned Leudast that they were coming, but he was not disturbed, and went on conversing with the merchants under the wooden portico which ran all round the square and served as a lobby for the various shops.[17] Although Fredegund had no reason to expect that she would encounter her enemy there, with the piercing gaze of the bird of prey she espied him among the crowd of strollers and shoppers. She kept walking, so as not to startle the man whom she wanted captured without fail, and as soon as she had set foot across the palace threshold, sent several of her retainers, bold and clever men, to catch Leudast unawares, take him alive, and bring him to her securely bound.

In order to get near him without in any way arousing his suspicions, the queen's servants put down their weapons (swords and shields) behind one of the pillars of the portico; then, distributing the roles each was to play, advanced in such a manner as to make it impossible for him either to escape or resist. But their plan was poorly executed, and one of them, too impatient to act, laid hands on Leudast before the others were near enough to surround and disarm him. The ex-count of Tours, guessing what peril loomed over him, drew his sword and struck his attacker. The man's companions fell back several paces, then, running to pick up their weapons, came towards Leudast with swords and shields raised, furious with him and determined to spare his life no longer. Assailed simultaneously from front and rear in this unequal fight, Leudast received a slash across the head which practically scalped him. Despite his wound, he succeeded in beating off the enemies in front of him and fled, covered with blood, towards the bridge onto which the southern gate of the city opened.

This was a timber bridge, and its dilapidated condition testified to the decline of the municipal authorities—or to the exactions and depredations of the royal tax collectors. There were spots where the planks, rotten with age, left gaps between the joists of the framework and obliged passers-by to tread with caution. Hard pressed in his flight and compelled to cross the bridge at full speed, Leudast had no time to avoid the bad places; one of his feet, slipping between two badly joined beams, got caught in such a way that he was hurled backwards and broke his leg in the fall. His pursuers, having overcome him by accident, tied his hands behind his back and, since they could not present him to the queen in such a state, flung him across a horse's back and took him to the public jail to await further instructions.

Orders came from the king himself, who, eager to get back into Fredegund's good graces, strained his ingenuity to do something wholly agreeable for her. Far from having any pity on the wretch whose presumptuous illusions and crazy fecklessness had been fostered by his own act of forgiving and forgetting, he cast about for some mode of execution for Leudast to suffer, mentally calculating the strong and weak points of every type of torment in order to find the one most apt to assuage the queen's vengeance. After carefully thinking it over in the most appallingly cold-blooded way, Chilperic considered that the prisoner, gravely wounded as he was and weakened by massive loss of blood, must of necessity succumb to the slightest tortures, and so resolved to have him cured and put in shape to endure to the bitter end the agonies of a long-drawn-out execution.

Entrusted to the care of the best physicians, Leudast was removed from the unwholesome prison and carried out of the city to one of the royal estates, so that the fresh air and the amenities of the place might speed up his recovery. Perhaps, by way of a subtly barbarous precaution, they let him believe that his good treatment was a sign of clemency, and that he would regain his freedom on recovering his good health; but all was to no avail: his wounds turned gangrenous and his state became hopeless. When news of this reached the queen, she could not bring herself to let her enemy die in peace; and while there still remained a little life that she could take from him, she commanded that he be made to die a bizarre death that, to all appearances, she herself took pleasure in contriving. The dying man was dragged from his bed and stretched out on the stone floor, the nape of his neck resting on an enormous iron bar; then a man with another bar struck him on the throat with it, and kept on striking until he breathed his last.

So ended the adventurous existence of this sixth-century parvenu, the son of a Gallo-Roman serf who was raised through a stroke of royal favor to the same rank as the leaders of the conquerors of Gaul. If the name Leudast, barely mentioned even in the most voluminous of the histories of France, is little worthy of being rescued from oblivion, his life, which was closely interwoven with those of several famous persons, presents one of the most characteristic episodes of the general life of the period. Problems on which scholarly opinion has been much at variance are, so to speak, resolved of their own accord by the facts of this strange story. What could be the fortunes of a Gaul of servile condition under Frankish rule? How were the diocesan cities administered, placed as they were under the twofold authority of their counts and their bishops? What were the mutual relations between these two naturally hostile (or at least rival) powers? These are questions clearly answered by the mere telling of the adventures of Leocadius's son.

Other controversial historical points will have been—at least, I hope so—similarly settled beyond all serious argument by the preceding Episodes. Although filled with details and marked with fundamentally individual touches, each of these Episodes has a general meaning, which is easily put into words. The story of Bishop Praetextatus is the description of a Gallo-Roman Council; that of young Merovech reveals the life of the outlaw as well as the interior of religious sanctuaries; that of Galswinth portrays conjugal life and domestic customs in the Merovingian palace; and, finally, the story of Sigibert's murder presents, at its very outset, the increasingly nationalistic hostility of Austrasia towards Neustria.

SEVENTH EPISODE
Revolt of the Citizens of Limoges—Great Epidemic—
Fredegund's Maternal Sorrows—History of Clovis,
Third Son of King Chilperic (580)

Fredegund had received her share of profit from the conquests of her husband, the king of Neustria; it appears that several Aquitanian cities were allocated to her in usufruct, that is to say with the right of collecting all taxes due there in cash and in kind.[1] Anxious to increase this revenue as much as possible, owing it as she did to the fortunes of war, which might well take it away from her again, she suggested to King Chilperic the idea of a new ruling for his enlarged realm with respect to the establishment and rate of the property tax. The land tax, which had been set up in Gaul by the Roman administration, was still, in the sixth century, being levied on the basis of land-survey registers modeled on the old imperial rolls. Only Gallo-Roman landowners paid it, and free men of Germanic descent were exempted therefrom through primordial custom and a stubborn resistance against which the treasury agents' every endeavor—ranging from violence to guile—came to grief.

This example was not without influence on the native-born property owners who, supported by the bishops and the higher diocesan clergy, used all sorts of subterfuges to evade the demands and inquiries of the tax gatherers. Moreover, the ever-increasing decay of administrative competence made the actual collection of taxes very erratic, and the receipts very uncertain. Property and population censuses were only partial and were becoming more and more uncommon. So far as taxation was concerned, there was a tendency for custom to replace law. About the year 580, when Fredegund—whose action was inspired not by political considerations but by innate greed—took it into her head to counsel that a general census be taken, taxes on buildings in the kingdom of Neustria were still adjusted on the same footing as in King Lothar's day, which meant that for the past twenty or thirty years, at least, neither the establishment nor the rate of taxation had changed.

The advice given by the queen was of a kind that King Chilperic could hardly fail to receive with delight. It was decided that the entire Neustrian tax system would be overhauled, and the king gave the responsibility for the execution of this great scheme to his Gallo-Roman officials, the preservers of traditional administrative ability and avidity. Proceeding along lines followed in the times of the emperors, they made a plan which distinguished and classified cultivated lands and subjected them to different rates and different types of taxation. Next, a royal decree ordained that this plan be applied to all territories subject, whether of recent date or of old, to the king of Neustria. The tax rates which, for more than half a century, had been imposed on the indigenous landowners were all at once vastly increased; new taxes, not unskillfully diversified and graduated, were levied on every kind of crop and on the very agricultural implements. There were taxes on fields, woods, houses, cattle, and slaves; but the main surcharge was incurred by vine-growing lands. For the first time ever, they were assessed at the rate of one amphora, that is to say at half a hogshead of wine per half-acre, which would seem to show that at that time Chilperic, in his materialistically covetous way, was thinking above all of the prosperous vineyards of Aquitaine.

The task of going from city to city to take the census of property and persons subject to taxation—a difficult and possibly even dangerous one in those days—fell to the referendary Marcus, who was a Gaul, and very zealous in the interests of the Treasury as well as very adept at deducting for himself a portion of the monies which he collected. His commission was twofold, and there were two ways of carrying it out, one applicable to Neustrian lands of long standing, the other to the recently conquered territories. In the towns which had belonged to the kingdom of Neustria since the latest partition and whose land-survey registers were in the keeping of the royal Treasury, Marcus, carrying copies of these rolls with him, was supposed to amend and complete them through his investigations. As regards the cities which had been taken away from Austrasia or from Guntram's kingdom, he was to seize their municipal survey rolls and, after checking their accuracy, send them to the Treasury. Such were the duties assigned to the Gallo-Roman commissioner, together with orders to expedite the collection of the new taxes to the limits of his ability.

He set out from the palace of Soissons (or from some nearby royal residence) in the winter of 580 and, whether he began his tour with the northern towns or reached the southern country directly, he was in Limoges by the end of February. This city, captured and recaptured so many times, had belonged legitimately to King Chilperic before becoming his by conquest,[2] and its survey rolls had long since been deposited in the royal archives of Neustria. It was numbered among the cities where the new system of taxation could be set up by a simple checking of the rolls—a task which, however, was possible only through public inquiry and statements made by the landowners before the curia[3] or the municipal senate. The Calends, i.e., the first day of March, were apparently set aside for a solemn assembly and judicial hearings by the curia of Limoges. On that day the municipal magistrates and the corps of decurions[4] would sit on the bench or deliberate in council, and the country people, both landowners and tenant farmers, would flock into town for their lawsuits or their business affairs. This was the day chosen by Marcus for his first transactions, which consisted in giving a public reading of the king's commands; in obtaining the collaboration of the municipal authorities whether they liked it or not; and finally, in beginning an investigation regarding the state of property located in the then very vast district comprised within the city's jurisdiction, the exact area of these properties, their sundry crops, and the transfers of property effected since the previous census.[5]

Early in the morning of March 1st, the city of Limoges was in an uproar, and townspeople of every class were crowding thickly around the approaches to the place where the curia was to convene. The city magistrates, the decurions, the Defender, the bishop and the higher clergy took their places on the seats and benches of the senate-house. Referendary Marcus entered the assembly with an honor-guard, followed by men carrying his survey books and his tax rolls. He presented his commission, sealed with the impress of the royal signet ring, and proclaimed the rate and nature of the taxes decreed by the king. In Roman times, the Defender would have been the man who raised his voice to make objections and protests, the law under which he was appointed giving him that prerogative; but since the outset of the reign of the Barbarians, this lay leader of municipal authority had taken a back seat to the bishop, who alone was capable of seeing to the protection of the city's interests. Ferreolus, the bishop of Limoges, did not shirk this duty. Making a kind of case for the defence against the new tax, he said that the city had been assessed in King Lothar's time and that this assessment was binding; that after Lothar's death, the citizens having sworn allegiance to King Chilperic, he himself had promised and vowed to impose neither new law nor custom on them, nor to make any ordinance aimed at despoiling them, but to maintain them in the state in which they had lived under his father.[6] These words, a calm expression of public discontent and inclinations to resist which were even then smouldering in the town, were followed by murmurs of approval from the benches of the curia, and perhaps there was, after the Roman fashion, a chorus of acclamations from all sides, such as: "That's true! That's right! That's what we all think! Yes, all of us!"

Full of the arrogance of power and impatient of the delays which this opposition might cause him, Marcus made a sharp and haughty rejoinder; he said he had come to act, not to argue, called upon the city to obey the king's decree, and added threats to his demands. His voice was at once drowned in a general uproar, and, the commotion in the assembly spreading to the outside, the densely packed crowd around the doors could no longer be restrained and poured into the curia. Moderate resistance then gave way to the rage of the common people, and the chamber echoed with cries of: "No new assessment! Death to the extortioner! Death to the despoiler! Death to Marcus!" Accompanying these outcries with meaningful gestures, the mob moved towards the place where the commissioner was sitting by the bishop. At that critical moment, Bishop Ferreolus for the second time performed the noble role of protector attached to his title; he told Marcus to stand up and, taking his hand, held the flood of insurgents in check by his tone and manner: surprised and respectful, they stopped while he reached one of the exits and led the referendary to the nearest basilica. Having reached this place of refuge where his life was now secure, Marcus looked to ways and means of getting out of Limoges with all possible speed; he succeeded, aided once again by the bishop, and possibly by a disguise.

Meanwhile, in the hall of the curia, the hubbub went on; the magistrates and senators, laymen and clerics alike, remained mingled pell-mell with the people, some of them dejected and uncertain what they should do, others giving themselves up to all the excitement of political enthusiasm. Among the latter group, apparently, some priests and abbots were conspicuous. Briefly at a loss, and as it were amazed at having allowed the man on whom they wished to avenge themselves to get away safe and sound, the people turned their anger against the land registers abandoned by the fleeing Marcus. The wilder spirits seized them in order to tear them to pieces; but a different counsel prevailed, which was to carry these records to the marketplace and there to burn them with due pomp, signalling the victory of the citizens of Limoges and their determination not to endure the levying of fresh tributes. They hurried off to search the house which had been occupied by the referendary, and removed everything in the way of registers and scrolls intended for different cities. A bonfire was built amid the gleeful shouts of the multitude, intoxicated by its own rebellion. High-ranking citizens in its midst became excited just like the rest and applauded to see the flames destroying the books brought by the royal official. Before long nothing but ashes remained. But these books were mere copies, and the originals reposed safely in the coffers of the Treasury; the kind of deliverance which the city of Limoges deluded itself it had won could not be of long duration; it did not in fact last long, and its consequences were deplorable.

From the first town in which he thought it was safe to make a halt, Marcus sent a message to King Chilperic informing him of the serious events which had just taken place in Limoges. Sedition, with threats of death against a royal official and destruction of public records, was one of the crimes for which, under the Roman Empire, the emperor (no matter what his character) could have neither pardon nor clemency. In determining the king of Neustria's conduct in this case, there was added to the imperial tradition the wrathful and personally vengeful spirit of Barbarian kingship, as well as the instinctive avarice aroused by such an opportunity for making handsome profits out of confiscations and fines. To all appearances, these diverse motives played a part in the drastic decision immediately arrived at by the king. He dispatched from his palace, on extraordinary commission, officers charged with going to Limoges, entering the city with or without its consent, and dealing harshly with its inhabitants by executions, by a terrifying array of tortures, and by an increase in taxes. The order was carried out in every particular; the royal commissioners arrived in Limoges, and the people who had recklessly rebelled either dared not or could not do anything to defend themselves. After a summary investigation into the circumstances of the revolt, a kind of proscription engulfed the senators of Limoges and, together with them, every citizen of note. Abbots and priests, accused of having incited the people to burn the survey books, were subjected to various kinds of tortures in the marketplace. All the property of those who had been executed or outlawed devolved to the Treasury, and an exceptional tribute, much more burdensome than the taxes which it had previously refused to pay, was imposed on the city.

While the Limousins were being so cruelly punished for their one-day rebellion, referendary Marcus was proceeding with his administrative tour, which he completed unmolested. Six or eight months after his departure, he returned to the palace of Braine, bringing with him the money collected as first installment of the new tax and the census rolls and tax assessments decreed for every city of the kingdom. The tax records of the cities whose revenues belonged to Queen Fredegund were handed over her to be kept in the chests where she locked up her gold, her jewels, her precious fabrics, and the title-deeds to her estates; the remainder were returned to storage or took their place for the first time in the royal Treasury of Neustria. Marcus derived immense, more or less illicit, profits from this vast financial transaction; his wealth was the object of the hatred and execration of his brother Gallo-Romans, who were sick at heart and ruined by the new tributes. Either because these charges were of themselves intolerably heavy, or because their weight was increased for the majority of the taxpayers by an inaccurate land classification and by inequitable assessments, many families preferred to abandon their heritage and leave the country rather than endure them. During the course of the year 580, a host of emigrants left Neustrian territory to go and settle in the cities owing allegiance to Childebert II or to Guntram.

That same year, during which King Chilperic's administrative measures fell like a scourge on Neustria, was marked throughout Gaul by natural calamities. In the spring, the Rhône and the Saône, the Loire and its tributaries, swollen by continual rains, overflowed their banks and created much destruction. The entire Auvergne plain was inundated; at Lyons, many houses were destoyed by water, and part of the city wall collapsed. In the summer, a hailstorm laid waste to the Bourges area; the city of Orléans was half destroyed by fire. An earthquake violent enough to shake city ramparts was felt in Bordeaux and the surrounding countryside: in the Pyreneees the shock, extending in the direction of Spain, broke off gigantic blocks of stone which crushed both the shepherds and their flocks. Last of all, in the month of August, a smallpox epidemic of the deadliest kind broke out at several places in central Gaul and, the infection spreading by degrees, swept through almost the entire country.

The notion of a secret poison, which in similar catastrophes never fails to occur to the imagination of the common people, was pretty widely accepted, and potions brewed from antidotal herbs played the principal role among the remedies which were tried. The death rate, which was frightening, was highest among children and young people. By far the most heartrending feature of these doleful scenes was the grief of the parents. It drew a cry of sympathy from a contemporary chronicler, who phrases it both gracefully and tenderly: "We lost," he says, "our dear, sweet children, whom we had cherished in our bosom, carried in our arms, and painstakingly fed with our own hands; but we dried our tears and said with the holy man Job: 'The Lord gave and the Lord hath taken away: blessed be the name of the Lord.' "[7]

When the epidemic, having ravaged Paris and the surrounding area, moved towards Soissons, closing in around the city and with it the royal residence of Braine, one of the first to be stricken was King Chilperic. He felt the serious symptoms of the early stages of the disease, but had, in his ordeal, the advantage of maturity, and made a speedy recovery. Scarcely had he become convalescent when Dagobert, the youngest of his sons, who was not yet baptized, fell ill. Through a religious presentiment and in the hope of calling down the divine protection upon him, his parents hurried to have him christened; the child seemed to feel a little better, but before long his brother Chlodobert, aged fifteen, was also stricken by the prevalent disease. At the sight of both her sons in danger of death, Fredegund was gripped by the cruel pangs which nature inflicts on mothers, and, beneath the weight of her maternal concern, something strange occurred in so savagely egotistical a soul. She suffered twinges of conscience and feelings of kindness; she began to think remorseful thoughts, thoughts of pity for the sufferings of others, fearful thoughts of God's judgment. The evil that she had done or advised others to do, and especially the melancholy events of that year,

the blood spilled at Limoges, the miseries of every kind caused throughout the realm by the creation of the new taxes, all these things came into
her mind, troubled her imagination, and caused her repentance mingled
with dread.

Perturbed by her maternal fears and by this sudden fit of self-criticism,
Fredegund was with the king one day in the palace room where their two
sons were lying in bed, prostrated with fever. There was a fire burning in
the hearth to guard against the first cold spells of September and to
prepare the draughts administered to the young patients. Chilperic was
silent and displayed few signs of emotion; the queen, on the other hand,
sighing, letting her eyes roam about her, staring now at one of her
children, now at the other, showed by her attitude and her gestures the
intensity and the agitation of the thoughts which haunted her. In such a
state of mind, Germanic women used often to begin to speak in extem-
pore verse, or at any rate in a more poetic and more modulated language
than ordinary speech. Whether it was because they were overcome by
violent emotion or because they wished to diminish the weight of some
mental suffering by an outpouring of the heart, they would instinctively
resort to this more solemn mode of expressing their feelings of every
kind, grief, joy, love, hate, indignation, scorn.[8] Fredegund herself was
so inspired; she turned to the king and, fixing him with a look which
commanded attention, she uttered the following words:

> Long have we done ill, long has God in his goodness endured us;
> Oft has he chastised us with fevers and other afflictions,
> But we have not amended our ways.
>
> Lo! we are losing our sons;
> Lo! the tears of the poor, the widows' complaints, and the sighs of the
>   orphans now slay them;
> No more may we hope to have someone to save for.
>
> We hoard treasure and know not for whom we amass such a store;
> See now our riches bereft of their owners, all brimful of rapine and
>   curses.
>
> Yet did not our store-rooms run over with wine?
> Our granaries, were they not bursting with wheat?
> Then were not our coffers all bulging with treasure?
> With gold and with silver, with gemstones, with collars, with other
>   kingly adornments?
> But of all our belongings, lo! now we lose the most lovely.[9]

At this point, the tears, which ever since the beginning of her lament
had been flowing from the queen's eyes, and which had become more
abundant at every pause, choked her. She fell silent and remained with
drooping head, sobbing and beating her breast; then she drew herself

up, as though filled with a sudden resolve, and said to the king: "Now then, if you will take my advice, come here and let us throw all these iniquitous tax rolls into the fire; let us be satisfied for our revenues with what sufficed your father, King Lothar." And she at once gave orders for the registers which Marcus had brought from the towns belonging to her to be fetched from her coffers. As soon as she had them, she took one roll after another and threw them into the broad fireplace, right into the middle of the blazing logs. Her eyes lit up on seeing the flames engulf and consume these documents obtained with such difficulty; but King Chilperic, who was far more astonished than happy at this unexpected act, looked on without uttering a single word of acquiescence. "Do you hesitate?" said the queen imperiously. "Look at me and do as I do, so that even if we lose our sons we may at least escape eternal punishment."

Yielding to his wife's prompting, Chilperic went to the room of the palace where the collection of public records was kept; he had all the rolls which had been drawn up for the gathering of the new taxes taken out, and ordered that they be thrown into the fire. Next, he sent men into the different provinces of his realm with instructions to proclaim that the previous year's decree concerning the land tax had been rescinded by the king, and to forbid the counts and all revenue agents to enforce it in future.

Meanwhile the fatal illness ran its course; the younger of the two children was the first to die. His parents wanted him to be buried in the basilica of St. Denis, and they had his body carried from the palace at Braine to Paris without themselves accompanying it. All their care was then lavished upon Chlodobert, whose condition left little room for hope. Despairing of any human aid, they laid him on a stretcher and went with him, on foot, into Soissons, to the basilica of St. Médard. There, following one of the religious practices of the age, they exposed him (that is, they left him lying in bed near the saint's tomb), and made a solemn vow for his recovery. But the sick boy, spent with fatigue after a journey of only a few miles, entered upon his last agony that very day, and expired about midnight. The entire population of the city was deeply moved by his death; in addition to feeling the usual sympathy for the untimely end of persons of royal estate, the people of Soissons were reflecting upon their own misfortunes. Almost everyone had some recent loss to weep for. They flocked to the obsequies of the young prince and followed his body in procession to the place of his burial, the basilica of the martyred Saints Crispin and Crispinian. The men shed tears and the black-clad women acted as grief-stricken as at the funeral of a father or a husband; it seemed to them, as they accompanied this cortege, that they were mourning all their families.

As a token of his paternal sorrow, Chilperic made large donations to the churches and the poor. He did not return to Braine, which had become hateful to him and where the epidemic was continuing its ravages; instead, having left Soissons with Fredegund, he went with her to live in one of the royal houses on the edge of the vast forest of Cuise, not far from Compiègne. It was then October, the season of the autumn hunt, a kind of national ritual to the enjoyment of which any Frank would devote himself passionately enough to forget the greatest affliction. The movement, the noise, the appeal of a violent and sometimes dangerous sport allayed the king's melancholy, and now and then restored him to his old self: but for Fredegund's grief there was neither distraction nor respite. Her pain as a mother was intensified by the change that the death of her two sons would necessarily bring about in her situation as queen, and also by her fears for the future. There remained but one heir to the kingdom of Neustria, and that was Clovis, the son of another woman—the very wife whom she had once supplanted—and the man that a recent conspiracy had just brought to her attention as the object of the hopes and intrigues of her enemies. [10] The prospect of widowhood, a misfortune which she was every day obliged to dread, appalled her; she saw herself, in her fearful imagination, degraded from her rank, stripped of honors, power, and wealth, and subjected by way of reprisal to cruel treatment or to humiliations which she feared worse than death itself.

This new form of mental anguish did not inspire her with the same kind of thoughts as had the first. Momentarily taken out of herself by the noble and tender yearnings characteristic of motherhood, she had fallen back into her own true nature—unbridled egotism, guile, and cruelty. She began to look for methods of setting a fatal trap for Clovis, and in this intrigue she counted on the same pestilence which had just robbed her of her sons to destroy her enemy. The young prince, having been absent from Braine, had escaped this sickness; she resolved to suggest to his father—on a false pretext—the idea of sending him to the place where the contagion was proving ever more deadly. The reason she invented for persuading her husband was doubtless the desirability of finding out, through the eyes of a trustworthy person, a member of the family, what was going on in that royal house, suddenly deserted by its owners and consequently open to all manner of pilfering and peculation. Suspecting nothing of her secret reasons for this advice, Chilperic thought it well worth taking; he sent word to Clovis, ordering him to proceed to Braine, and the young man complied, with that filial obedience typical of Teutonic mores.

Not long after, the king left the forest of Cuise for his estate of Chelles on the Marne, [11] to make a personal inspection of the harvest, or else to vary his distractions. While there, he fell to thinking of his son, who, to please him, was exposing himself to almost certain danger at Braine, and he recalled him to his side. Clovis returned safe and sound from his perilous mission; full of himself and of his good fortune in outliving his younger brothers, he inflamed Fredegund's grief and hatred as though wantonly. He would flaunt his scornful pride before her and would make remarks to all and sundry such as: "Now that my brothers are dead, the kingdom is left for me alone; all Gaul will be subject to me, fate has reserved paramount rule for me. Now that my enemies are in my hands, I shall deal with them as I think fit." Often, to this puerile boasting he would add offensive remarks about the queen; his vanity was swollen by the pride the Neustrians took in their recent conquests, which gave them hopes of reuniting Frankish sovereignty to their own benefit.[12]

Fredegund kept well informed of every trifling thing her stepson said, and in her extremely preoccupied state, these idle words would make her shudder with fright. To begin with she was given accurate reports; next the truth was mixed with falsehood; and finally, outright fiction was supplied by her followers, trying to outdo one another in zeal. One day, somebody came and told her: "If you are left without sons, it is the result of Clovis's plots. The daughter of one of your serving-women is his mistress, and he has made use of the mother's black magic to kill your children. I warn you, expect nothing better for yourself, now that you have lost what gave you hope." This false accusation electrified the queen, revived all her old energy, and drove her from dejection to fury. She had the two women who had been pointed out to her apprehended in her house and brought before her, tightly bound. At her command, Clovis's concubine was beaten with rods and all her hair was cut off, a mark of infamy inflicted by Germanic custom on the adulteress and the wanton before any other penalty; then the wretched girl was exposed in the palace courtyard, her body squeezed between the two halves of a split stake which had been erected in front of the young prince's quarters to put him to shame and grieve him at one and the same time. While the daughter was undergoing this punishment, the mother was being put to the question; and a false confession of the sorceries imputed to her was extracted under torture.

Furnished with this proof, which seemed to be unanswerable, Fredegund went to find the king, told him what she had just learned, and asked for revenge on Clovis. Her story, artfully sprinkled with innuendoes likely to make Chilperic afraid for his own life, made such an impression on him that without any investigation, without questioning anyone else, without even hearing his son's defense, he decided to hand him over to the justice of his stepmother. Having become fainthearted through his own gullibility, crediting Clovis with thoughts of usurpation and parricide over and above the crime of which he was accused, he dared not have him arrested in the palace, but wanted to get his hands on him by means of a kind of ambush. On the day in question, there was a hunting-party in the nearby forest of Chelles; the king went to it accompanied only by a few devoted leuds, among whom were prominent Duke

Bob,[13] or Baudeghisel, and Duke Desiderius, the able and successful commander of the army of invasion which was even then pursuing the conquest of Childebert's and Guntram's cities in Aquitaine. Having come to the court of Neustria in the interval between two campaigns, one might say that he just happened to be there at the right moment to lend a hand in the father's senseless anger against his own son, and to fill the role of fate's minister which the Gallo-Roman lords played more than once in the domestic catastrophes of the Merovingian dynasty.

At one of his halts in the forest, Chilperic sent word to Clovis, ordering him to come before him for a secret interview. Perhaps the young man believed that this mysterious rendezvous had been arranged by his father to give him the opportunity of explaining himself, of speaking freely, and of proving his innocence; at any rate he obeyed without hesitation, having no suspicion of what lay ahead. When he reached the forest, he soon found himself in the presence of his father and of Dukes Bob and Desiderius, who were standing near him. We do not know how the king received his son; perhaps he burst out with reproaches and curses, or perhaps he merely gave a nod of command in gloomy silence, whereupon Desiderius and Bob approached the young prince and, seizing him by the arms, held him by main force while his sword was taken away from him. When he was disarmed, they stripped him of his fine clothes and put coarse ones on him; in this get-up, bound like a base felon, he was taken before the queen and left at her mercy.

Although Fredegund had long since thoroughly made up her mind what she wanted to do when she had the life of the last of her stepsons in her power, she was in no hurry; and acting in conformity with her perennially calculating and farsighted mentality, she kept Clovis a prisoner in the palace of Chelles in order to interrogate him herself and to extract from his answers either evidence against himself or information concerning his relationships, both self-seeking and personal. For three days, these domestic proceedings brought face to face in unequal contest two human beings of utterly different temperament; the woman as shrewd as she was ruthless, a most accomplished deceiver, iron-willed; the young man foolhardy, scatter-brained, open-hearted, and given to saying the first thing that came into his head. The interrogation of the prisoner turned on three points, which were put to him in every possible way: What had he to say concerning the circumstances of the crime with which he was charged? From whom had he received suggestions or advice? With whom was he particularly friendly?

No matter what devious methods were tried to catch him out, Clovis stoutly denied all the alleged facts; but, unable to resist the pleasure of glorying in the power and devotion of his friends, he named a large number of them. This information was all the queen needed, and she brought her investigation to an end, going on to do what she had already determined to do. On the morning of the fourth day, Clovis, still bound with ropes or chains, was taken from Chelles to Noisy, a royal domain not far off on the opposite bank of the Marne. Those who conveyed him thus (as though for a change of prisons) were under secret orders; a few hours after his arrival he was stabbed to death (the knife being left in the wound), and buried in a grave dug beside the wall of a chapel belonging to the palace of Noisy.

When the murder had actually been committed, men schooled by Fredegund went to the king and reported that Clovis, driven to despair by the enormity of his crime and the impossibility of obtaining pardon, had died by his own hand; as evidence of suicide, they added that the fatal weapon was still in the wound. The unshakeably credulous Chilperic did not entertain the smallest doubt, and performed neither inquest nor investigation. He regarded his son as a guilty man who had punished himself, shed no tears for him, and did not even give orders for his burial. This omission was turned to account by the queen, whose enmity was insatiable; she lost no time in commanding that her victim's body be disinterred and thrown into the Marne, so that it would be forever impossible to give it decent burial. However, this barbarous calculation was wasted; instead of vanishing at the bottom of the river or being carried far away by the current, Clovis's remains drifted into a net spread by a neighboring fisherman. When this man came to pull in his nets, he dragged a corpse out of the water, and recognized the young prince by his long hair, which no one had thought to cut off. Moved by respect and compassion, he took the body to the river bank and buried it in a grave which he covered over with turf so as to be able to find it again, keeping to himself the secret of a pious deed which could well cause his ruin.

No longer did Fredegund have to fear that one of Chilperic's sons by another wife should inherit the kingdom; in this respect her security was complete: but her fury was not yet at an end. Clovis's mother, Audovera, the wife Fredegund had had repudiated, was still living in a convent in the city of Le Mans; this woman had her to thank for her own misfortune and for the death of two sons, the first hunted down like a wild animal and compelled to commit suicide,[14] the second murdered. Whether Fredegund really believed that Audovera, shut up in her cloister, could be fostering schemes and looking for ways to be revenged, or whether her hatred had no other reason than the harm she herself had done her, this hatred was now at its peak, and a new crime soon followed the murder of Clovis.

Some of the queen's men, acting on her orders, set out for Le Mans and, when they arrived there, forced their way into the abbey where Audovera had been living in retirement for more than fifteen years, and where her daughter Hildeswinde, called Basine,[15] had grown up at her side. Both of them were taken care of, each in her own way, by Fredegund's horrible commission: the mother was put to death, and the daughter—and this would be hard to believe were it not for the testimony of a contemporary—King Chilperic's own daughter was raped, and suffered this outrage during his lifetime. The estates which Audovera had once received by way of consolation for her divorce, her other property, as well as all that of Clovis and his sister, became Fredegund's. As for the unfortunate girl who was left alive, dishonored, with no family—although she had a father, and her father was king—she went away to shut herself up in the abbey of Poitiers, placing herself under the maternal care of the foundress of that house, the gentle and noble Radegund. [16]

The woman who, under torture, had been compelled to make statements incriminating herself and Clovis was sentenced to be burned at the stake. On her way to execution she retracted her confession, screaming that everything she had said was a lie; but the man who should have been startled by these words, Chilperic, was not awakened from his mental torpor, and the protestations of the doomed woman died away unavailingly amid the flames. There were no more executions at the palace of Chelles; Clovis's friends and servants, schooled by the example of what had happened to his brother's comrades three years before, had taken to their heels at the right moment, scattering in different directions and hurrying to get out of the kingdom. [17]

Orders dispatched to the border counts enjoined them to block the fugitives' way, but only one—Clovis's treasurer—was arrested, just as he was entering the Bourges area, which was in King Guntram's territory. As he was being brought back through the city of Tours, Bishop Gregory, the narrator of these lamentable scenes, saw him passing by with his hands tied, and learned from his guards not only that they were taking him to the queen, but also what fate was in store for him. Moved with compassion for this unfortunate man, Gregory gave his escort a letter asking the queen for his life. At this entreaty from a man whom she revered in spite of herself, Fredegund was filled with salutary astonishment, and, as though a mysterious voice had said "Enough," she stopped short. Her feverish cruelty ceased; she displayed the clemency of the lion, disdain for pointless murder; and not only did she spare the prisoner torture and execution, but she even left him at liberty to go wherever he liked.

Five years later, Chilperic was dead, murdered, leaving as heir to his kingdom a son four months old; and Fredegund, unable to hold out against her insurgent enemies, had placed the child and herself under the protection of King Guntram, who had come to her in Paris. During this journey, which was about to give him the upper hand in Neustrian affairs, Guntram was a prey to very diverse feelings: joy at being able to get even for the wrongs Chilperic had done him, and sadness, which as a good brother he felt for his death; mistrust aroused in him by friendship as treacherous as Fredegund's, and satisfaction at thinking how he must benefit by doing her a good turn which would secure for himself both the guardianship of her son and the regency. On the one hand, ambition detained him in Paris; on the other, a vague sense of dread urged him to cut as short as possible a stay which he believed to be dangerous; he was playing the part of Fredegund's patron and protector, but he was on his guard against her. His anxieties brought vividly to his mind the violent ends of his brother and his nephews Merovech and Clovis. The two latter, especially, dead in the flower of youth without ever having done him any harm, were the object of his reveries, which were a mixture of fears for himself and sorrow for his kinsmen. He constantly spoke of them and lamented the fact that he could not even give them honorable burial, ignorant as he was of the places where their bodies had been flung. Such thoughts led him to make inquiries, and soon the news of his pious investigations had spread far and wide around Paris. Acting on this report, a countryman came to the king's lodging, asking to speak to him; and, when he had been admitted to his presence, he said: "If it won't be used against me later on, I will show you where Clovis's body is."

Happy at what he had just heard, King Guntram swore to the peasant that no harm would come to him, and that, quite the reverse, if he could give proof of what he was saying he would be handsomely rewarded. The man then replied: "Sire, I'm telling you the truth, the facts will bear me out. After Clovis had been killed and buried beneath the porch of a private chapel, the queen, afraid that he might some day be found and buried with honor, had him flung into the Marne. I found him in the nets I had prepared for my trade, which is catching fish. I didn't know who it could be, but I saw by the length of his hair that it was Clovis. I took him on my shoulders and carried him to the river bank, where I buried him and made him a tomb covered with turf. His remains are in a safe place; so now do whatever you want."

Guntram, on the pretence of going hunting, had the fisherman take him to the spot where he had raised a mound of sods. A hole was dug and Clovis's body was found lying on its back, almost intact; part of the hair, which was underneath, had become detached from the head, but the rest of the long, flowing tresses were still attached. By this mark, which left no room for doubt, King Guntram recognized his brother's son, one of the men whose remains he had so greatly desired to find. He gave orders for a spendid funeral for the young prince and, with himself as chief mourner, had the body carried to St. Vincent's basilica, now Saint-Germain-des-Prés. Some weeks later, Merovech's body, which had been discovered in the Térouanne area, was brought to Paris and buried in the same church, where King Chilperic also lay.

This church was the common grave of the Merovingian princes, above all of those who, carried off by violent deaths, could not choose their own place of burial. Its paved floor survives to this day and, within the walls of the edifice, rebuilt several times, still keeps the dust of the descendants of the conqueror of Gaul. If these Tales have any merit, they will increase the respect that our age bears the ancient abbey, nowadays a mere Parisian parish church, and perhaps they will add one more emotion to the thoughts inspired by this place of prayer consecrated thirteen hundred years ago. [18]

NOTES

INTRODUCTION

1. Unhappily, the promised continuation of the book was never undertaken.

2. By, among others, Charles Claude Hamilton (London, 1825); William Hazlitt (London, 1847, reprinted 1881 and 1885); and J. Arthur Price (London and New York, 1907, reprinted 1927).

3. In the series "Le Monde en 10/18." Paris: Union générale d'éditions, which follows the text of the sixth edition (Paris: Furne et Cie, 1859).

4. *Mimesis: The Representation of Reality in Western Literature*, trans. Willard R. Trask (Princeton, 1968 [1946]), 86.

5. Cf., e.g., Third Episode, 60, where Gregory expresses his prim disapproval at hearing Prince Merovech call his stepmother "an infamous whore" and his father "an imbecile husband." "Although there was a good deal of truth in all this . . . I do not think that it was pleasing to God that such matters should be divulged by a son." Thierry's own narrative contains similar strictures, of an unmistakably Victorian tenor, e.g.: "While Lothar's three older sons were living in such debauchery *and marrying domestics . . .*" (my italics, First Episode, 13).

PREFACE

1. M. de Chateaubriand: *Les Martyrs*, livre VI et VII; *Etudes ou discours historiques*, étude sixième, Moeurs des Barbares.

2. [Jean Froissart (C. 1337- c. 1410), possibly the most celebrated and attractive of the medieval French chroniclers.

3. *Nouvelles Lettres sur l'Histoire de France.*

4. *Abrégé de l'Histoire de France á l'usage des élèves de l'école royale militaire,* a part of the *Cours d'études rédigét imprimé par ordre du roi,* 1789, v. I, pp. 5 and 6.

5. *Les Martyrs,* book VI.

6. *Les Martyrs,* book VI.

7. [In 1840, Thierry had been totally blind for some years.—J.]

FIRST EPISODE

1. [Here Thierry justifies the adoption of Teutonic spellings of names in order to contribute "à la vérité de couleur dans ces récits" and to contrast and separate Frank from native Gaul. However, I think that for the modern English-speaking reader such names as Chilperic, Fredegund, Lothar, etc. are already sufficiently exotic in their "usual" forms.—J.]

2. [Thierry gives *lites. Liti* is the Latin form.—J.]

3. [Southwest Gaul.—J.]

4. [Vassals, liegemen.—J.]

5. *Koning* means *king* in the Frankish dialect.

6. [A people of ancient Germany.—J.]

7. [The river Waal is the southern branch of the Lower Rhine in the Netherlands.—J.]

8. [I.e., on the Ile de la Cité.—J.]

9. [A German tribe; cf. modern Burgundians.—J.]

10. [Thierry says "your fellow-godparent (commère) and godmother," etc., which doesn't really make sense, as Chilperic is not the godfather of the child.—J.]

11. [Actually Visigoths.—J.]

12. [The mayor of the palace was a very important official in Frankish times.—J.]

13. [Cf. modern Bavarians.—J.]

14. This monastery, the earliest convent established in Frankish Gaul, had been founded at the beginning of the sixth century by Bishop Caesarius, or St. Césaire.

15. [Venantius Fortunatus.—J.]

16. [The fundamental law of the Salian or Merovingian Franks, the best-known provision of which (not pertinent here, however) in the English-speaking world is the ban on succeeding to the throne through the female line. (Cf. Shakespeare, *King Henry V*, Act I, Scene ii).—J.]

17. *Handelang or handelag*, from the word *hand*, expressed in the Teutonic language the action of handing over, giving, transmitting (something) by hand.

SECOND EPISODE

1. This class of men is also denoted in the laws and public records by the name of *Rachinburgii, Racinburdi (Rekinburghe)*, powerful guarantors.

2. The word *trustee* survives in English.

3. [Cf. modern Lombards.—J.]

4. *Mark*, march, frontier; *graf*, district chief, governor, judge.

5. [Since the Romans.—J.]

6. [The Franks were Catholics; the Visigoths were Arians.—J.]

7. [Unless otherwise stated, "the contemporary narrator," "the chronicler," "the historian," etc., is, without exception, Gregory of Tours.—J.]

8. Man of no account, *Nithig, Nithing, Niding* in the various Teutonic dialects: this formula was used in challenges and proclamations of war.

9. Rumor had it that Guntram-Bose killed him with his own hand, or let him be killed by his (Guntram's) soldiers when he might have taken him prisoner. See below, Third Episode.

10. According to certain Teutonic roots, the mouth was the symbol of authority for the ancient Germans, the ear that of dependence.

11. The learned authors of the collection of *Historiens des Gaules et de la France* have erroneously attributed this letter to the year 574.

12. The *Brynhilde* of the Scandinavian Edda, and the *Brunhilt* of the *Nibelungen*. The likeness of the names is purely fortuitous.

13. [Proverbs 26:27.—J.]

THIRD EPISODE

1. [I.e., second (now oldest surviving) son of Chilperic by Queen Audovera.—J.]

2. [Not strictly true; Fredegund was behind the murder of Sigibert.—J.]

3. *Sig* is a familiar diminutive. [Referendary—court official who received petitions, kept the seal, etc.—J.]

4. See below, Fourth Episode.

5. *Bose*, in modern German *Boese* [böse], means cunning, wicked.

6. [According to Webster, *eulogia* is bread blessed but not consecrated, distributed in small pieces to those present at mass who have not communicated. The custom still survives in the Eastern Church and as a local practice in the Western Church, especially in France.—J.]

7. See below, Fourth Episode.

8. Law of the Emperor Leo concerning asylums (466).

9. [Proverbs 30:17. Unless otherwise stated, all Biblical passages are cited from the King James Bible.—J.]

10. [I Kings 9:9.—J.]

11. [Psalms 73:18-19.—J.]

12. [Matthew 26:2.—J.]

13. [The murderers of Sigibert were from Térouanne. See Second Episode.—J.]

FOURTH EPISODE

1. The objection has been raised against this double enumeration that in the sixth century the Roman or Teutonic appearance of proper names is not always a sure sign of a person's origins; that already some Germanic names are appearing in Gallo-Roman families. I am well aware of this, but they are rare exceptions which do not invalidate the rule. If one may not (until the contrary be proved) take for Franks people from the Merovingian Age who bear Germanic names, and for Gauls those bearing Roman names, it is impossible to write the history of the period.

2. [Ezekiel 33:6.—J.]

3. [Psalms 109:8–13; this is Psalm 108 in the Vulgate.—J.]

FIFTH EPISODE

1. [The ancestor of our *marshal*.—J.]

2. [*Comes stabuli*, constable.—J.]

3. See Second Episode.

4. See Third Episode.

5. See Third Episode.

6. Samson, born in Tournai during the siege of that city, had died in 577.

7. See Third Episode.

8. [From Auvergne.—J.]

9. [Psalms 78:52–53; Vulgate, Psalms 77:52–53.—J.]

10. See Fourth Episode.

11. Lothar I is estimated to have had five wives, among whom Radegund's place in chronological order is not easy to determine; some assign her first place, others third, others again, fifth. Mabillon was of this last opinion.

12. This fact is given by St. Radegund's biographers as being later than her entry into convent life, and St. Germain already appears there as bishop of Paris, which was not the case prior to 555. Such an act of passion, if belonging (as it is believed to do) to the year 559, the fifteenth after the divorce, proves that the king's regrets must have appeared no less expressively on several earlier occasions. I have placed it here, not being able to insert it at its correct date. It is, I hope, a pardonable anachronism.

13. On St. Radegund's learning and wide reading, see the poems of Fortunatus. She sedulously read St. Gregory of Nazianzus, St. Basil, St. Athanasius, St. Hilary, St. Ambrose, St. Jerome, St. Augustine, Sedulius, and Paulus Orosius (Lib. V, cap. 1).

14. See above, First Episode.

15. See Fourth Episode.

16. [Isaiah 5:8.—J.]

17. [Luke 23:34.—J.]

SIXTH EPISODE

1. [Very briefly, according to Arius (d. 336), God is alone and unknowable, and Christ a created being. Sabellius (fl. 220) held that Father, Son, and Holy Spirit are different manifestations of the one divine essence.—J.]

2. [Psalm 109: 3, Vulgate (Knox translation). The King James Bible reads differently: "Thy people shall be willing in the day of thy power, in the beauties of holiness from the dew of the morning; thou hast the dew of thy youth." (Psalm 110:3).—J.]

3. [Psalm 107:20; in Vulgate, Psalm 106: 20.—J.]

4. Isaiah 66:9.

5. [Baruch 3:36–38; Vulgate only.—J.]

6. [This quotation is actually taken from St. Matthew (1:23) who is, however, repeating Isaiah (7:14): "Behold, a virgin shall conceive, and bear a son, and shall call his name Immanuel."—J.]

7. [Psalm 22:16–18; in Vulgate, Psalm 21:17–19.—J.]

8. [Psalm 69:21; in Vulgate, Psalm 68:22.—J.]

9. Isaiah 53:5.

10. Isaiah 53:12.

11. Isaiah 53: 7, 8; 54:5.

12. Genesis 49: 8–9.

13. [Genesis 32:26.—J.]

14. See Third and Fifth Episodes.

15. On the distribution of *eulogias* to nonexcommunicated persons, see Third Episode.

16. [Paris being then located on the Ile de la Cité.—J.]

17. The absence of any trace of foundations made of Roman masonry allows us to conjecture that the buildings of this marketplace were of wood, which was moreover very common then in the towns of northern Gaul. Timber construction, often used in the erection of churches and other sizable edifices, was lacking neither in artistry nor tastefulness.

SEVENTH EPISODE

1. Here one will recall the five cities forming Galswinth's dower.

2. [He had given Limoges to Galswinth (First Episode) as part of the morrow-gift, then taken it from Sigibert (and lost it again). See Second Episode.—J.]

3. [Court.—J.]

4. [Members of a municipal senate.—J.]

5. Several facts mentioned by Gregory of Tours prove that questions relating to the establishment of the tax were dealt with in each city by the royal commissioners and the municipality, without the intervention of the count.

6. The promise which King Charibert made in 561 to the cities of his portion must at the same time have been made by Lothar's other sons in their respective kingdoms. What holds good for the city of Tours may therefore be admitted for Limoges, aside from the difference that Tours claimed, as a privilege, a total exemption from taxes.

7. [Job 1:21.—J.]

8. A host of examples of this kind are to be found in the *Sagas,* which are the most complete memorial to ancient Teutonic custom. The characters in these narratives, men and women alike, frequently improvise; improvisation by women is heralded by the following forms of words: *"Tha kvad hun visu thessa; Hun svarar og kvad visu; Enn hun kvad visu* (then she spoke these verses; she made answer and spoke these verses; she spoke to him in verse, etc.).

9. It is hard to believe that this speech, so full of emphasis and movement, is a rhetorical amplification composed by the historian; Gregory of Tours does not have the fault of making speeches in the name of his characters; he has them speak the words which he himself had heard, or which contemporary opinion ascribed to them. Now, if Fredegund's speech was, as there is every reason to believe, based on hearsay evidence, its character can only be explained by the inductive reasoning which precedes it.

10. The conspiracy of Leudast and the priest Rikulf. (See the Fifth Episode.) Clovis was then about twenty-five years of age.

11. Chelles is in the department of Seine-et-Marne, between Bondy and Lagny, fifteen miles east of Paris.

12. The expansion of Neustria had been proceeding since the year 577, by the occupation, one after another, of all the Aquitanian towns belonging either to Austrasia or to Guntram; this invasion was complete by the year 582. (See Third and Sixth Episodes).

13. The syllables *Bob, Bab, Bod, Bad, Bat* were often substituted by way of a nickname for the Teutonic names formed with the component *Bald* or *Baud* and any other word. (See Third and Sixth Episodes.)

14. Merovech: see Third Episode.

15. See First Episode. *Basine* means *the good;* the root of this noun, *bas* or *bat,* depending on the dialect, is still found in modern German and English in the comparatives *besser* and *better,* and in the superlative *best.*

16. See Fifth Episode.

17. See, Third Episode, the death of Merovech's companions.

18. [Written before 1840.—J.]

INDEX